A New Paradigm:
Perspectives on the Changing
Mediterranean

Edited by
Sasha Toperich and Andy Mullins

Center for Transatlantic Relations
Paul H. Nitze School of Advanced International Studies
Johns Hopkins University

Sasha Toperich and Andy Mullins, *A New Paradigm: Perspectives on the Changing Mediterranean*

Washington, DC: Center for Transatlantic Relations, 2014

Center for Transatlantic Relations
The Paul H. Nitze School of Advanced International Studies
The Johns Hopkins University
1717 Massachusetts Ave., NW, Suite 525
Washington, DC 20036
Tel: (202) 663-5880
Fax: (202) 663-5879
Email: transatlantic@jhu.edu
http://transatlantic.sais-jhu.edu

ISBN 13: 978-0989-02948-3

Cover background: Laurin Rinder, www.rinderart.com

Contents

Part IV: Migration and Diaspora

Part V: Women and the Mediterranean: Opportunities and Challenges for Gender Equality

Acknowledgments

This book would not have been possible without the support and input of our colleagues in Washington and around the Mediterranean Basin, who contributed significantly to the success of the Mediterranean Women in Leadership and Civil Society Conference in Sarajevo in November 2013, where this project was announced.

In particular, we would like to express our gratitude to our SAIS colleagues Daniel Serwer and Michael Haltzel for their valuable insights at our Economic Fora, panel discussions and other venues dedicated to the Mediterranean Basin Initiative.

America-Bosnia Foundation Fellow and Project Coordinator of the Mediterranean Basin Initiative Dajana Džindo worked tirelessly to organize the Sarajevo conference and follow-up activities, and we are thankful for her tremendous efforts.

Our special thanks go to Hanna Engblom for her dedication to timely and incisive edits in the last phase of production.

As always, we are grateful to Peggy Irvine and Peter Lindeman for working out the publishing details of this and many other CTR publications.

The opinions expressed in the following essays are the authors' alone, and do not necessarily represent the views of any government or institution, or those of their fellow contributors.

SASHA TOPERICH
Senior Fellow, Center for Transatlantic Relations SAIS
ANDY MULLINS
Visiting Scholar, Center for Transatlantic Relations SAIS

Preface

The Mediterranean Basin Initiative, launched in 2013 by the Center for Transatlantic Relations at Johns Hopkins University's Paul H. Nitze School of Advanced International Studies, has capped several years of work in the Balkans and the Mediterranean area.

Working with our partners in the Mediterranean, we strive to promote a stronger relationship with the countries and peoples of North Africa and Southeast Europe.

The Mediterranean Basin Initiative aims to focus the attention and support of the international community on the complicated transitional processes in North Africa, where experience from Southeast Europe over the last two decades informs our understanding of the longer-term nature of transition; the countries of the Basin have something to offer one another in several fields.

The Initiative is a collaborative, issue-focused framework built around the themes of stronger transatlantic economic cooperation, empowering civil society and women in leadership, and political and academic dialogue throughout the Mediterranean.

To date, we have convened two major international conferences under these auspices: the Transatlantic Economic Forum in June 2013 in Washington, and the Mediterranean Women in Leadership and Civil Society Conference in November 2013 in Sarajevo, Bosnia and Herzegovina. In the interim, we have regularly hosted lectures and panel discussions featuring U.S., European, and North African business leaders, policymakers, and officials.

All of the authors whose work is contained in this collection were participants in one or more of these events, helping to shape the conversation about the changing nature of the Mediterranean and what role the transatlantic community can play in it.

This book represents many important threads in that conversation, the direction of which, in many places—Syria, Egypt, Libya, and elsewhere—remains very much unsettled. Future Mediterranean Basin events will produce different discussions, and as in this case, discussants will not always achieve common viewpoints. But taken as a whole, the book offers a compelling vision for closer transatlantic cooperation in the Mediterranean Basin.

Enjoy the reading.

DANIEL HAMILTON
Austrian Marshall Plan Foundation Professor
Executive Director, Center for Transatlantic Relations

Introduction

Sasha Toperich and Andy Mullins

The Mediterranean is changing. Political tremors that began in Sidi Bouzid, Tunisia in December 2010 have shaken the entrenched order and toppled leaders in Tunisia, Libya, and Egypt. Governments around the Mediterranean are struggling to deal with flagging economies, growing unemployment, security threats, migration, and other human security challenges.

Simultaneously, the Arab Spring has brought an unprecedented opportunity for democratization and inclusive growth to millions more Mediterranean citizens than ever before. Long-standing social stagnation, gender inequality, and human rights violations stand ready to be addressed by reconsidering the relationship between states and citizens, by enhancing the rule of law and prioritizing individual rights. New constitutions in Morocco, Tunisia, and Egypt (and forthcoming in Libya) spark hope for increased liberty across the region.

As each of the popular movements that toppled long-standing regimes in Tunisia, Libya, and Egypt encountered severe difficulties, most observers realized that the transition process toward vibrant, democratic societies would take much more than the genuinely inspirational "will of the people." It will require much more time and effort.

Even as the revolutions that overthrew Ben Ali, Mubarak, and Qaddafi faltered, however, they created possibilities for future progress in the form of a number of new political parties and civil society organizations. New outlets in mainstream print and electronic media and on the Internet were also established, breathing fresh air into their societies. New political parties declared an end to oppression in all segments of life, pledging either to rewrite constitutions, or to pass new legislation to fight corruption, protect the rule of law, and guarantee judicial independence.

But a lack of experience and political know-how on the part of the reformers, a widespread thirst for power and influence, obstructionism—usually triggered by domestic and regional special interests, and a re-assertion of power by the armed forces, especially in Egypt, have severely dampened the optimism of the Arab Spring.

And as it is always easier to criticize than to praise, in all fairness, newly-formed governments worked tirelessly to bring about needed changes. But in many instances, they were faced with the simple question: Where do we begin?

Previous regimes held a tight grip on their countries and had a very limited circle of trusted people that actually governed the state. To redirect governance and real responsibility to not only the respective ministries, but all other agencies, committees, and departments takes time to adjust and make functional. In the meantime, the economic climate took a huge toll as consumer prices rose, political parties entered into bickering power struggle games, and performance fell far too short of people's expectations.

However, good things were achieved that will certainly enter history. Libya held its first free elections after almost 60 years and formed its first National Assembly (General National Congress), dividing legislative and executive powers. Tunisia has launched a National Dialogue that brought together a broad cross-section of Tunisia's political life, setting an excellent example to other countries of how to work out internal differences and pathways to reconciliation in the nation-building process. This dialogue culminated in the adoption of a new constitution on January 26, 2014, hailed across the region and around the world as a model for other countries to follow.

Egypt held a free and fair presidential election in 2012 to bring Mohamed Morsi and the once-outcast Muslim Brotherhood to power; after a year of teetering on the brink of economic collapse and increasing repression, Morsi was ousted by the military and, at the time of this publication, is on trial for incitement of violence. While Egypt is moving unmistakably away from democratic rule again, we can hope that fresh memories of an energized population, taking to the streets *en masse* and demanding good governance twice in four years, will encourage leadership in Cairo to listen more closely to the people.

And as we have learned from the Balkans, although with a different set of issues and problems, the transitional process after the fall of one long-lived regime will take much longer than anticipated, with many ups and downs. Protests across Bosnia and Herzegovina in early 2014 reminded us that transitions in the Balkans are still unfinished.

Ultimately, it will be on the political leaders in these countries themselves to make it possible for their countries to thrive, but the influence of the international community is as crucial as it can ever be. Much is at stake in North Africa that would have serious impact beyond the borders of these countries. Beyond even the immediate security concerns (covered in-depth by several of our contributors), the prospect of missed opportunities for marked improvement in the social, economic, and political spheres across the Mediterranean could have a chilling effect on democracy promotion at large. Not to mention, of course, poor and worsening life chances for hundreds of millions of people.

In spite of this, the tone of this publication is cautiously optimistic. We do not intend to argue that the daunting present challenges facing these countries have turned the Arab Spring into an "Arab Winter," as some analysts suggest.[1] Indeed, inspired by the French historian Fernand Braudel—whose seminal works on the Mediterranean inspired an ongoing conversation at our Center, indirectly leading to this book—and by our experiences in the Balkans, we see the need for an emphasis on the *longue durée*, that is, the long term evolution of political, social, and economic structures in what we hope is a freer direction.

To date, our Center has organized two major international conferences to consider the changing Mediterranean and how to encourage this evolution. The first, the Transatlantic Economic Forum held in Washington, DC in June 2013, welcomed business leaders, academics, and policymakers from North Africa, Europe, Turkey, and the U.S. In dynamic discussions on transatlantic cooperation, fostering better business environments, improving transport and trade networks, and the relationship between democracy and prosperity, participants in the

---

[1] The poetry of the phrase "Arab Spring" almost demands such a contrarian complementary response, as the 76.8 million results Google returns on a "Arab Spring to Arab Winter" search suggest.

Forum pointed the way toward setting a common agenda for the countries of the Mediterranean and their international partners.

In November 2013, in partnership with the Agency for Gender Equality of the Ministry of Human Rights and Refugees of Bosnia and Herzegovina, we organized the Mediterranean Women in Leadership and Civil Society Conference in Sarajevo. Women's activists, civil society leaders, politicians and policymakers, academics, and private sector elites from 15 countries gathered at the Parliament of Bosnia and Herzegovina to tackle issues such as gender equality, empowering youth in the economic and political spheres, combatting violence, and political participation. The spirited and oftentimes courageous participants, many of whom had been on the front lines of revolution and its aftermath in North Africa, gave lie to the notion that apathy was taking root in the populations of their countries.

The core takeaway from these two conferences is this: energizing Mediterranean cooperation will significantly help countries of the greater Mediterranean Basin to move forward faster.

Enhancing trade, expanding business partnerships, grassroots-level cooperation, bringing civil societies together to learn from each other experiences, encouraging young entrepreneurship, promoting and highlighting positive steps and achievements are part and parcel of the mission we embarked on with the Mediterranean Basin Initiative.

We looked at the friendly, strong and dynamic relationship between the countries of the Western Balkans and other Mediterranean countries with the Maghreb nations, bonds built by Tito's, Nehru's and Nasser's Non-Aligned Movement founded in Belgrade in 1961. They remained strong even after Yugoslavia dissolved into the now seven independent states while Qaddafi, Mubarak and Ben Ali firmly ruled Libya, Egypt and Tunisia.

This collection of essays authored by colleagues and participants from our two major conferences covers a wide range of topics. As Braudel said, "There are ten, twenty, a hundred Mediterraneans, each one sub-divided in turn."[2] As we consider the new and evolving dynamics of the Mediterranean, we are aware that the perspectives

---

[2]Braudel, F. (2001.) *Memory and the Mediterranean*. New York: Knopf, 22.

collected here are another sub-division, one united by a common autocratic heritage, a history of trans-Mediterranean economic and social cooperation, and the prospect or reality of troubled transitions. There are "other" Mediterraneans that one could comfortably merge with the set presented here, the subjects of future publications.

Of note, Syria's tragic three-year civil war has killed over 150,000 people and has made refugees of more than half of its population. Over one million Syrians are in Lebanon, 670,000 in Turkey and 600,000 in Jordan, to say nothing of the nine million internally displaced persons.[3] Little can be said further with respect to the comprehensive ongoing effort by the U.S. Secretary of State, John Kerry, to bring about a framework to end the Israeli-Palestinian conflict. At the time this volume is published, circumstances in this part of the Mediterranean will be already different. We will be discussing these countries in our next volume on the region.

We start with a look at opportunities for greater economic cooperation in North Africa. Ghazi Ben Ahmed, executive director of our partner NGO the Mediterranean Development Initiative, puts forward a recommendation for closer economic cooperation in the Maghreb, arguing that expanded trade links between Tunisia and the EU and U.S. would unleash the full potential of the private sector. The U.S.-Tunisia Strategic Dialogue, announced by Secretary of State John Kerry in Tunis in February 2014, enhances Tunisia's standing as a leader in North African development and democratization. (It also encourages observers concerned that the old saw about America's Mediterranean policy being no more or less than the Sixth Fleet would continue to ring true.) Border regions in North Africa offer a stepping stone to enhanced trade and economic relationships.

Ben Ahmed and Slim Othmani consider the failures of the Arab Maghreb Union process and attribute its shortcomings primarily to the top-down approach employed by North African leaders. The active exclusion of civil society, lack of synchronicity in economic policies from country to country, and nationalist rivalries helped sink the AMU in the 1990s. The authors find reason for new hope in the Arab Spring and an invigorated business community, willing to work

---

[3]Leila Hadj-Abdou considers Syrian refugee movement in brief in Chapter 9.

together to establish a Maghreb Common Market as a first step toward greater regional integration. The article highlights the role a Business Advisory Council, comprising business leaders from across the Maghreb, could play in guiding necessary reforms and promoting a better investment climate.

Adel Dajani and Ben Ahmed examine the precariously intertwined economic and political situation in Libya. They argue that there is an urgent need for UN mediation, including a High Commissioner for the country not unlike the High Representative in Bosnia and Herzegovina. Libya experienced this form of conservatorship in the 1950s when Dutch diplomat Adriaan Pelt supervised the drafting of a constitution and the declaration of an independent constitutional monarchy under King Idris in 1951. Further, national reconciliation dialogue (advised by the South African model), economic reforms and diversification away from hydrocarbons, and regional integration with Tunisia are sensible recommendations to improve the climate in the country. Dajani and Ben Ahmed stress the role that the government of Libya would do best by getting out of the way of these sorts of innovations, by encouraging and facilitating but not leading cooperative efforts.

From Turkey, Aylin Ünver Noi offers an alternative for improving human security in the Middle East and North Africa, recognizing the successes of the Council of Europe in protecting human rights and proposing an expansion to include the Southern Mediterranean, or the establishment of a Council of the Middle East and North Africa (MENA). She looks at the successes and failures in the development of the Council of Europe and considers how best to guard human rights in an international framework.

The security situation in North Africa is in flux and certainly one of the international community's top priorities for the region. Olivier Guitta analyzes the declining security picture in Libya and wonders whether the country is on the cusp of becoming a failed state. The dismissal of Prime Minister Ali Zeidan following the failure of Libya's navy to halt the departure of an unregistered oil tanker in March 2014, as this book went to print, offers a stark example of how central this problem is to addressing the country's other challenges.

As mentioned earlier, Egypt continues to struggle with societal shifts brought about by the revolution and the subsequent tumult of Muslim Brotherhood rule. As Field Marshal Abdel Fattah al-Sisi consolidates the army's hold on the levers of power in 2014, whither the revolution, and what does it mean for women in Egypt? Emily Dyer argues that sexual harassment and violence has become a tool of repression by Egypt's rulers, first with the Muslim Brotherhood and the subsequent al-Sisi coup. The aims of the revolution—"bread, freedom, and social justice"—are not much closer than they were under Mubarak, and time is running out.

Edward Joseph finds lessons learned from previous transitions that could help guide the way for North Africa in the Balkans, but also looks for ways the Arab Spring could inform our understanding of the "crisis of democracy" today in the Balkans. Noting the shared Ottoman legacy and potential for ethno-religious conflict in Southeast Europe and North Africa, Joseph highlights promoting dialogue as the best entry point for international efforts to support transitions in both cases. Finding consensus on difficult topics, as Belgrade and Pristina did in 2013 and Tunisians have done with their new constitution, is the best way forward.

Rupert Sutton reminds us that perhaps the best comparison case is another Mediterranean state, Lebanon, whose Cedar Revolution in 2005 can inform our understanding of the pitfalls still facing North African countries. Sutton argues that in spite of the unsettled political scene after the assassination of Rafic Hariri in 2005, Lebanon was able to stabilize its economy, reach an agreement to end factional street violence in 2008, and saw significant GDP growth until the Syrian conflict next store restored the divided atmosphere. Were it not for the Syrian morass next door, Lebanon would offer a qualified but hopeful picture for other post-revolutionary Mediterranean countries.

The sea itself is at the heart of life on the Mediterranean, and one of its most important roles is as a facilitator of movement of peoples. Perhaps more than any other field, migration in the Mediterranean shows the contrast between the international community's rhetoric on assisting the peoples of North Africa and a sometimes decidedly different practice. Leila Hadj-Abdou documents the recent history of North African migration to Europe to determine how the EU has handled the aspirations of the peoples of its neighborhood to access the economic and social benefits of residence. She finds that the EU has enlisted non-member states to act as buffers for irregular migration and argues that "Europe seems to remain locked into a wrong and misleading dilemma of irregular and regular migration, which is embedded in a one-sided discourse of security."

Even when peoples are free to relocate to better socioeconomic situations in other countries, they frequently maintain ties with co-nationals and their homelands. Diasporas can be positive drivers of development and capacity-building in their new countries and old; they may also be destabilizing factors, carrying memories of conflict out of the homeland. Andy Mullins considers the role diasporas are playing in transitioning states in the region, and suggests free movement—and the remittances it enables—is an underappreciated pathway to prosperity compared to more traditional development aid.

Intisar Azzuz explores the history of Libyan women to highlight the challenges facing them in political structures and society. She draws hope from the Tunisian example, but argues women must remain vigilant and proactive in pursuit and defense of their rights, especially as Libya's newly-formed constitutional committee goes to work on the country's foundational document.

The Agency for Gender Equality of Bosnia and Herzegovina is a leader in developing gender equality strategies in the Mediterranean, and led the effort to draft and sign a multinational memorandum of understanding among women's groups at the Mediterranean Women in Leadership and Civil Society Conference. The Agency's director, Samra Filipović-Hadžiabdić, summarizes Bosnia and Herzegovina's National Action Plan to harmonize the country's laws with the 2000 UN Security Council Resolution 1325, "Women, Peace, and Security." She emphasizes the Agency's search for lessons learned and examples from cases as diverse as Sweden and Liberia, arguing that North African women can learn from Bosnia and Herzegovina's experiences as well.

Dajana Džindo also looks to the Balkans for successes and failures in promoting women's entrepreneurship. Examining the characteristics of women-owned businesses around the Mediterranean, she finds similarly low labor force participation and a lack of state encouragement for entrepreneurs. Dzindo argues that "no single policy can effectuate women's entrepreneurship in transitional countries," something demonstrated by two decades of halting attempts in the Balkans. From this background, she offers timely and actionable recommendations to policymakers in North Africa.

Many regard the Nordic states as the vanguard of gender equality globally, with a high degree of parity between men and women and a number of prominent women business leaders. Marianne Aringberg Laanatza and Camilla af Hällström deconstruct the "Nordic model" of women's empowerment to derive lessons and best practices for Arab countries in transition, especially in the field of entrepreneurship. They note that the starting point for women in these countries does not compare favorably to women's position in the Nordic states, but opportunities are better than commonly believed. In particular, technology startups are a promising avenue in many MENA countries. Additionally, there is direct engagement between Nordic governments and MENA women entrepreneurs through direct development aid, providing another example of successful international engagement in the region.

Turning to civil society and institutional roadblocks on women's political and social participation in Bosnia and Herzegovina, Valery Perry points to the post-war constitutional structure of the country as the main culprit. An overly-bureaucratized state with multiple levels of governance and an electoral system that fails to hold politicians accountable for responding to citizens' needs is a recipe for social and economic stagnation. Despite international and domestic efforts, Perry writes, "it is clear that neither structural incentives nor cultural encouragement are resulting in more women in state-level government." One of the most important takeaways of Bosnia and Herzegovina's experiences is the dangers of placing women in the "pink ghetto," where women tackle women-only and children's issues and men engage in constitutional reform and governance efforts. The success of Tunisia's constitution-drafting process, for one example, signals that this is not a guaranteed dead-end for transitional processes, but remains a worrisome possibility throughout the region.

In some cases, state institutions are more than an impediment to women's empowerment—they can actively facilitate gender inequality. Anissa Naqrachi highlights the example of early marriage in Morocco. In the Fez region, the average age of a woman on her wedding day is 15 years old. UNICEF research indicates that 11 percent of Moroccan women between the ages of 15 and 19 are married; 64 percent of Moroccans in this age group believe husbands are justified in physically abusing their wives under certain circumstances. The legality of early marriage is both a symptom and a cause of these and other problematic phenomena. Naqrachi offers recommendations to the Moroccan authorities to harmonize the Criminal Code and Family Code of Morocco with international conventions ratified by the state as a starting point to rectify these abuses.

Najla Abbes of the League of Tunisian Women Voters presents a history of women's political participation pre- and post-revolution. She finds that women were underrepresented in the first freely-elected National Constituent Assembly, with the Islamist Nahda party bringing the most to the chamber. There was a "risk of regression for women's rights emerging, in particular from the general political context and the profile of the election winner"—yet, thanks to pressure from the League of Tunisian Women Voters and other women's activists, a progressive constitution resulted in gender parity enshrined in law.

Nadia Ait-Zai contributes an analysis of women's political participation in Algeria, the Maghreb country least radically affected by the Arab Spring. Parties have not made credible efforts to promote women in Algeria, so Ait Zai argues "they will soon be relegated to subordinate positions... if they have no desire to fight for their place and defend their ideas." She suggests non-party avenues, such as women's organizations, may offer better advocacy outlets for women.

In sum, while there is no "magic answer" to how long the transitional processes in countries can take, we believe enhanced grassroots-level cooperation between the United States and the greater Mediterranean Basin, supporting women's empowerment organizations, civil society groups, advocating reforms to reflect freedom and justice for all, promoting laws that would make commerce and investments more vibrant, assisting the private sector to work together to further build trust, friendship and create mutually beneficial business opportunities, and promoting the countries of the Mediterranean in Washington, DC will help them overcome the problems they are facing these days.

We believe inclusiveness is the key word and our continued message to the leadership in the Mediterranean region.

Each country has its own set of issues and particular set of obstacles: whether tribal relationship issues and security problems in Libya; the struggle between the secular versus Islamist parties in Tunisia; or supporters of the Egyptian military versus Muslim Brotherhood supporters. But they all have one thing in common: the political key to moving forward is *inclusiveness*.

This volume addresses a number of important issues, from national security, economic cooperation, gender equality, to ideas of various aspects for Mediterranean cooperation and lessons learned from the Balkan transitional processes. Future publications, conferences, and discussions in the framework of the Mediterranean Basin Initiative will doubtless take us to different Mediterraneans. With our partners in Europe and North Africa, we are dedicated to building a collaborative network among them.

And as we all know, by the time this volume is published, many things will already have changed. But we are confident the ideas stated here by scholars, researchers, and activists from both sides of the Atlantic and the north and south shores of the Mediterranean will be relevant for some time to come.

Part I

Regional Integration and Cooperation in North Africa

Chapter One

Tunisia's Awakening Economy: A Trilateral Vision

Ghazi Ben Ahmed

One has to acknowledge that the circumstances are tougher for MENA than they were when Eastern Europe went through its historic transition. In the early 1990s, the world economy was booming, Europe was keen to embrace the transition economies and provide a policy anchor, and external financing was readily available. That is not the case today and we will need different approaches to this transition.

Nemat Shafik, Deputy Managing Director, IMF, May 10, 2012

And today, as the Arab Spring unfolds... some principles of the [Marshall] plan apply again. As Marshall did in 1947, we must understand that the roots of the revolution and the problems that it sought to address are not just political but profoundly economic as well.

U.S. Secretary of State Hillary Clinton, June 2, 2011

The Swerve, or How Tunisia Became a Model for Democracy and Modernity

The swerve is a good metaphor for the unexpected process of political as well as historical change, where a small event—the self-immolation of a street vendor in a small Tunisian village—can have far-reaching and unintended consequences. As a matter of fact, the spark ignited by Tunisia with the so-called Jasmine Revolution inspired protests from Egypt to Libya and Yemen, and in doing so has irretrievably changed the future course of the countries in the Middle East and North Africa (MENA). It offered—initially—new hope for an inclusive and sustainable development that has not before been seen in the region. But the unfolding of the situation is now affecting the MENA countries differently. Only Tunisia seems well engaged to break with the past and set course in a newer direction. Each country in the region will eventually make the transition towards democracy in its own way and at its own speed.

Tunisia's success matters to the community of democracies and across the Middle East and North Africa, as it sets a powerful and positive example. The recent political developments, especially the ratification of the new constitution and the approval of a new government of technocrats, are a decisive milestone in Tunisia's democratic transition and a prerequisite for it to stay on the right path.

Tunisia seems now on track to succeed in its revolution, which aims at freedom, dignity and job opportunity. The path has not been easy and the journey is not finished yet. But three years after the start of the uprising, thanks to their pugnacity and courage, Tunisians stand closer to realizing the promise of their revolution. They are sending a powerful message to the rest of the region, a message of hope based on a remarkable spirit of compromise and inclusiveness. This political success calls for an "economic spring" and a debate to rethink the region's economic future.

In fact, while the new government has been appointed to prepare the ground for the next elections according to an agreed roadmap, which stresses the need to review partisan appointments in the Tunisian administration, disband the "Revolution Protection Leagues" that are accused of violence, and fight terrorism, it is crucial now to take advantage of the positive momentum and start immediately tackling the economic reforms needed to resume and boost economic growth.

Organizing the next elections before the end of 2014 will put an end to the period of uncertainty that is undermining the country's economic recovery and hindering the confidence of traditional donors and investors. However, some common issues will have to be addressed immediately: How can Tunisia move away from generalized subsidies to those targeting exclusively the poor, in order to free up resources and invest in productive projects and infrastructure? How to reshuffle the tax system to be fairer in order to enhance the standard living of the poorest? How will the private sector be induced to create 1,350,000 jobs in the next decade (650,000 currently unemployed plus 70,000 new job seekers every year)?

Incremental changes to the existing economic model will not deliver this outcome. A qualitative and quantitative increase in the pace of economic growth is needed, and it calls for new policies, inclusion and economic reforms. While there is willingness from the international community to help, resources are limited. Most of the economic transition in Tunisia will have to be financed through domestic resources. Only Tunisians can navigate the path ahead, but as they do so, they need a vision that will give them incentives to implement tough reforms, and inject a new dynamic to satisfy the rising expectations and hopes of the people. Hope gives direction and so inspires confidence.

Tunisia needs a trilateral vision. (i) A reinvigorated and integrated Maghreb open to the rest of the Mediterranean region and to the Gulf Cooperation Council, (ii) A committed EU "sharing everything but institutions," adopting for this the "much more for more" policy, and (iii) a fully-fledged U.S.-Tunisia Free Trade Agreement (FTA) open to the rest of North Africa.

Reinvigorate North African Regional Integration

Unleash the Full Potential of the Private Sector...

In order to improve considerably the socio-economic situation across the region, there is a need to promote the expansion of the private sector, notably micro-, small- and medium-sized enterprises (SMEs) and their participation in value chains as a powerful engine of economic growth and the main source of job creation.

North African value chains would be a powerful vehicle for SMEs to diversify and innovate, offering new opportunities for the region to become part of the global factory. Modern international trade has split the production of goods and services among many countries, creating supply chains that reduce overall costs by trading in tasks across borders. By locating activities and tasks in the different North African countries according to their comparative advantages, the total costs of production can be reduced. Successful exporting countries in Asia and Eastern Europe have become active participants in supply chains. An important pre-condition for the participation in regional and global value chains is good infrastructure, transportation, access to trade finance, trade barriers and border policies.

An empowered private sector can serve as an interface with North African governments and international organizations to help devise and prioritize economic reforms and structure policies in support of private sector development, with a particular focus on border regions and SMEs.

A better business climate helps to promote efficient domestic investment, attract foreign direct investment and increase productivity, thereby raising income and employment opportunities. There is a need for sensitization of people and NGOs about the importance of speeding up the reforms and further liberalize the market. Emphasis should be put on reducing administrative and regulatory barriers for business, building capacities in relevant ministries, and reviewing existing legislation and policies.

This should be complemented by a support for business development services such as training, advice and information services which aim at improving technical and managerial skills and encourage the transfer of know-how and technologies.

...Promoting Border Regions as New Engines for Growth and Regional Integration

The success of the democratic transition in Tunisia requires vigorous economic growth. At this critical time, the private sector can play an essential role in creating economic gains focusing on border regions such as El Kef on the Algerian frontier and Ben Guerdane on the Libyan frontier. Border region co-development strategy could be elaborated as a pilot case and broadened later to the whole country. This strategy of focusing on border regions could pave the way for regional integration.

Significant cross-border trade already takes place in the informal sector, which represents in Tunisia about 40 percent of GDP. Cross-border enterprise zones would seek to formalize and expand economic activity by fostering the growth of small and medium enterprises operating in these border areas.

It is very relevant that people engaging in business activities on either side of the border often have more in common with each other than with their respective capitals. Formalizing, regulating and expanding this type of activity could help anchor economic integration in these border zones.

Efforts should be made to learn from earlier attempts at sub-regional economic integration. In particular, the case of Souk Ahras—Le Kef on the Tunisian-Algerian border area is worth examining. The initiative was undertaken by public companies and ultimately failed. However, a renewed attempt at this type of sub-regional cooperation should instead focus on the private sector. The example of the Tunisian company Poulina's operations in Ben Guerdane and its cross-border operations in Libya may be instructive and worth replicating.

Similarly, the creation of an economic corridor between Algeria and Morocco has also been under consideration. Two years ago, discussions of an economic corridor between Algeria and Morocco was modeled on a similar plan developed in China. In the case of Algeria and Morocco, frontier passage points would be established to allow the flow of goods between the countries. (Currently the Algerian-Moroccan border is closed.) The movement of goods would be monitored to determine whether the cross-border trade has a negative or positive impact on each country's economy.

Existing literature on regional integration focuses predominantly on supranational levels of integration such as the European Union and North American Free Trade Agreement (NAFTA) to the exclusion of sub-national regions at the borders of nation-states.

Theoretically, integration, i.e. the opening of the border for trade and factor mobility, may significantly change the economic situation of border regions. The reduction of border impediments decreases access costs with respect to foreign markets especially in border regions.

However, this is not straightforward. Trade in the EU has been essentially free of tariffs since the late 1960s. But significant barriers to cross-border trade remain due to differences in technical standards or bureaucratic impediments. The Single European Act aimed at a completion of the internal market in 1992 via a reduction of non-tariff barriers to trade.

The literature emphasizes also the differentiation of regional development paths in East Central Europe, contrasting a "high road" and a "low road" to development. This is explained by the "endogenous influences," i.e., the communication barriers and a "low trust environment" that are rooted in the particular development history of the European regions and are a hindrance to regional integration. However, this is absolutely not the case for El Kef and the other border-regions in North Africa. The inhabitants of El Kef, for instance, feel very close to their neighbors in Algeria, and are often related. There was always a high trust environment that could be conducive to joint venturing in the new settings. The same applies for the Tunisian-Libyan border region. It was very clear following the Libyan revolution where the neighboring region offered spontaneously hospitality to more than 300,000 Libyan refugees. The integration of power networks and the joint oilfield exploitation could be an engine for growth and development for the south of Tunisia and a win-win strategy for both countries.

Consolidate the Partnership with the EU

The EU to Act as a Responsible Neighbor...

> Our response ... is built on the need to acknowledge past mistakes and listen without imposing. We are doing exactly that and it requires perseverance and sustained commitment. Success should translate into what I have called "deep democracy."

> Baroness Catherine Ashton, the EU's High Representative for Foreign Affairs and Security Policy, in 2011

The European Union first responded to the Arab Spring by issuing a joint communication on 8 March 2011 titled *A Partnership for Democracy and Shared Prosperity with the Southern Mediterranean*. In this document, the EU expressed its intention "to support wholeheartedly the wish of the people in our neighborhood to enjoy the same freedoms that we take as our right." It further outlined a new "incentive-based approach based on more differentiation ('more for more')" for its partners in the region, promising that "those that go further and faster with reforms will be able to count on greater support from the EU.

In May 2011, the European Commission issued the results of its review of its European Neighborhood Policy, which drives its relations with its southern and eastern neighbors, including Tunisia. The review entails a new partnership with the EU based on greater economic integration, trade and increased funding for the Southern Neighborhood. As part of this offer, the EU allocated an extra €1.24

billion in funding for the region, on top of €11.5 billion already allocated for the period 2007–13. It also announced that the European Investment Bank had been authorized to increase its lending by €1 billion for Mediterranean countries undertaking political reform, as well as the creation of several funding tools, including a European Endowment for Democracy, a Civil Society Facility, and a €26 million 'umbrella' programme named SPRING (Support for Partnership, Reform and Inclusive Growth), to supplement reform efforts in existing country programmes in the region.

A third Communication[1] was published by the EU in 2012: "*Supporting Closer Cooperation and Regional Integration in the Maghreb.*" This new flexible institutional framework is supposed to allow progress at different speeds (based on variable geometry) and enable the Mediterranean partners to carry out the remaining reforms.

However, in front of the economic challenges facing Tunisia and the region, there is growing concern that the EU lacks ambition and the means to implement its vision and incentivize its reforming southern partners. And even more so when we compare with the amount the EU is offering to support Ukraine, i.e., an overall support of at least €11 billion over the next couple of years, from the EU budget and EU-based international financial institutions

However, the EU proposals are not enough to address the important breakthrough made by Tunisia and clearly needs a bold vision from the EU member states. The EU needs to institute a new and inclusive regional approach that would help keep and promote peace and foster stability and security throughout the continent, ultimately promoting the emergence of democracy and better global governance.

…Tunisia's Candidacy for European Economic Area Membership

Tunisia was the first country to sign an Association Agreement with Europe and the first also to put in place a free trade zone for industrial products back in 2008. The level of trade and EU investment in Tunisia and the level of intra-regional trade in North Africa remained below expectations, despite several tentative attempts to reinvigorate

---

[1]"Supporting Closer Cooperation and Regional Integration in the Maghreb" (17.12.12), JOIN(2012) 36 final.

the Barcelona process with the European Neighborhood Policy and the Union for the Mediterranean.

The Arab Spring, initiated by Tunisia at the end of 2010, posed several challenges to Europe and marks a new phase in the political and economic relationship between the EU and Tunisia. It is not clear today whether there is a clear European strategy for cooperation and work with the new Tunisia in the short and longer term.

The Deep and Comprehensive Free Trade Agreement (DCFTA) is the long-term incentive on offer by the EU to those countries that are moving towards "deep democracy," an upgrade compared to the Free Trade Areas that were the ultimate aim of the Association Agreements set in motion with the Euro-Mediterranean Partnership.

In the short term, Tunisia was granted "advanced status." It was a good start, but clearly not enough, especially now after the adoption of the new constitution. The advanced status was supposed to provide a framework for a deepening of the free trade area in order to unlock growth potential and consequently to raise living standards and to create jobs for a rapidly growing population. However, there are doubts that it might not be enough as an incentive.

The EU support is based on an assessment of the country's progress in building democracy and applies the "more for more" principle, which means that the more a country progresses in its democratic reforms and institutional building, the more support it can expect from the EU. However, there is not much to incentivize a country to undertake painful reforms. To be truly effective, "more for more" should be "much more money, for much more reform" in order to have an impact. It was the case with Central and Eastern European countries after the fall of the Berlin Wall.

EU membership prospects and huge financial aid enabled Central and Eastern European governments to have a clear vision and to implement the necessary reforms to resume growth and reinvigorate their economies. Only this prospect sustained the reformers in their efforts to overcome nationalist and other resistance and fears of change and modernization.

One of the weaknesses of the translation of EU successful experience from accession countries into the Neighborhood partners rests on the absence of the final "carrot." While developing countries are more dependent on EU aid and accession countries are prized for their efforts with final membership, the EU has much less to offer to the Mediterranean countries.

Tunisia should be "upgraded" and granted explicitly the "everything but institution"[2] status, and should become a member of the European Economic Area (EEA) after a transition period. The Agreement on the European Economic Area, which entered into force on January 1, 1994, brings together the EU Member States and the three EEA EFTA States—Iceland, Liechtenstein and Norway—in a single market, referred to as the "Internal Market." They share one single market, which is governed by the *acquis communautaire*. The single market entails all four freedoms: the free movement of persons, goods, services and capital. If a country has reached this level, it has come as close to the EU as it is possible to be without being a member.

This might take a long time for Tunisia. But it would help to carry out the necessary reforms and take the right measures because it would have an objective to aim at. And it would clearly bring mutual benefits, and consequently mutual incentives, to both the Union and its neighbors.

The main aim is to respond to the pressing socio-economic challenges that Tunisia and other countries in the Mediterranean region are facing and to support them in their transition to democracy.

The European Union should have a real strategy vis-à-vis the Mediterranean region in response to the Arab Spring. It is time for EU Member States to be bold, ambitious and coherent. EU must "give every incentive to countries in the region to make decisions that bring freedom and prosperity" and to "marshal its resources to act as a magnet for positive change in the region."

There is now growing hope that the forthcoming Italian Presidency of the EU will put the Mediterranean region at the center of its six-month program. This was highlighted by the Italian Premier Matteo Renzi during his visit to Tunis in March 2014. He also stated that

---

[2]"Everything but the institutions" was one of the slogans advanced by Romano Prodi who was President of the European Commission until November 2004.

"the Mediterranean will not be a border but the center of Europe." We thus hope that he will base his approach on the nature of existing challenges rather than on the instruments available.

The quality of the relations between Arab Spring countries and the EU should largely depend on the performance and the political will on either side on the basis of "shared principles and values." Therefore, if the EU's aim is genuinely to extend to its neighboring region a set of principles, values and standards that define its very essence, then it needs to upgrade substantially the nature of its partnership with the new Tunisia, enhance its interdependence with a changing Mediterranean region and identify the common interests and concerns that correspond to the demands of the people in the Mare Nostrum.

Further enhancement of the EU-Tunisia relationship will depend on Tunisia's commitment to actively pursuing the transition to democracy and clearly outlining and implementing reform to create jobs and achieve inclusive growth. The new European Commission, backed by EU Member States, will have to pursue its engagement to develop dialogue, explain better its incentive-based offer (everything but institutions) and explore options to foster regional integration in North Africa and improved access to the EU internal market.

U.S.-North Africa Trade and Development Agreement

> *Our message is simple: if you take the risks that reform entails, you will have the full support of the United States.*
>
> President Obama, *A Moment of Opportunity*, May 19, 2011

The Middle East and North Africa today is going through complex historical transformation, and demands greater diplomatic and economic American engagement.

The Arab Spring, Vali Nasr writes, was a ray of hope in a troubled region. But a brave call for freedom cannot alone change the reality of economic stagnation, social misery, and political frustration. Not without outside support.

The international community would have to come up with a new Marshall Plan to bring about change of that magnitude, and that requires American leadership, to rally donors, mobilize funds and convince the region's capitals to undertake the necessary economic reforms.

President Obama acknowledged it in his speech on the Arab Spring:

> Our support for these principles [human rights and democratic, peaceful demands for political freedom and economic opportunity, and legitimate aspirations of people] is a top priority and central to the pursuit of other interests in the region. The U.S. will marshal all our diplomatic, economic and strategic tools to support these principles.

The new Tunisia should be viewed by the U.S. as its best ally in the region to spread these principles, fight against terrorism and enhance trade exchanges. Tunisia should be seen as a free trade partner, as well as a model for democracy and modernity in the region. Ties between the U.S. and Tunisia could only increase after the very sad events that saw the storming of the U.S. embassy in Tunisia (and the torching of the American School) on September 14, 2012, as the two countries begin a Strategic Dialogue (announced by Secretary Kerry during his visit to Tunisia in February 2014) to identify issues and define modalities for greater collaboration.

What makes the Strategic Dialogue so important, especially at this time, is that it reflects the recognition of Tunisia's importance as a pillar of shared interests and values in a very challenging region.

As a short-term economic strategy, there is a need to set up a new form of U.S. trade preferences, exclusively for post-revolution countries, in addition to the already existing Generalized Systems of Preferences (GSP). It would expand North African exports to the U.S., increase foreign direct investment, and create new employment opportunities in North Africa.

However, a strategic partnership should go eventually beyond simply creating another set of trade preferences akin to the African Growth and Opportunity Act. That means setting up a U.S.-Tunisia Free Trade Agreement entailing trade liberalization on both sides, accompanied by a commitment in terms of financial assistance dedicated to building the physical and institutional infrastructure and creating the human capital to make the underlying trade agreement work.

It is one of the most effective ways the United States can offer support to Tunisia in this critical phase of transition to solidify democratic gains by expanding trade and commercial ties. Spurring faster economic growth through increased trade would bring the necessary resources for sustainable democratic development and prosperity in Tunisia, which counted the United States among its top five trading partners in 2010.

In 2012, U.S. Congressmen David Dreier, Gregory Meeks and Erik Paulsen introduced a bipartisan resolution (H. RES. 719, June 29, 2012) calling for a free trade agreement with Tunisia, and the Office of the U.S. Trade Representative relaunched the Trade and Investment Framework Agreement (TIFA) talks with Tunisia.

In the meantime, Tunisia must speed up reforms such as investment regulations, border controls, and other regulatory changes that could help facilitate trade between the U.S. and Tunisia. By taking some of these steps earlier on, Tunisia might get some of these trade benefits sooner than if they were wrapped into one large negotiation for a free trade agreement.

Further, the U.S.-Tunisia Strategic Dialogue provides both parties with opportunities for greater cooperation and collaboration on issues ranging from economic growth and jobs promotion to promoting the establishment of a Tunisia-U.S. Free Trade Agreement and a Millennium Challenge Corporation Compact. The first meeting, coming at a time of many transitions and challenges in the region, indicates the pivotal role that Tunisia does and can play as a leader in the region for democracy and development, as well recognition of the importance of the adoption of the new constitution.

The Strategic Dialogue should therefore:

- Enhance U.S. support for the ongoing political, social, legal, judicial, and economic reforms.

- Expand military-to-military exercises and training with Tunisia and increase opportunities for greater intelligence sharing.

- Assist and promote Tunisia's successful model of consensus building and religious tolerance to encourage moderation and peaceful dialogue in the Arab world.

- Commit to structure a trilateral U.S. relationship with Tunisia, as the anchor, and the region to boost political and economic security through greater regional integration.

- Support the need for additional economic reforms that will advance Tunisia's economic freedom and be able to fully reap the benefit of a U.S.–Tunisia FTA. This FTA would establish the basic underpinnings of market economies capable of pulling those in the informal sector into the formal sector and linking the countries of the region through linkages between local markets, with regional markets, and, eventually, to global markets. The goals of establishing those underpinnings would be twofold. The first is to provide assurance to potential investors. The second is to build a strong set of economic institutions that reinforce political pluralism.

It is important to have a successful model in North Africa for the other countries struggling with democratic reform. Tunisia could be a critical ally for the U.S. to help set up the comprehensive trade and investment partnership initiative with the Middle East and North Africa announced by President Obama on May 19, 2011. The commitment is part of a new approach to promoting democratic reform, economic development, and peace and security across this region, in the midst of significant changes.

President Obama said it will be the policy of the U.S. to promote political reform and support transitions to democracy across the MENA region. Because successful democratic transitions depend on an expansion of growth and broad-based prosperity, "the goal must be a model in which protectionism gives way to openness, the reins of commerce pass from the few to the many, and the economy generates jobs for the young. ... America's support for democracy will therefore be based on ensuring financial stability, promoting reform, and integrating competitive markets with each other and the global economy." This will need substantial financial means as well as innovative ideas such as the LEND (Leaders Engaged in New Democracies) Network which brings together key leaders from the world's newest democracies and the Network's advisors, through peer-to-peer exchanges, to facilitate constant exchange of knowledge and experience, with the vision that a global virtual forum for exchanging information and expertise on democratization shall support leaders as they work to build strong, accountable institutions and establish the rule of law.

Conclusion

Tunisia is a modern, pluralistic, civilized place. It is a moderate country that recognizes the equality between men and women and respects its minorities, and is recognized as such. The first Arab nominated for recognition as Righteous Among the Nations by Yad Vashem, Israel's official Holocaust memorial, is a Tunisian who risked his life to save Tunisian Jews from Nazi persecution in Mahdia (Tunisia), during World War II.

Tunisia's constitution is an important milestone to consolidate these characteristics and the foundation of a thriving democracy that strengthens the voices of those who are advocating for democracy, dignity and freedom in other MENA countries.

The new constitution goes even further than many in Western countries concerning the equality between female and male citizens in rights and duties as it enshrines the commitment of the State to ensure gender parity in all elected assemblies.

Tunisia remains a source of inspiration for people across the MENA region. It stands as an example of what dialogue and compromise can achieve. And it reminds us that despite all the challenges and the uncertainties of change, a better future is still very much within reach.

However, Tunisia's lagging economy and threatened security must be addressed or they will risk derailing the democratic transition, putting an end to the Arab Awakening. The EU and the U.S. should therefore enable joint policy approaches and new instruments to support the country (at least) proportionally to its already substantial achievements.

Furthermore, the EU-U.S. trade deal, known as the Transatlantic Trade and Investment Partnership, or TTIP, will bring additional opportunities for Tunisia and thus, this is an additional incentive for a transatlantic cooperation that would enable Tunisia to fully benefit from the TTIP. Increased trade between the two economic giants will raise demand for raw materials, components and other inputs produced by Tunisia and the other Mediterranean countries.

Therefore, the debate on the strategic vision to be adopted by Tunisia should be launched immediately and engage the different sub-regions (that have been marginalized for too long) as well as the youth whose economic futures are at stake—both their job prospects and the debt they will have to repay if the transition fails.

Chapter Two

Libya Deserves Better

Ghazi Ben Ahmed and Adel Awni Dajani

The Libyan Constitution aimed at democracy and the respect for human liberties. Some might object that it contains articles more suitable for the highly developed democratic countries. Therefore, they argue, this Constitution does not suit the Libyan people at this stage of their development. I do not share this opinion. For, when the newly independent people are governed under a constitution, it is wise to widen the scope of their political activities and not to restrict it.

Adrian Pelt, UN Commissioner for Libya, in an article that appeared in the newspaper *Barqa Algadida*, December 25, 1953

Undertaking such wide ranging reforms is primarily the responsibility of the countries themselves. It will require difficult choices and trade offs often for new government keen to deliver on past promises, but faced with limited resources. But given the magnitude of the problems, domestic efforts and resources alone are not sufficient. Therefore, it is very important that the region and the international community at large rally to support domestic efforts.

Nemat Shafik, Deputy Managing Director, IMF, May 10, 2012

Libya is on the brink of a precipice. Its politicians and both the Interim Parliament and the Acting Government have failed: They have talked the talk but not walked the walk and have been guided by narrow self-interest rather than national interest.

Gross mismanagement and incompetence in dealing with the security and economic challenges have now combined in a perfect storm, causing the country to face for the first time severe liquidity problems compounded by armed militias controlling the economic pulse of the country. Nothing better illustrates this point than the recent debacle over the North Korean ship loading illegally the country's only national liquid asset and sailing into international waters amidst feeble excuses by the Government blaming adverse weather conditions! The Libyan population has been patiently observing this façade, but is now angry and clamoring for action: security in its cities, empowerment of the army and police and an economic policy to tackle both the short term and long term challenges of daily life in Libya from electricity black-outs, shortages of fuel to basic needs for infrastructure, housing, health and education.

In the absence of a unifying vision, Libya is heading into a zero-sum battle for oil wealth among militias, with a very high risk of negative spillovers to the region via renewed conflict and smuggling, and to the world via disruption of hydrocarbon production, massive migration and terrorism.

A deadlock situation needs decisive action and bold initiatives to build modern institutions, repair infrastructure, and diversify the economy.

The Need for an Honest Broker for the Resolution of the Political and Security Impasse

Rationale for UN Mediation

The Libyan people want revolutionary change that requires dramatic reforms in order to break the zero-sum politics of factions fighting for national resources. Success depends on leadership and consensus building. The Tunisian model may not apply in the Libyan case, but doing nothing is not a solution and at least Libya can learn from the Tunisian experience.

Tunisia also faced the precipice, but unlike Libya, where the previous regime made it a state policy of not building institutions, Tunisia did have state institutions: a functioning state bureaucracy, a functioning judicial system, powerful trade unions and a relatively educated population with professional confederations. When it was clear that the Tunisian politicians, whether Islamists or liberals, would face the wrath of the people and an economic meltdown, both competing parties were guided both by self-preservation and national interest. In this process they were actively assisted by a coalition of the trade unions and representatives of civil society that knocked politicians' heads together and brought up a consensus for the way forward, namely the establishment of a government of competences.

In the Libyan case, a neutral and trusted leadership is needed to tackle the short-term challenges of managing the political transition, normalizing the security situation, and addressing the severe institutional capacity constraints. A possible solution would be a coalition headed by the United Nations, a solution that was already tested successfully more than 60 years ago. The UN mission in 1950 headed by the Dutch diplomat and Assistant Secretary-General of the United Nations Adrian Pelt supervised the formulation of the constitution. On December 24, 1951, Libya was proclaimed an independent and sovereign state with King Idris as the first monarch of a unified and federal Libya. Adrian Pelt became very popular in Libya because of his success in bringing together the peoples and tribes from Tripolitania and Cyrenaica, administered by the British, and the French-administered territory of Fezzan to form a new state and to draw up a constitution with his help.

The UN High Commissioner for Libya would be helped by selected representatives of Libyan civil society and professional associations who must be mandated and empowered by the Parliament for the selection of an emergency government of national competence. A working committee of representatives from the Islamic, liberal and independent parties together with Libyan civil society and professional associations under the chairmanship of the UN and endorsement by the Parliament would then need to be urgently constituted. The committee would be given a deadline for the appointment of a new government and the criteria would be independent Libyan technocrats not belonging to any political party and with proven technical competences, and the key prioritization would be security and the economy.

The success of the Tunisian model and the processes used would serve as a model, although there are obviously specificities for the Libyan case. The Tunisian political precedent of involving the civil society and the population at large in the debate on the nature of the country and the constitution was the right priority. This model needs to be followed in Libya and this kind of popular and engaging debate on the nature of the country and constitution is a much more effective national strategy than superficial popular elections for a President, which are scheduled in Libya for the summer of 2014.

National Reconciliation Conference

Simultaneously and also under the auspices of the UN and representatives of Libyan civil society and professional associations, there needs to be convened a National Reconciliation Conference for the settlement of all outstanding matters including displaced people inside and abroad. For example, the dispute between the people of Misrata and the people of Tawergha needs to be resolved. The main goals of the conference would be to agree on the basic principles of citizenship and equality, which can be done with the help of the UN, and other countries that have experienced change through armed conflict and succeeded in reaching political stability by use of a national reconciliation plan.

There are many country precedents for national reconciliation processes, and perhaps the South African model can be an appropriate one to which Libyans can relate. However the critical point is the need for an honest broker, as otherwise the exercise is academic and will lead nowhere. The UN can provide a multilateral and historical legitimacy for the exercise.

Security and Disarmament

The need for security is paramount in stabilizing the country and is a *sine qua non* for any economic resurgence. All the governments since the revolution have postponed taking decisive action to disarm the militias and the public at large, and to empower the Army, which has been neglected as a working force for mostly political reasons. This is a national priority, which has public endorsement; and the "carrot," in spite of any inflationary effects, needs to be financial.

Libya needs to have a special tribunal (criminal court) to judge any violation of the basic human rights, similar to the one formed in the Hague for the former Yugoslavia.

There have been numerous road maps setting out in details the steps that need to be taken but again this seems to be highly unlikely to be achieved without international support and without the UN auspices. In relation to the proposed government of competences, the posts for the Ministers of Defense and Interior should be strictly based on technical merit and credibility.

Economic Vision for a United Libya

Over the medium term, and once the country is stabilized, the authorities will have to address issues including the capacity to build institutions, improving the quality of education, rebuilding infrastructure, putting in place an efficient social safety net, financial market development, and reducing hydrocarbon dependency through private sector-led growth.

Libya is dependent on hydrocarbons, which account for over 65 percent of GDP and 96 percent of revenue. To quell discontent, the Gaddafi regime used oil revenues to provide grants and expand subsidies. This policy has been continued and expanded since the Revolution with a common mantra by the politicians in charge being "let's pay to solve problems." The total wage bill for the 2013 fiscal year is around LD 22 billion and with the decrease of the daily oil production to less than 200,000 barrels from a high of 1.6 million barrels after the Revolution, Libya is facing an acute liquidity problem which needs immediate fixes as the security and economic problems have become interlinked and this is a combustible combination. Again the mantra that Libya is rich needs to be adjusted to say Libya is asset rich but cash poor!

As of year-end 2010, unemployment was 13.5 percent with youth unemployment estimated at 25 to 30 percent, according to the 2013 IMF Article IV Consultation Concluding Statement. It further indicates that the lack of employment opportunities for nationals can be traced back to a mismatch between the skills of workers and the demands of the private sector, as well as insufficient labor productivity, which limits demand for Libyan workers. In this connection, the authorities agreed with the mission that private sector investment is necessary to sustainably create employment opportunities.

Against this backdrop, Libya needs an economic vision that calls for economic diversification to create employment opportunities in the private sector and reduce hydrocarbon dependency. This economic vision that will bring sustainable and inclusive growth should not be implemented by politicians but by a technocratic and apolitical team comprising the Ministries of Economy, Finance and the Chairman of the Central Bank of Libya. The economy of a country like Libya is not difficult to fix, but needs a clear strategy and prioritization.

Several factors could provide the necessary means to dynamically improve the economy. For instance, the banks in Libya have enormous liquidity and the deposits of the commercial banks with the Central Bank of Libya amount to a total of LD 35.6 billion as of March 31, 2013. The cost of capital to the banks is virtually nil, but there is a clear problem in the banking intermediation process in Libya, which has been inherited from the Gaddafi era. The country has one of the lowest loan deposit ratios in the MENA area and this liquidity has not been channeled into lending, which would be a huge boost to the economy and be the beginning of a public-private partnership. However, before this can take place, the impediments that are preventing the Libyan banks from playing the role of financial intermediation need to be fixed, such as:

- The closure of the Property Registry and the urgent need for structural reform of the whole property ownership in Libya. As during Gaddafi's time, the property land registry was burnt, and there were laws that banned renting and gave legal rights to squatters and only permitted one home for each family, i.e., fairly draconian property laws. In addition, mass nationalization of property assets took place; and therefore, given this state of affairs, banks are very reluctant to lend, as title deeds are often forged and the real ownership of property assets is difficult to ascertain;

- The need to establish a centralized Credit Bureau;

- The need for a government guarantee to the banks for local SME lending;

- The rush to Islamic banking curtailing the lending appetite of the banks with the process being politically rather than economically driven. This "rush" follows a move of the Parliament, which passed a law effective next year banning all banking not in accordance to Islamic law;

- The lack of an interbank market and the nonexistence of capital markets, which could also channel the liquidity into productive sectors of the economy, as there is no interbank lending in Libyan dinars between the banks.

The economic legacy of the Gaddafi era will take time to unravel, but there needs to be a vision and a game plan. Ambitious plans for the free convertibility of the Libyan dinar should be an objective over the mid-term, but in the interim, concrete steps need to be taken to make the private sector a stakeholder in the development of the country with Libyan banks and capital markets playing a meaningful role in the process.

Regional Integration

The Maghreb Union is another example where the politicians have been unable to implement a clear popular clamor for closer regional integration. In the case of Libya, a step-by-step approach towards closer integration with neighboring Tunisia has obvious synergies for both countries.

Several elements are in favor of an enhanced relationship between Libya and Tunisia. A semi-skilled and skilled workforce, a cultural and historical affinity, two-way trade and investment flows, and most recently the revolutions of January 14 and February 17, 2011 and the post-revolutionary era.

Economic integration will widen the range of traded goods, enhance the local impact of trade and will affect positively employment, particularly among the youth, who are the most likely to take up the challenges if equipped with adequate skills. Trade expansion and diversification need to be accompanied by increased overall investment in the informal economy as well, and especially in the border regions. The informal economy engages a large portion of the working population in Libya and Tunisia, including unskilled and young people. The need to create productive employment throughout all sectors of the economy represents a real challenge but also an important opportunity if ways can be found for the young to contribute effectively to development.

Privileged economic integration between Libya and Tunisia will contribute to producing the desirable outcomes that are difficult for individual countries to achieve on their own. Enhanced competition, trade, and productivity can result from creating a rules-based preferential regional market conducive to export diversification, economies of scale, greater specialization, productivity enhancement, attraction of foreign direct investment, and generation of national and regional investment. Most importantly, successful integration between Libya and Tunisia will pave the way for Maghreb regional integration, which would be an effective tool to deal with the vulnerabilities created by greater openness, such as the contagion of financial crises and large fluctuations in commodity prices. In addition, regional integration is increasingly perceived as part of the solution to long-standing development problems across a wide range of sectors, such as value-added upgrading, infrastructure and acquisition of skills for entrepreneurship and employment.

The weight of commercial exchange between Tunisia and Libya has been intensified during the political tensions in Libya and confirm once again how regional integration can play a leading role in increasing trade potential for the two countries. However, the increasing exports to Libya have not been only positive, as it has been a source of high inflation that may be increased with the expected flows of Tunisian workers to Libya. Given the high degree of linkages between the two economies, analyzing the impact of a Free Trade Agreement between Tunisia and Libya would be useful.

Safety and security of the borders between Tunisia and Libya are also important because these would facilitate investment and entrepreneurship on the border regions and beyond that the return of expatriate workers. Security of the borders may require the establishment of joint military task forces between Libya and Tunisia aided if necessary by multilateral specialists.

Sustainable growth requires a business environment that is conducive to private sector development and practical issues, which will further deepen the regional integration, such as the issuance of IDs for border crossings and easing the lengthy border crossings (to wit, security issues), bank convertibility of Tunisian and Libyan currency, ability and ease of citizens to invest and purchase property and to work freely in either country, and tariff-free borders for goods. On the investment side, the establishment in the border region of joint projects between the Libyan and Tunisian private sector has to be encouraged, such as a private hospital for instance. For example, given the acute shortage of hospitals in Libya, a state-of-the-art hospital managed by a specialized hospital management company would be an excellent beginning of cooperation between the future generations of Libyans and Tunisians. The role of both governments in these kinds of projects should be minimized and should be limited to facilitation and providing the proper legal and fiscal environment.

Given its abundant resources, Libya does not need financial assistance, but rather technical assistance to build capacity and better manage its wealth. Initiatives such as Leaders Engaged in New Democracies (LEND) help address priorities identified by countries that are in the midst of promising transitions. Tunisia and Moldova were selected as the first two countries to participate in the initiative, but Libya could be invited as an observer and eventually become a member of the LEND network. The government has already requested assistance in reforming the system of untargeted subsidies.

Conclusion

Libya will need to build its institutions and respond to the demands and aspirations of its population. To achieve this, Libya needs to diversify its economy away from oil dependence and thus create an enabling business environment that will facilitate private sector–led growth and job creation.

Enhanced economic integration and cooperation with Tunisia could help unleash Libya's huge economic potential by promoting greater inclusiveness and transparency, as well as enhanced governance. Moreover, it could pave the way for Maghreb regional integration and leverage the region's inherent strengths: a dynamic and young population, abundant wealth (oil and gas and phosphates), as well as an attractive destination for eco-tourism.

The Libyan public has been incredibly patient suffering for 42 years under the dictatorship of Gadhafi and now enduring the instability of the post-revolutionary era. Let that patience not be tested to its breaking point. The Libyans deserve a much better future.

Chapter Three

An Alternative for Improving Human Security in the Middle East and North Africa

Aylin Ünver Noi

The Arab uprisings indicated that people are seeking human rights and democracy that has been lacking in the Middle East and North Africa (MENA) for decades. Yet the post-Arab Spring developments did not help to change human security conditions. Polarization in the societies and the violence spreading in the region have further jeopardized human security in the MENA region. In this article, the Council of Europe, which is guardian of those rights and developments in the MENA region focusing on the concept of "human security," will be evaluated in order to find an answer to the following question: Is it possible to improve human security conditions by establishing a "Council of MENA" or expanding membership of the Council of Europe to the MENA countries?

Council of Europe: Guardian of Human Rights and Democracy

Although documents asserting individual rights go back to the *Magna Carta* (1215) and the English Bill of Rights (1689), the idea of human rights, which is closely related to natural rights, were conceptualized by the Enlightenment philosopher and political theorist, John Locke (1632–1704) as natural and inalienable rights given to men by God that government could not take away.[1,2] Locke advocated the view that men have rights by their nature, and natural rights of the people should be protected by the government.[3] His ideas, which are

---

[1]Patterson, John (2004). *The Bill of Rights: Politics, Religion, and the Quest for Justice*, Universe Inc., p. 52.

[2]The *Magna Carta* limited powers of the King to tax and issue fines by those who were being governed. English Bill of Right is one of the significant charters of English liberty which eliminated the methods kings used to suppress Parliament. The English Bill of Right promoted the God-given rights of English speaking people. Patterson, *op. cit.*, p. 1, p. 40.

[3]Patterson, *op. cit.*, p. 52.

the basis of human rights and classic liberalism, are still used to pro-claim moral inviolability of men in the face of oppressive government today.[4]

The idea of human rights, which underlay the American Declara-tion of Independence in 1776 and the French Declaration of the Rights of Man and of the Citizen in 1789, re-emerged and developed strength after the Second World War following the experiences of Nazism and Fascism.[5] The calls for human rights standards to protect citizens from abuses by their governments gained enormous impor-tance. The International Bill of Human Rights: the 1948 Universal Declaration of Human Rights and the two international covenants, on Civil and Political Rights and on Economic, Social and Cultural Rights are the basic international framework for the protection of human rights declared after the Second World War. The Genocide Convention and the Convention against Torture are other important treaties in terms of human rights. Yet committees monitoring their implementation cannot force a state to comply.[6]

The idea of establishment of a Council of Europe was first voiced by the Prime Minister of the United Kingdom, Winston Churchill on a radio broadcast at the time of Second World War. He repeated his view on the establishment of a "United States of Europe" in a speech he made at Zurich University in 1946. The major reason lying behind his idea was not only to provide a reconciliation among the people of Europe that would prevent the re-emergence of a conflict, but also to protect individuals in the continent by establishing common institu-tions, standards and agreements. The Council of Europe thus was established on May 5, 1949 by 10 countries to develop democratic principles based on the European Convention on Human Rights (1950) and other reference texts on the protection of individuals throughout Europe. The Council of Europe has 47 members today.

---

[4]Simmons, A. John (1983). "Inalienable Rights and Locke's Treatises," *Philosophy and Public Affairs*, Vol.12, No. 3, p. 175.

[5]The Declaration of the Rights of Man (1789) has the goal of granting individuals natural, sacred and inalienable human rights—freedom, property, safety and right to resist oppres-sion. Yale Law School (2008). *Declaration of the Rights of Men-1789*, The Avalon Project Doc-uments in Law, History and Diplomacy.

[6]Smith, Karen E. (2003). *European Union Foreign Policy in a Changing World*, Cambridge: Polity, p. 98.

The European Convention of Human Rights (ECHR) lays down a number of civil and political rights, including freedom from torture and slavery to freedom of religion and expression. Under the ECHR, an individual can file a complaint against his or her own state alleging violations of the convention. Contrary to other international treaties on human rights, the judgment of the European Court of Human Rights is binding on the state. All EU member states that ratified the ECHR indicated their willingness to protect human rights strongly. This reflects the need for making human rights issues that happen within state boundaries subject to international scrutiny.[7]

Human Security

The concept of human security, which was first introduced in the United Nations Development Program's (UNDP) 1994 Human Development Report, is closely related to the respect for human rights and for democratization.[8] In contrast to earlier state-centered security understanding, which focuses on protection of the state, the concept of human security emphasizes the protection of individuals. It comprises everything that is "empowering" for individuals: human rights, including economic social and cultural rights, access to education and health care, equal opportunities, good governance, etc.[9] Extreme poverty, inequalities among and within countries, environmental damage, pandemics, discriminations, and human rights violations, which transcend national frontiers, cannot be handled by traditional military security understanding. Hence, the military conception of security had been superseded by a global conception of the democratic security of populations.[10]

Despite the debates among scholars, there is no real consensus reached on what should constitute the focus of human security studies, which led to three distinct conceptions of human security. The first conception of human security is related to the basic individual rights to

---

[7]Smith, *op. cit.*, p. 99.

[8]UNDP (1994). *Human Development Report 1994*, New York & Oxford: Oxford University Press.

[9]UNESCO (2008). *Human Security: Approaches and Challenges*, p. 3.

[10]Ibid., p.xiv; p. xviii.

life, liberty and the international obligation of the states to protect those rights.[11] The second conception of human security is humanitarian, which focuses on international efforts to deepen and strengthen international law, particularly related to genocide and war crimes, and to abolish weapons that are harmful for civilians and non-combatants.[12] It is mostly related to humanitarian interventions directed at improving the basic living conditions of refugees.[13] The third conception of human security suggests that human security should include economic, environmental, social and other forms of harm to the overall livelihood and wellbeing of individuals, in contrast to the other two conceptions, which focus on basic human rights and their deprivations.[14]

The emergence of the concept of human security reflects the impact of values and norms on international relations. Human security argues that there is an ethical responsibility to reorient security around the individual. Not only the emergence of new threats, which led to international norms and values superseding national ones, but also targets became global.[15] A transition from a security that has been identified solely with defense issues to a multidimensional human security based on the respect for all human rights and democratic principles has been realized. Some steps were decided to be taken for contributing to sustainable development and especially to the eradication of extreme poverty, which is a denial of all human rights. Furthermore, steps for reinforcing prevention at the root of different forms of violence, discrimination, conflict and internal strife, mainly on civilian populations in all regions of the world were taken.[16] There has been

---

[11]Morsink, Johannes (1998). *The Universal Declaration of Human Rights*, University Park: University of Pennsylvania Press; Lauren, Paul Gordon (1998). *The Evolution of Human International Rights*, University Park: University of Pennsylvania Press; Alston, Phillip (1992). The Commission on Human Rights in Phillip Alston (Ed.) *The United Nations and Human Rights*. Oxford: Clarendon.

[12]Hampson, Fen Osler (2008). *Human Security*, in *Security Studies: An Introduction*, Paul D. Williams (Ed.) New York: Routledge, p. 279.

[13]Kaldor, Mary. (2007). *Human Security: Reflections on Globalization and Intervention*, Cambridge and Malden: Polity Press.

[14]Hampson, *op. cit.*, p. 280.

[15]Newman, Edward. (2001). *Human Security and Constructivism*, International Studies Perspectives, Vol. 2, p. 242.

[16]UNESCO, *op. cit.*, p.xx, p. xxi.

an internationalization of ethical standards that has increasingly impinged upon "national" laws and norms.[17]

As a result of these developments, forms of government, human rights and gender equality have all become international issues. Democracy is no longer an issue confined to territorially enclosed communities. The human needs and rights that comprise human security are slowly becoming part of decision-making relating to security. People's awareness and expectations of rights has an impact. Similarly, people's expectations and attitudes toward governance and authority have evolved.[18] In the following section, the first two conceptions of human security related to basic human rights and their deprivations in the MENA region, particularly focusing on the post-Arab Spring developments, will be evaluated.

The Arab Spring and Human Security

The Arab uprisings, which commenced with the "Jasmine Revolution" in Tunisia on December 17, 2010, following the self-immolation of Mohammad Bouazizi, indicated that people of this region are seeking human dignity, human rights, fundamental freedoms and democracy that has been lacking in the Middle East and North Africa for decades. In other words, the Arab uprisings were prompted by the same universal values such as fundamental freedoms, human rights, dignity and equality that are upheld by the Council of Europe and shared by its member states. Free and fair elections followed some of the uprisings. As stated by Mignon, free and fair elections do not on their own guarantee the success of democratic transition. Consensus on constitutional reform, promoting equality between men and women, empowerment of women both in the public and private sphere, ensuring respect for human rights including personal freedoms and against the risk of religious fundamentalism, protecting the rights of religious minorities, freedom of the media, fighting corruption, empowering civil society, and fighting terrorism are *sine qua non* of the success of democratic transition.[19]

---

[17]Newman, *op. cit.*, p. 242.

[18]Ibid.

[19]Mignon, Jean-Claude (2012). *Conclusions of the President of the Parliamentary Assembly*, European Conference of Presidents of Parliament, Strasbourg, 20–21 September 2012, p. 4.

The right of all citizens to be represented in the political decision-making process as well as the representativity of elected bodies are core principles of democracies. Political composition of the electorate as well as other significant aspects like gender, ethnicity or other group identities, including age or specific vulnerability, should be reflected in an elected assembly. The legitimacy of a democratic system depends upon the conviction of all sections of society. These sections should have adequate access to decision-making institutions. Excluding sections of the population from the right to be represented is detrimental to a democratic system.[20]

As stated in Resolution 1888[21] of the Parliamentary Assembly of the Council of Europe, "Sound states are based on strong democracies. Strong democracies are possible with the inclusion of direct democratic elements designed to increase citizens' participation as well as the promotion of active citizenship."[22] Accordingly, sound states should be guided by the public interest and capable of maintaining a high level of trust amongst their citizens, need to be made strong against the abuse of political, administrative or judicial power, unethical behaviour such as corruption, favoritism and undue influence by the media or interest groups. If a state cannot achieve these, citizens' confidence in decision-makers will further decrease.[23]

Egyptian President Hosni Mubarak's authoritarian regime, which had been charged with corruption, human rights abuses, implementation of a state of emergency for decades, and anti-democratic acts such as restriction on opposition parties, ended with his overthrow. The democratically elected government of Mohammed Morsi came to power in Egypt in the post-Arab Spring era. However, Egyptians experienced decreasing confidence in their new leader after Morsi's effort to enhance his power by initiating legislation that would put

---

[20]Parliamentary Assembly, Doc.12107 (2010). *Thresholds and Other Features of Electoral Systems Which Have an Impact on Representativity of Parliaments in Council of Europe Member States*, Parliamentary Assembly, Political Affairs Committee, Rappoteur: Henrik Daems, Alliance of Liberals and Democrats for Europe.

[21]Parliamentary Assembly, Resolution 1888 (2012). *The Crisis of Democracy and the Role of the State in Today's Europe.*

[22]Ibid.

[23]Ibid.

him above the rule of law. Moreover, closing ears to Christians', liberals' and women's demands during the constitution drafting process in Egypt led to disappearance of a nationwide consensus, which is vital to the success of a pluralistic representative democracy.

According to the Muslim leaders Sheikh Muhammad al-Ghazali and Sheikh Yusuf al-Qaradawi of Egypt and Rashid al-Ghanouchi of Tunisia, prevention of arbitrary rule and making government accountable, protection of the rights of minorities, protection of the citizens from the abuse of power by government, holding free elections, peaceful transition of power are among the universal principles which are also must be respected under an Islamic democracy.[24] Despite the claims of Muslim leaders who advocated the compatibility of Islam and democracy, tactical alliances of the Muslim Brotherhoods on some issues in practice led to criticism of the "Salafization of the Muslim Brotherhood" which means less room for human rights, women's rights and minority rights.

Lowering the marriage age for girls to nine or ten and attempts to de-criminalize female genital mutilation (FGM) in Egypt after years of efforts to pass a ban on FGM are some examples to those backwards steps lawmakers attempted to take. Women who fought for their freedoms during the uprisings still have continued to face an increasing number of threats to their security in the post-Arab Spring era. Harassing women for their style of dress, attacking secular intellectuals, assaulting women activists verbally and physically, beating women wearing short dresses in the countries of the MENA region in the post-Arab Spring era are some examples of increasing Salafi violence against women in the region.[25]

Since the Egyptian Revolution, religious minorities' role, and particularly Coptic Christians' role within the governance of the nation has dwindled further, and violence against them has increased, although Coptic Christians joined with Muslims in Tahrir Square to overthrow Mubarak. Moves made to introduce Islamic-based laws into Egyptian society have further isolated Coptic Christians. Moreover,

---

[24]Dorraj, Manuchehr. (2002) *Islam, Governance and Democracy*, in *Human Rights and Religion: A Reader*, Liam Gearon (Ed.), Brighton & Oregon: Sussex Academic Press, p. 149.

[25]Marwan, Asma (2012). *Tunisian Women Slapped by Salafists for Wearing Trousers and Skirts.*

the Coptic Christians' participation in the removal of President Morsi by military coup d'état made them victims of Sunni reprisals through violent attacks to their churches, houses and businesses.[26]

The assassinations of Chokri Belaid and Mohammed Brahmi, the political leaders of secular opposition parties in Tunisia, and increasing Salafi threats to people's freedoms are some of the developments that occurred in Tunisia in the post-Arab Spring era, leading to a decrease in citizens' confidence in the ruling party, Ennahda, and mass anti-governmental protests in the streets of Tunisia. Ennahda was accused of not protecting secular politicians and allowing the rise of armed Salafists and Ansar al-Sharia in Tunisia.

The question of whether these Arab uprisings represent a step forward or backward for human rights and democracy came to the agenda because of marginalization of those rights by some fundamentalist religious political groups and their efforts to impose their own variant of totalitarianism under the pretext of protecting Islamic sanctity and truth in the post-Arab Spring era.[27] *Sharia* law thus as a source of legislation became a contentious issue between Islamists and liberals/secularists/Christians. People in Tunisia and Egypt were disappointed with the newly elected Islamist governments, owing to their failure to implement economic, social and political reforms intended to increase the welfare of the public and liberties.[28]

Similar and even worse experiences have been experienced by the people of Libya and Syria. The uprising in Syria began similarly to other uprisings but turned into a civil war. Tens of thousands of Syrians have died, tens of thousands of protestors have been imprisoned and tortured, hundreds of thousands became refugees, and millions of Syrians were left in poor living conditions as a result of this war, which also has transnational effects. The involvement of *jihadist* and Al Qaeda affiliated groups in the civil war in Syria radicalized and complicated the situation in Syria.

---

[26]Benham, Peter (2013) *Christians in the Middle East and Their Fate in the "Post Arab Spring World*," Conflict & Security.

[27]Dorraj, *op. cit.*, p. 154.

[28]Kienle, Eberhard (2013). *The Security Implications of the Arab Spring*, Geneva Center for Security Policy, p. 20.

The Libyan assembly voted to make *sharia* law the foundation of all legislation and state institutions in the country despite the secular-leaning National Front Alliance, which called for a more liberal position. This step has the potential to deteriorate the chaotic transition period in Libya.

Democratic transition in the MENA region was frustrated by increasing authoritarian tendencies of democratically elected governments. Disappointment of the people in the post-Arab Spring era led to a new wave of anti-governmental protests. The Arab Spring that made democratic elections possible in the MENA region turned into an anti-democratic form through the military coup d'état and toppling of Mohammed Morsi in Egypt, and call for the resignation of the democratically elected ruling party, Ennahda in Tunisia.

Furthermore, the outbreaks of clan, community, sectarian and street fighting in Libya and Yemen, and civil war in Syria which led to an increasing number of refugees lacking humanitarian conditions, Islamic radicalization and terrorism, sectarian conflicts, polarization of societies as secular versus Islamist, Salafist versus Sufi, Muslims versus Christians, discrimination against women and minorities, which all represent principal threats to human security, became prevalent instead of the realization of pluralistic representative democracies in the MENA region. Contrary to the expectations of the people, post-Arab Spring developments did not help to change human security conditions. Moreover, increasing polarization in the societies and the violence spread in the region have further jeopardized human security in the MENA region.

Council of Europe in the MENA Region

In the post-Arab Spring era, the Council of Europe followed the developments in the MENA region and put some effort into preventing human rights violations. Following the violence against Christians in the Middle East, the Council of Europe took the following measures to hinder these violations against Christians living in the region. The Parliamentary Assembly of the Council of Europe called on the European Union to enhance its monitoring of the situation of Christians and other religious communities in its political dialogue with the countries of the Middle East and to link its European Neighborhood Policy, including financial aid, to the degree of human rights protection and awareness in those countries.[29]

Moreover, following the countries of the MENA's interest in strengthening cooperation with the Council of Europe, the Council of Europe as an organization has worked with countries from the MENA region for many years and launched the "South Programme" in January 2012 in order to identify priority lines of cooperation. Hence, this joint programme, also known as "Strengthening Democratic Reform in the Southern Neighborhood" was initiated by the Council of Europe and the European Union.[30]

This joint program focuses on the following objectives:

1. To enhance efficiency and independence of the judiciary by improving courts' performance and by facilitating judicial reform, using as a reference relevant Council of Europe standards.

2. To promote good governance through increased prevention of corruption and money laundering on the basis of the relevant Council of Europe standards, mechanisms and instruments, and to improve the basic framework for regional cooperation.

3. To strengthen and protect human rights, in particular through the prevention and control of trafficking in human beings in line with the provisions of the Council of Europe Convention on Action Against Trafficking in Human Beings and other international standards.

4. To promote democratic values in the region, building on the Council of Europe's existing networks such as those developed by the North-South Centre, the Youth Department, the Pompidou Group, the Venice Commission, the School of Political Studies and the Parliamentary Assembly of the Council of Europe.[31]

---

[29]Parliamentary Assembly, Recommendation 1957 (2011). *Violence Against Christians in the Middle East*, Parliamentary Assembly of the Council of Europe.

[30]Council of Europe and European Union Joint Programme. *Strengthening Democratic Reform in the Southern Neighborhood.*

[31]Ibid.

The areas of cooperation with the countries in the Southern Neighborhood are decided in accordance with the specific needs expressed by each country, with reference to shared values of human rights, the rule of law and democracy. Some activities were planned for implementation over the period 2012 to 2014 throughout the region.[32] In comparison to other initiatives, this initiative has a tailor-made approach to the countries of the North Africa. Given the reactions of the Council of Europe to the developments in the MENA region and its joint actions with the European Union, it is significant to mention the EU's foreign policy in the MENA region and its limits in the post-Arab Spring era. The following section focuses on these areas.

Democracy and Human Rights Promotion Efforts in the EU Foreign Policy

The promotion of respect for human rights in third countries is one of the objectives of the EU's foreign policy. The EU assumes that the protection of human rights and democracy is a distinctive feature of the EU's international identity.[33] As a part of this understanding, protection of human rights has been included as a significant goal of the EU's foreign policy since the 1990s. The Council, Commission and European Parliament set up committees or working groups to monitor human rights situations in third countries.[34]

The EU applies sanctions on third countries that abuse human rights and democracy. Its weakest form is to condemn violations of human rights in common declarations, which is the traditional tool of the EU's Common Foreign and Security Policy (CFSP). The other forms of sanctions and coercive measures that the EU applies are diplomatic sanctions, arms embargoes and approving military interventions to end human rights abuses. The EU uses its financed pro-

---

[32]Ibid.

[33]Panebianco, Stefania (2006). "The Constraints on EU Action as a 'Norm Exporter' in the Mediterranean." In *The European Union's Roles in International Politics: Concepts and Analysis*, Ole Elgström and Michael Smith (eds.), London & New York: Routledge, p. 137.

[34]Sedelmeier, Ulrich (2006). "The EU's Role as a Promoter of Human Rights and Democracy: Enlargement Policy Practice and Role Formation." In *The European Union's Role in International Politics: Concepts and Analysis*, Ole Elgström & Michael Smith (eds.) London and New York: Routledge, p. 119.

grams designed to promote human rights to achieve this end. The EU also uses asymmetrical interdependence to attach conditions related to democracy and human rights to its offers of membership or trade agreements with third countries.[35]

However, as stated by Balfour,[36] promoting human rights and democracy issues even in the EU's neighbors was not so simple due to different member states' opposite policies or the EU's hesitance or fear that these acts further leads to the emergence of new ruling governments with anti-democratic and anti-EU agendas.[37] Moreover, promoting human rights in third countries could undermine other fundamental norms: sovereignty, inviolability and non-interference in the domestic affairs of other states.[38] One of the main challenges confronting the promotion of human security is that it may be perceived as a means of intervention of the developed nations in the affairs of developing ones as an imposition of Western values upon other sets of values.[39] The underlying suspicion the concept represents a Western agenda, centered as it is on such liberal values and approaches as human rights and humanitarian intervention, while giving short shrift to regional economic and developmental priorities.[40] Universality of human rights is another criticism on this issue.[41]

Despite these critics, the EU aims to export to third countries the EU-principled norms that inspired the EU's creation—democracy, the rule of law, the universality and indivisibility of human rights and fundamental freedoms, respect for human dignity, equality and solidarity, and respect for the principles of the United Nations (UN) Charter and international law.[42] Kagan describes the EU's role in world poli-

---

[35]Ibid.

[36]Balfour, Rosa (2007). *Promoting Human Rights and Democracy in the EU's Neighborhood: Tools, Strategies and Dilemmas.* In *Reassesing the European Neighborhood Policy,* R. Balfour and A. Missiroli (eds.), Brussels: European Policy Center.

[37]Ünver Noi, Aylin (2013). Introduction. In *Islam and Democracy: Perspectives on the Arab Spring,* Aylin Ünver Noi (ed.), New Castle: Cambridge Scholars Publishing, p. 1.

[38]Smith, *op. cit.,* p. 98.

[39]UNESCO, *op. cit.,* p. 4.

[40]Ibid.

[41]Smith, *op. cit.,* p. 98.

[42]Panebianco, *op. cit.,* p. 137.

tics: "Europe is turning away from power, or it is moving beyond power into a self-contained world of laws and rules and transnational negotiation and cooperation. It is entering a post-historical paradise of peace and relative prosperity, the realization of Kant's perpetual peace."[43] The EU aims to promote norms and values in the international system by embracing the Kantian goal of perpetual peace[44] with its "normative power." Attempts to realize this happened through the EU enlargements or regional cooperatives and partnerships.[45] Central and Eastern European Countries (CEECs), Euro-Mediterranean Partnership (EMP), European Neighborhood Policy (ENP), and the Union for the Mediterranean (UfM) can be given as examples of such attempts of the EU. These norms are particular to the EU or are universally acceptable.[46]

Kagan[47] claims that "every international order in history has reflected the beliefs and interests of its strongest power, and every international order has changed when power shifted to others with different beliefs and interests.... The better idea does not have to win because it is a better idea. It requires great powers to champion it."[48] The continuity of postwar liberal international order went beyond the Wilsonian vision in its more expansive embrace of universal human rights and its liberal internationalist agenda for spreading liberty and democracy worldwide related to the Great Powers' ability to champion it.[49]

Yet, French Professor Guy Hermet claims that "democracy is spreading at the peripheries of the world, but exhausted in the center,"

---

[43]Kagan, Robert (2002). *Power and Weakness: Why the United States and Europe See the World Differently*. Policy Review.

[44]Ibid.

[45]Sedelmeir, *op. cit.*, p.119.

[46]Sjursen, Helene (2006). "Values or Rights? Alternative Conceptions of the EU's 'Normative' Role," In *The European Union's Role in International Politics: Concepts and Analysis*, Ole Elgström & Michael Smith (eds.), London and New York: Routledge.

[47]Kagan, Robert (2013). *The World America Made*, New York: Vintage Books, p. 5.

[48]Ibid., p. 21.

[49]Ikenberry, G. John (2009). Introduction. In G. John Ikenberry, Thomas J. Knock, Anne-Marie Slaughter and Tony Smtih (eds.) *The Crisis of American Foreign Policy: Wilsonianism in the Twenty-first Century*, Princeton & Oxford: Princeton University Press, pp. 19–20.

and explains the basic reason of the decline of political democracy thus: "Our societies came to their material limits.... The petrol of democracy is material promises... the welfare state is now sitting on the sand, unable to finance any promises anymore.... The hope, upon which democracy was based, has been destroyed."[50] Furthermore, the correlation between economic development and democracy, which was made by American sociologist Ronald Inglehart, has been eroded today. The rise of the BRICS can be given as an example to the erosion of the correlation between economic development and democracy.

Developed democracies might not only lead to a change of parties in the next election or to protests against the president, but also lead to lack of trust and increased disinterest of citizens in current institutionalized procedures of democracy. It also affected the EU's "normative power," which is its ability to spread its norms and values to other states, and its "soft power," which is its ability to attract others to its point of view.[51] The trust of their citizens in democratic institutions that is the basis of their legitimacy has been fading, owing to the apparent failure of the northern Mediterranean countries' social model—the welfare state. The democratic model, which took shape and came to the fore in the 19th century in Europe, is being eroded and is perceived as outdated.[52]

Howorth[53] argues that in the emerging environment, the rising powers will be persuaded to embrace the existing international order in its current form or the great powers will agree to devise a new global order which better manages and harmonizes the multiplicity of preferences, the diversity of cultural realities and governance systems.[54] Whatever the outcome, human security is a significant issue with transnational effects and should be taken seriously by everyone.

---

[50]Parliamentary Assembly, Doc. 11623 (2008) "The State of Democracy in Europe: Specific Challanges Facing European Democracies: The Case Diversity and Migration," p. 99.

[51]Parliamentary Assembly, Doc. 12498 (2012) "Austerity Measures-a Danger for Democracy and Social Rights".

[52]Parliamentary Assembly, Doc. 12279 (2010). "Democracy in Europe: Crisis and Perspectives."

[53]Howorth, Jolyon (2012). "Developing a Grand Strategy for the EU." In Thomas Renard & Sven Biscop (eds.) *The European Union and Emerging Powers in the 21st Century: How Europe Can Shape a New Global Order*. Burlington: Ashgate.

[54]Ibid., p. 119.

It does not change the reality that there is a need for international organizations such as the Council of Europe to provide people who suffer from anti-democratic practices in their countries with a second chance to demand justice.

Democracy in the European Union member states is in crisis today. Their efforts to find a remedy to their own democracy crisis should not be ignored. Moreover, this does not mean that basic values and norms such as respect for fundamental freedoms, human rights, minority rights, the rule of law, and democracy are not universal norms that should be respected by all states. Democracy is still the best system of governance in the world. The situation of Europe might be interpreted in other ways, even as an opportunity to rebuild a strong democracy and universal values and norms—respect for human rights, fundamental freedoms, the rule of law etc.—together with the countries of the MENA region. Their partnership and possible achievements might give a new impetus to the European institution known as the guardian of democracy and human rights, adapting itself to the emerging needs and demands of the people of both Europe and the MENA region.

Conclusion

The Arab Spring was ignited by the human security goal of achieving freedom from want, freedom from fear and freedom to live in dignity.[55] People deprived of human rights and freedoms demonstrated against their authoritarian regimes to change their human rights and security conditions, which were undermined by their former regimes. Yet democratic transition efforts that will guarantee the security of all have failed. The actors defined their own security in the light of their respective position, interests and concerns with only little regard for their counterparts, disappointed popular expectations and weakened state capacity for improving human rights and security[56]. Hence, the goal of achieving human security could not be realized in the MENA region in the post-Arab Spring era. The negative citizen-state relationship that leads to human rights abuses not only damaged the

---

[55]Nuruzzaman, Mohammed (January 4, 2013). "Human Security and the Arab Spring," *Strategic Analysis* Vol. 37, No. 1.

[56]Kienle, *op. cit.*, p. 7.

human security but also the state itself, since states, for ensuring their own legitimacy and state security, need human security as well.[57]

Some potential models on the way of achieving this goal should be considered. The first is to initiate the establishment of a Council of MENA, which will become the protector/guardian of human rights in the MENA region. There are some former attempts to establish a human rights regime in the MENA region. The Cairo Declaration on Human Rights in Islam, which was adopted by the Organization of the Islamic Conference in 1990, and The Arab Charter on Human Rights adopted by the League of Arab States in 2004, are examples of those attempts. Yet these initiatives are criticized as introducing discrimination against both non-Muslims and women; threatening intercultural consensus; containing restrictive character in regard to certain fundamental rights and freedoms; being below the legal standards in effect in a number of Muslim countries; and its confirmation under *Sharia* law of the legitimacy of practices such as corporal punishment that attack the dignity of the human being.[58]

The second model might be extending geographic areas of the existing Council of Europe to the countries of the MENA region by accepting them as new members of the Council of Europe. Widening of the membership of the Council of Europe to the countries of the south and the east of the Mediterranean, which might help to build a basis of shared values through the progressive implementation of the European Convention on Human Rights, has been voiced in some platforms.[59] However, no concrete step has been taken in this respect, at least up to now.

Following the accession of the countries of the MENA region, their citizens would be able to petition the European Court of Human Rights directly.[60] In other words, membership of the MENA countries in the Council of Europe gives their citizens who believe their rights

---

[57]Morris, Kieran (2012). "The Arab Spring: The Rise of Human Security and the Fall of Dictatorship," *Internet Journal of Criminology*.

[58]Littman, David (1999). *Universal Human Rights and "Human Rights in Islam"*. Midstream.

[59]Executive Summary: Report of An Expert Group EuroMed-2030. (2010). *Long Term Challenges for the Mediterranean Area*.

[60]Massias, Jean-Pierre (2007). *Russia and the Council of Europe: Ten Years Wasted?* Russia/NIS Research Program, p. 9.

curbed or paralyzed or to be used or treated unequally or unjustly a second chance to seek their right to demand justice after they exhaust all the judiciary options in their respective countries. The decisions of the European Court of Human Rights might be treated as binding precedents by the MENA Constitutional Court and other courts. The principles carried by the Convention for the Protection of Human Rights and Fundamental Freedoms might serve as point of reference in these countries. This might lead to the promotion of progressive propagation of European standards and the convergence of legal regulations.[61] The existence of such a control mechanism and its binding force have the potential to prevent and hinder the member countries from continuing their human rights abuses.

Their membership will be an opportunity for the countries of the MENA region to emerge with a call for democracy, since they will have a chance to show their willingness to consolidate their alignment to the universal values upheld by the Council of Europe and to gain international respectability and a good image internationally. Their membership will be interpreted as an encouraging and productive factor in their democratic transition, since it will not only raise awareness in human rights and democracy, but also the continuity of condemnation for violating rules might force them to adopt a series of measures to improve human rights conditions. Joining the countries of the MENA region to the Council of Europe might not only test the credibility and capability of the Council of Europe, but also give it a new impetus as an international organization that is the guardian of human rights and democracy.[62]

The lack of a reward of EU membership, resistance to wholesale import of Western-style democracy, attempts to make *Sharia* law a source of legislation or perception of Western initiatives as an imperial ambition of the Western powers are some of the challenges that might lead to deceleration of such a process. On the other hand, some representatives in the Council of Europe might have reservations against the danger of opening the doors of the Council of Europe, which has the institutional responsibility to defend human rights and the rule of law, to countries that leave much to be desired in those respects, as we have witnessed in Russia's case.[63]

---

[61]Ibid., p. 10.

[62]Ibid., p. 4.

[63]Ibid., p. 5.

Despite these challenges listed, the Council of Europe might have more of a chance to improve human security conditions and democratic transitions in the MENA region in comparison to other Western-sponsored initiatives that have institutionally imbalanced partnership, lack of co-ownership and invisibility in the daily lives of people of the MENA region. In this respect, it is important to consolidate the Council of Europe's role as the "guardian" of democracy within the wider Europe by expanding its membership to the MENA region.[64] A willingness to submit national human rights practices to some international review is necessary to achieve the goal with respect to improvement of human rights internationally. Although traditions, cultures and religious background may be different, human nature is universally the same. Any attempt to bring in cultural and religious particularisms would simply remove the specifically universal character of human rights and fundamental freedoms.[65] The Council of Europe is far from this particularism.

In conclusion, the people of this region needs a protector of human rights, democracy, fundamental rights and freedoms in their respective countries. The need to expand the role of international organizations that maintain human security is undeniable.[66] As Professor Daniel Serwer said, "Transitions need a destination, since they gave the countries direction and impetus. Otherwise, countries would have wandered aimlessly." Despite the difficulties that Western democracies suffer today for being a force of attraction, the values they embrace are still the best option among others. It provides ways to rescue people who suffer from anti-democratic practices in their countries and maintain the human dignity they seek. In this respect, an expanded Council of Europe would give the countries of the MENA region a destination for both the governments expected to meet the human rights standards and their citizens to provide a second chance to demand what they deserve as human beings.

---

[64]Parliamentary Assembly, Resolution 1888, *op. cit.*

[65]Littman, *op. cit.*

[66]McDonald, Matt (2002). "Human Security and the Construction of Security," *Global Society* Vol. 16. No. 3, p. 279.

Chapter Four

North Africa Awakening: New Hopes for Faster and Inclusive Growth

Ghazi Ben Ahmed and Slim Othmani

Empower the private sector. Business communities must be on the front lines of trade liberalization. In South Asia, economic relations are better served by the action-oriented, proactive, problem-solving approach favored by the private sector than by the more plodding, reactive, and bureaucratic style associated with governments. Additionally, the private sector is a powerful shaper of public opinion on trade (popular support for trade normalization increased in Pakistan after its business community became convinced of India's willingness to move forward). Public-private partnerships, particularly those that facilitate more interconnectivity through infrastructural improvements (such as by upgrading highways), should also be embraced.

Michael Kugelman, *The Pakistan-India Trade Relationship: Prospects, Profits, and Pitfalls*

Maghreb Integration, a Series of False Starts

By taking the initiative to create the Arab Maghreb Union (AMU) in 1989, the five North African countries (Algeria, Libya, Mauritania, Morocco and Tunisia) took the first concrete step towards the realization of the historic declaration of Tangier 1958, whose vision remains a reference for all North Africans. But the process they had planned in order to establish a Maghreb Common Market by 2000 has derailed. Six AMU summits were held in the last 23 years, equaling one about every four years. For many observers, the reasons behind such a stalemate are to be found in the Western Sahara conflict between Morocco and Algeria. However, the root causes have not been clarified with the care they deserve in terms of fundamental issues of the project, the enormous cost of "non-Maghreb" and the "nobility" of the project. Today, more than twenty years since its creation, and amid profound political changes in the region, the Maghreb could well now find a new impetus allowing the hope for a resumption of Maghreb process on new bases and in new forms.

Assessment and Evaluation of the AMU Project

Maghreb construction never took off. Several attempts were made to achieve political integration in the Maghreb since its inception in 1989. A comprehensive strategy was adopted in the town of Ras Lanuf, Libya, in 1991. It planned for the following steps, as agreed in the treaty: a free trade area, including the dismantlement of all tariff and nontariff obstacles to trade; a customs union with a common external tariff with the rest of the world; and a common market with no remaining restrictions on the movement of production factors.

This strategy aimed to intensify trade among member countries in order to enable the creation of a North Africa customs union by 1995 and an economic common market by 2000. This plan failed amid political tensions between member states and strong resistance to trade liberalization.

The first step was not reached until the Arab Free Trade Area was set up and the accession of Algeria to it in 2009, which allowed a very basic form of economic integration to be established between the five North African countries.

Since 1994, when the last AMU Heads of State summit—the union's decision-making body—was held the North African construction is stalled and each country has been acting alone in economic openness and trade agreements with the EU and the rest of the world.

The cost of a non-Maghreb is considerable and has been evidenced in several articles and studies. On the economic front, the bulk of the Maghreb's trade is with the EU. The level of intra-Maghreb trade is lower than that of many of the world's trading blocs. Intra-Maghreb trade does not exceed 3 percent of consolidated foreign trade.

Although trade with the EU—both import and export—remains predominant, there is a growing trend in trade between Maghreb countries and the rest of the world. This is a positive movement towards a wider diversification of origins and destinations of traded goods. This movement should be the subject of a deeper analysis in order to identify which sectors (or at least which types of products) and what partners are concerned, and what are the consequences on Maghreb economies.

The absence of such economic integration entails a loss of two to three percentage points of GDP in the Maghreb countries, as well as lost opportunities for job creation in the region. In fact, unemployment rates, although declining, remain very high: 18 percent in Algeria, 11 percent in Morocco (19 percent in urban areas), and 16 percent in Tunisia, with youth unemployment exceeding 20 percent in the region. North African countries need to build up momentum in policy reforms to make a sustained reduction in unemployment by accelerating growth.

This also extends to many areas of insufficiently exploited cooperation that need to get organized and leverage the exchange of skills and expertise available in a variety of sectors, sharing and capitalizing on cross-peer experiences in areas that are similar, increased bargaining power in areas of common interest vis-à-vis the rest of the world, etc.

Recurrent Obstacles Encountered by the AMU Project

The reasons for the failure of AMU have been extensively discussed here and there, but in superficial terms that sometimes reflect national biases. Basically, these reasons revolve around issues that are not specific to the Maghreb. The European construction, which is recognized as the most accomplished and most successful integration, was also facing similar challenges. But unlike the Maghreb, Europe has addressed them through a rational political process centered on the strategic interests of the collective project and not on positions and calculations of short-sighted politicians.

Two subjects come back repeatedly to explain the non-Maghreb:

- Firstly, the clenched relations between Morocco and Algeria. Even though it is true that the relationship between the two countries is a drag for the entire Maghreb, it seems that by repeating it, we ended up giving undue importance, without realizing that it is this detail that is actually preventing the big picture from being grasped. How can we possibly explain otherwise, that the axes of intra-trade between Maghreb countries with excellent relations are also far below their potential? With regard to Algeria and Morocco, we would rather "incriminate" political or even cultural incapacity of the authorities of these two countries to even out their differences and settle old liabilities in order to be able to consider a common regional future.

If European integration was carried out successfully, it is in great part because the member states have managed to turn the page on the Second World War, the bloodiest conflict of all time. In 1954, less than ten years after the end of military hostilities and the Paris Agreements, Germany and Italy were fully integrated in the process of European integration. This is a masterful political lesson that demonstrates that in the Maghreb, major historical choices may remain hostage to narrow-mindedness based mostly on irrationality than to actual foreign policy vision. The obstacle to Maghreb construction does not lie in actual political disputes that arise between the states, but to the failure of the latter to solve them or at least to avoid that they interfere with strategic options of common interest.

- Second, using a different approach, the failure of the AMU project is explained by the lack of political will of the authorities to echo the aspirations of the people of the entire region, who feel committed to building a Maghreb entity, as was formally confirmed by field surveys. In other words, the non-Maghreb is attributed to a deficit of democratic political regimes, specifically on the issue of regional integration.

Thus, the Marrakesh Agreement of 1989 is merely a hint of nationalist reflexes, irresistible, narrow and rigid that would have quickly taken over anyway. This step backward could find easy excuses, between the desire of some to preserve the sovereignty of their national choices, and the fear of others to be overwhelmed by new leadership or hegemony of one country in the region—naturally at their expense.

Once again, the European example demonstrates that some very real national rivalries such as the ones between France and Germany have not adversely affected their involvement in the regional integration process. In a rational way, cooperation and solidarity prevailed over defection, and the Franco-German couple ended up playing a leading role in this process, without anyone losing sight of their own national interests. Second masterful policy lesson! The obstacle to the Maghreb construction, therefore, does not lie in the preservation of the national interests of states, but in their disabilities to articulate these national interests in a well-understood manner, with a regional dynamic in the service of all.

By placing the experience of the AMU back in context, it appears that it was unable to succeed due to nationalist narrow-mindedness overfilled with irrationality. But apart from these considerations, we must also admit the existence of several other constraints mentioned very little because of their latent character:

- The Maghreb civil society was considered as a beneficiary and not as active agents of the project, and was therefore kept away from any possibility of initiative or influence. The only actors involved were the governments of member countries;

- The governments of the Maghreb countries did not have synchronized policies regarding economic openness; the openness was in reality related to cycles of economic crisis differed from one country to another.

Notwithstanding the narrowness and the nationalist rivalries of the governments, the monopolization of the Maghreb project by them and the asynchronous nature of their openness policies may mainly explain why the realization of the AMU project in the context of the 1990s was impossible.

Reactivation of the Maghreb Integration Agenda

Recently, due to the increasingly heavy cost of the non-Maghreb and the Arab Awakening, there is a renewed interest at different levels in a revival of the Maghreb process. Thus, the second half of the 2000s saw the launch of remarkable initiatives by government agencies as well as the business community of the three central Maghreb countries. These initiatives were supported, encouraged or tolerated by the governments in the region. This is heralded as the start of a recovery in the Maghreb process. The emerging route is the combination of three conditions that are more or less now in place:

- The first is that the Maghreb ideal, far from being reduced to an idea defined by a visionary elite, or even a formal official document, should be internalized in the consciousness of the entire civil society, ready to move as involved in the realization of this ideal. It now seems possible and promising to build on the setting in motion of the community of North African businessmen and other components of forces in the region, such as youth, senior managers and associations, intellectual elites, researchers, experts, etc.

- The second condition is that national policies are in phase with each other in terms of economic opening to the outside, which is now ascertained that the five Maghreb countries are part of the Arab Free Trade Area, and various trade agreements have gone through all of them, even though in a broader context, as the Agadir Agreement of 2004. Moreover, the AMU countries are now either members of the WTO (Tunisia, Morocco, Mauritania) or candidates with observer status (Algeria and Libya).

- The third condition is that the governments seek to establish favorable conditions for economic dynamics within the Maghreb, encourage, support and assist initiatives within the Maghreb construction, and this in the context of their regular tasks of economic regulation. On behalf of the sovereign control, it is legitimate that each government retains the latitude to implement safeguard measures to counter the possible risks. Such risks, however, would not constitute grounds for withdrawal, but they will be monitored in order to start with the activities that have positive or at least neutral impact on their national economies.

Even if the three conditions for a revival of the Maghreb construction are met, we still need to define a strategy. A starting point would be to identify what sort of Maghreb we need and take it from there in order to conceive how to build it. In view of considerable shortfalls due to the deadlock that has prevailed for twenty years, and internal and external issues, common and country-specific issues, the only means of recovery that today are worthy of being retained are two in number:

- Catch up with the delay in the implementation of the regional project since its blockade in 1994, taking into account all the changes that have happened since then; and

- Release in a strictly win-win spirit, the full potential of regional integration that lies in the countries of the region.

A Maghreb Common Market in the Short Term

If we consider that the first step of the original strategy, i.e. the Free Trade Area, has been achieved with the establishment of the Arab Free Trade Area, it is clear that the Customs Union would bring nothing more than the adoption of a common customs tariff vis-à-vis third countries. A bold and effective move in the integration process would require the establishment of free movement of people, capital and possibly services. In a word, we should now be aiming at a Maghreb Common Market.

The Maghreb Common Market would be a step in the transition towards medium-term economic union, a more demanding stage, because it involves a degree of harmonization of national economic policies, up to monetary union, even up to the Maghreb single currency. Then, on a slightly more distant horizon, it is hoped that the Maghreb will move up to harmonize the unification of its national economic and social policies. If this ultimate challenge is met, the Maghreb Union will be born and will prevail alongside the European Union and other regional groupings as a major hub in the Mediterranean. Then the dream born in Tangier on April 30, 1958 would be completed.

Greater transatlantic engagement and focus on the topic of regional integration in North Africa will be essential. The U.S. and EU can serve as a catalyst for greater economic cooperation through their leadership and economic diplomacy. In particular, they can provide expertise and technical assistance to Maghreb governments and private sector actors.

They could push for further North African strategic cooperation on global food security and the role of phosphates in ensuring it. The importance of phosphates, a key component in fertilizers, is crucial to fight food insecurity and a key driver of the agricultural productivity gains. Given the cumulative market share of Morocco, Western Sahara and Tunisia, North Africa could become an important supplier of phosphates, but also a key part of the solution to addressing food insecurity given ever-present resource realities.

Phosphate, oil and gas could be for North Africa what coal and steel were for Europe. The European Coal and Steel Community was the first international organization to be based on the principles of supranationalism and ultimately led the way to the founding of the European Union.

Economic integration in North Africa will not see progress without support from average citizens, business leaders and policymakers throughout the region. That is why innovative programs like the one elaborated by the Mediterranean Development Initiative jointly with the Center for Transatlantic Relations at Johns Hopkins University seek to build this support on the ground starting in Tunisia though an education and awareness campaign. They will use radio interviews, opinion pieces and other media interventions in order to sensitize and to highlight how integration will benefit citizens, communities and countries, as well as "door-knock" efforts, and town halls or other face-to-face encounters, among other activities. This program will prepare the ground upstream for, among others, the European Commission, World Bank, USAID and North Africa Partnership for Economic Opportunity (NAPEO) activities.

Cross-Maghreb roundtables will complement country-to-country efforts and seek to bring people from across the region together for further dialogue and relationship building. A series of roundtables will gather different combinations of policymakers, civil society leaders, and businesspeople to discuss prospects of stronger regional trade integration among the Maghreb countries.

Immediate Release of the Integration Win-Win Potential

The business community will play a leading role in the Maghreb integration process. The first step in this direction would be for the business community to get structured in this perspective and establish the tools to provide insight and the necessary operational capability.

Much attention should be given to its coordination channels within countries and between them, and to the establishment of specific frameworks for consultation with the respective governments in each country.

There are several initiatives fulfilling this regional consultation mission, such as the Maghreb Employers Union and its Maghreb Entrepreneurs Forum. The objective of the Forum was to strengthen economic integration in the Arab Maghreb Union and promote intra-Maghreb exchanges. The Forum sessions paid particular attention to the important role of entrepreneurs and small and medium-sized enterprises to accomplish this objective in the region, and established the Maghreb Initiative on Trade and Investment (IMCI) to develop intra-Maghreb cooperation.

Other important initiatives include the North Africa Partnership for Economic Opportunity (PNB-NAPEO), which is a public-private partnership of U.S. and North Africa business leaders, entrepreneurs, civil society leaders, and governments with a mission to foster job creation, entrepreneurship, and education with a focus on youth.

The EU participated in two key meetings of the Western Mediterranean Forum (also known as the 5+5 Dialogue): a meeting of Foreign Ministers in Rome in February 2012 attended by Commissioner Füle, and the Summit in Malta held in October 2012, attended by President Barroso and Commissioner Füle. At both meetings, the EU underlined possible synergies between the 5+5 Dialogue and EU bilateral and regional cooperation and also with the Union for the Mediterranean (UfM). Informal meetings were held with the Arab Maghreb Union.

Last but not least, an innovative project, i.e. the Business Advisory Council for North Africa (BAC NA). This new platform will become a business-oriented body that will foster constructive public-private dialogue and advocacy aimed at realizing regional integration and economic growth in the Maghreb. A core activity within the platform will be to marshal support and buy-in for regional integration:

- Grow public awareness about the potential advantages integration will have for citizens through radio interviews, opinion pieces

- Engage specific communities on the borders through town halls or other face-to-face encounters

- Bring business associations from around the Maghreb to Tunisia or reach out to them to have a panel on regional integration, present the project goals, etc.

The large-scale exploitation and all forms of partnership opportunities between and among Maghreb enterprises—joint ventures, cross-ownership, outsourcing, co-sourcing, processing, BOT, syndication, banking, etc.—is the priority among priorities. This axis remains central and crucial to the extent that it fosters existing complementarities, synergies, brings job and wealth, and reduce substantially the costs lying with non-Maghreb and strengthens economically irreversible interdependency ties.

In this context, and until the reopening of land borders between Algeria and Morocco, land and sea trade corridors can be usefully arranged on an interim basis, at least for a pilot phase. Reserved only to the movement of goods, these corridors would be subject to a specific monitoring device, designed to maintain the facilitation of a win-win goods trade.

A similar agreement has been experienced successfully between India and Pakistan. They agreed to open a trade corridor allowing round-the-clock movement of trucks and containers through their main border crossing, i.e. the Wagah-Attari border. If it works between India and Pakistan (the goal is to reach 6 billion USD in 2014) it should work between Algeria and Morocco as a pilot experience with a daily monitoring of trade exchanges.

More generally, insofar as firms are normally required to assume the risks associated to their proactive initiatives, governments would benefit from developing a monitoring system enabling them to monitor the impacts of the Maghreb construction on their national economies and to propose fixes. They can also, by appropriate and agreed safeguards, ensure that the resulting externalities, in particular the trade balance, job creation and environmental protection, are positive.

Opportunities for public-public partnership, possibly involving the private sector—companies or associations—are not left behind. Just think of all the conventional cradles bringing together peoples, such as the restoration of the Maghreb Games or shared strategic issues beyond the scope of intervention of private initiatives, such as food security, long-term water supply, environmental protection, including in particular the fight against desertification, penetration of renewable energy, technology transfer in various sectors, human resources creation and training, academic and professional, regional substitution/preference to import, sub-subcontracting and regional co-contracting, empowerment of regional negotiation, and so on.

For many young people in the region who continue to face high levels of unemployment, change is long overdue. The Arab Spring is a wake-up call for North African countries to take on economic reforms that will get the economy growing faster and create the jobs and opportunities that the youth are demanding for so long. There is a renewed impetus for regional integration among North African countries and closer cooperation between them. This movement, led by the private sector with the support of the civil society, is strengthened by the firm belief that the objectives of promoting higher living standards, stability and democratic transformation at the national level cannot be fully realized in the absence of deeper integration between the North African countries.

Part II

Post-Arab Spring Security
Challenges and Responses

Chapter Five

Libya: The Major Security Concern in Africa?

Olivier Guitta

Having ruled Libya for 42 years, Muammar Gaddafi came to his final demise in October 2011, after a bloody eight-month civil war. The country was then governed for ten months by the National Transitional Council (NTC), until the elections for the General National Congress (GNC) were held. In November 2012, the new incoming Prime Minister, Ali Zeidan, was tasked to run the country in a very difficult climate: in fact, there has been a real political vacuum, which has been filled by the militias that de facto control Libya. The failure of the government to ensure security even just within the capital, Tripoli, as shown by Zeidan's kidnapping in October 2013 and his forced resignation in March 2014,[1] has made Libya a very unsafe place, where tribal conflicts are recurrent; al-Qaeda (AQ) has gained ground in the south; and militias are roaming free.

The Impact of Insecurity on the Oil Sector

Libya's economic structure makes it a rentier economy, because the exports of its main natural resource, hydrocarbons, constitute 90 percent of the state revenue.[2]

The revenues of exports should be injected into the private non-hydrocarbon sector, in order to further decrease the high rate of unemployment in the country. During the Gaddafi era, the ensemble of the imposed sanctions hampered the economy from reaching its economic potential. The conflict, furthermore, damaged the

---

[1]RFI, "La Libye n'a plus de Premier ministre," March 12, 2014, available at: http://www.rfi.fr/afrique/20140311-libye-premier-ministre-perd-confiance-deputes/.

[2]IMF (2012) "Libya Beyond the Revolution: Challenges and Opportunities" (Washington D.C., International Monetary Fund), p. 2, available at: http://www.imf.org/external/ pubs/ft/ dp/2012/1201mcd.pdf.

economy.[3] It is estimated that the economic cost of Libya's civil war has been around $15 billion.

The security situation (in this case, the heightened insecurity) is not conducive for Foreign Direct Investment (FDI). Interestingly enough, because of the rewards that the Libyan energy market can bring, some foreign oil companies have returned to Libya, including *Total* (France); *Repsol* (Spain); *Wintershall* (Germany); as well as *British Petroleum* (BP) (UK). However, the timing changed for some companies because of the security outlook (especially after the attack on the U.S. consulate in Benghazi on 11 September 2012, and the attack on the In Amenas gas facility in neighbouring Algeria in January 2013). In 2007, BP had signed an exploration-and-production agreement with Libya's National Oil Corporation, but suspended this contract in February 2011. This suspension was lifted in May 2012;[4] however, in May 2013, BP withdrew non-essential foreign staff from operations in Libya, following "UK government advice about uncertainty in the country."[5] In November 2013, BP stated that it was withdrawing investment in Libya, but not ceasing activity altogether.[6]

Oil has become a tool for political negotiations,[7] especially since summer 2013, and, to make matters worse, in April 2013, Libya announced that it was not going to allow foreign security forces to protect its oil fields. Why is that problematic? Because even though the Libyan security force around the oil facilities is 15,000-men strong, it is not up to the level it should be to instil any confidence in the minds of foreign oil executives. The infighting between the various militias, coupled with the lack of equipment and adequate training, makes this task almost insurmountable.

---

[3]Deveaux, J. (2013) "La Libye, 20 mois après Kadhafi," *Geopolis*, June 4, available at: http://geopolis.francetvinfo.fr/la-libye-20-mois-apres-kadhafi-17045.

[4]BBC, "BP to resume oil operations in Libya," May 29, 2012, available at: http://www.bbc.co.uk/news/business-18256587.

[5]BBC, "BP withdraws some Libya staff over security concerns," May 12, 2013, available at: http://www.bbc.co.uk/news/uk-22501901.

[6]Ash, N. (2013) "BP to slash Libyan plans—report," *Libya Herald*, November 6, available at: http://www.libyaherald.com/2013/11/06/breaking-news-bp-to-slash-libyan-plans-report/#axzz2sea2uNXM.

[7]Casalis, M. (2013) "Libye: les conséquences de la crise pétrolière," *RFI*, October 4, available at: http://www.rfi.fr/emission/20131004-libye-petrole-crise-budget.

Sabotage is also playing a big role in the major disruption that the oil sector is regularly witnessing. For instance, the Italian oil company, *Eni*, was forced to suspend gas exports to Italy in March 2013, because of a dispute between terror groups near its Mellitah facility.[8] Militias are using their full power to show how they are in control, in effect, of most oil facilities. In other words, nothing can be done without them, and that is one of the major signs of the state's total lack of control over its main resource.

There have been also some social grievances—demand for more jobs and increased salaries—which have resulted in strikes that paralysed oil production over the summer of 2013. As a result, the oil production fell to 250,000 barrels per day (bpd), from an average of 1.5 million: a drop of 80 percent.[9]

A Power Vacuum

The Gaddafi regime kept an artificial balance between the local and regional powers, as well as between the institutions. He imposed the authority of one militia over the whole territory therefore when the regime collapsed, there was a power vacuum. Numerous separate militias jumped in to fill that void and replace the weak and defective central authorities. Even though the government tried to integrate these militias in order to avoid a civil war, it is still lacking to control any of them.

The militias are used for securing/defending the country, most notably to control the borders. The problem is that the integration of armed groups (particularly those with a jihadist or regionalist logic) within the government is hostile to the establishment of a centralised authority.[10] Not all these militias work against the government; most of them been drafted by the authorities that require their services

---

[8]RT, "Libyan gas exports to Italy disrupted due to clashes," March 3, 2013, available at: http://rt.com/news/libya-gas-export-italy-744/.

[9]*L'Expression*, "Crise pétrolière en Libye: La production en chute de plus de 80 percent," November 5, 2013, available at: http://www.lexpressiondz.com/internationale/183922-la-production-en-chute-de-plus-de-80.html.

[10]*Le Monde*, "L"Europe face au désastre qui s"installe en Libye," October 15, 2013, available at: http://www.lemonde.fr/idees/article/2013/10/15/l-europe-face-au-desastre-qui-s-installe-en-libye_3495807_3232.html.

for policing, defence, and border-control purposes.[11] The process of slow integration has been preferred over forced disbandment of the militias, in order to avoid the throes of a civil war which the central power could not win. The downfall of this policy will be the rise of a bundle of armed groups with jihadist; regionalist; or mafia-like inclinations, and which are hostile to a strong state.

Gaddafi was using these conflicts, and had revived the social divisions, in order to establish his authority. Since his fall, no one controls the situation: the country's regions have never been so divided, and tribalism will continue to persist in the post-Gaddafi era,[12] presenting the risk of a fragile or failed state.[13]

The Libyan government is finding it hard to restore its authority over the multiple armed groups that are still active all over the country.[14] Despite the dismembering of some militias in Tripoli and Benghazi since September 2012, the security apparatus remains in the hands of some 300 brigades that have emerged from the ruins of the Gaddafi regime. These local brigades are attempting to establish their own authority, thereby replacing the redundant central authorities.[15] In fact, post-Gaddafi Libya suffers less of an institutional void than a cruel lack of centralisation. In Tripoli, two main militias—the katiba from Zintan (a city located in the north-west of the country), constituted of "mountain warriors", and the katiba of Misrata (east of Tripoli), dominated by the Muslim Brotherhood—ensure the security of the capital, with the help of several ex-rebel groups.

---

[11]*Le Monde*, "Libye: le premier ministre brièvement enlevé par d'ex-rebelles," October 10, 2013, available at: http://www.lemonde.fr/libye/article/2013/10/10/le-premier-ministre-libyen-ali-zeidan-a-ete-enleve_3492883_1496980.html

[12]Haimzadeh, P. (2012) "Scrutin libyen sur fond de chaos," *Le Monde Diplomatique*, July, available at: http://www.monde-diplomatique.fr/2012/07/HAIMZADEH/47931.

[13]El-Katiri, M. (2012) *State-Building Challenges in a Post-Revolution Libya* (U.S. Army War College, Strategic Studies Institute), p. 2.

[14]*Le Monde*, "Libye: le premier ministre brièvement enlevé par d'ex-rebelles," *op. cit.*

[15]Barulet, A. (2013) "Libye: des milices mafieuses occupent le vide laissé par l'État central," *Le Figaro*, October 10, available at: http://www.lefigaro.fr/international/2013/10/10/01003-20131010ARTFIG00445-libye-des-milices-mafieuses-occupent-le-vide-laisse-par-l-etat-central.php

The Militias

While Libya underwent a very violent civil war, compared to the other countries of the "Arab Spring", the violence did not stop on the day of Gaddafi's death. In fact, with the numerous attacks; violence; and thefts, Libya may follow the same path as Iraq.[16] For instance, Benghazi suffers attacks and violence on a daily basis.

The popular uprisings in the neighbouring countries have presented a further threat to the security of Libya. The absence of a strong state and clearly delineated border has allowed an increase in arms smuggling and proliferation. This is relevant because it threatens the security of Libya's neighbours and Europe. Libyan fighters have been shipping arms to Sinai, Gaza, and Syria, among many other places.

The revolutionary armed militias refuse to disarm, fearing a possible retaliation from an opposing tribe. In addition to the tension created by the tribal configuration of Libya, there is the contention between Benghazi (the focal point of the rebellion in the east) and Tripoli (the ex-Gaddafi stronghold in the west). This rivalry could result in a shift of power from Tripoli to Benghazi. Several regions in the country are pushing towards federalism, especially the regions that have oil fields (such as Ras Lanuf, Zueitina,[17] and the province of Cyrenaica).

Since the fall of Gaddafi, the victorious rebel groups have been taking revenge against the tribes that supported the dictator who ruled for 42 years. An example of this tribal violence is after the Misratans were allegedly tortured, massacred, and raped en masse by the pro-Gaddafi Tawerghans during the uprising;[18] the wind has turned and, now, the Misratans are violently attacking the Tawerghans.

When it comes to the largest concern regarding the country's stability, i.e. the militias, the situation is very difficult to assess and is

---

[16]*Jeune Afrique*, "La Libye est-elle sur la voie de l'irakisation?" November 21, 2013, available at: http://www.jeuneafrique.com/Article/ARTJAWEB20131121091114/.

[17]*Libya Herald*, "Libya's oil production at 233,000 b/d," December 23, 2013, available at: http://www.libyaherald.com/2013/12/23/libyas-oil-production-at-233000-bpd/#axzz2 sea2uNXM.

[18]Abrahams, F. (2013) "Why have we forgotten about Libya?" *Human Rights Watch*, March 25, available at: http://www.hrw.org/news/2013/03/25/why-have-we-forgotten-about-libya.

really a moving target.[19] All the issues and identities are murky, at best, between the "elected" militia groups; the revolutionary groups fighting against the political instability; the institutionalised armed groups who have integrated the official security forces; and the revolutionary and illegal ones.

The renewed fighting between militias, in January 2012, led the National Transitional Council (NTC) to warn of the risks of another civil war.[20] Dozens of separate armed groups took control of Tripoli's neighbourhoods and strategic infrastructures, including the airports. They used this as political leverage to make sure that they would not be excluded from power, as had happened in Egypt and Tunisia.[21] The militias are estimated to comprise around 140,000 to 150,000 men in Tripoli alone. Efforts were made to integrate militias into the Ministry of Interior's forces;[22] this act was an effort to curb violence in Libya. Militias would be removed from the capital, disarmed, and the men integrated into security forces.[23] The transitional government has integrated into the national security forces only 29 percent of the estimated 170,000 militiamen who fought Gaddafi.[24] Because of the lack of a police or military force able to maintain order and security, the Islamist militias are ruling and filling the security void. An estimated 200,000 armed men involved in militias rule over the territory and bring insecurity to the region:[25] they exert control over the administrations and ministries, organise drug and arm traffics, hold to ransom the population, and attack the various diplomatic representations.

---

[19]Lussato, C. (2013) "LIBYE. "Les milices se nourrissent de la faiblesse de l'Etat," *Le Nouvel Observateur*, October 10, available at: http://tempsreel.nouvelobs.com/monde/20131010. OBS0726/libye-les-milices-se-nourrissent-de-la-faiblesse-de-l-etat.html.

[20]El-Katiri., *op. cit.*, p. 18.

[21]Ibid., p. 19.

[22]Touchard, L. (2013) "Armée libyenne : le casse-tête de l'intégration des milices," *Jeune Afrique*, November 26, available at: http://www.jeuneafrique.com/Article/ARTJAWEB2013 1125163018/.

[23]*Al-Akhbar English*, "Libyan government reveals plan to integrate militias into armed forces," November 20, 2013, available at: http://english.al-akhbar.com/node/17658.

[24]*Al-Akhbar English*, "Libya violence killed 643 over 2013: report," January 23, 2014, available at: http://english.al-akhbar.com/node/18356.

[25]*Le Monde*, "L'Europe face au désastre qui s'installe en Libye," *op. cit.*

The militias' success is made all the more possible because of the lack of unity within Libya,[26] the fragmentation of the political landscape, and the regional divisions between the federalists in the east; the Amazigh in the west; and the border minorities of the west and south (the Berbers of the Nafusa Mountains) who demand the recognition of their culture and language in the future Libyan Constitution.

One of the largest and most powerful militias in the country is the Misratan Union of Revolutionaries, comprised of 40,000 members: a real state within a state. These brigades are said to control significant military equipment (heavy artillery, tanks, and vehicles mounted with machine guns).[27]

Although the group is based in the city of Misrata, it is also involved in central and western Libya.[28] Around 50 people were killed in Tripoli, on 18 November 2013, when Misrata militia opened fire on demonstrators protesting against their presence in Tripoli.[29] As a consequence, the Misrata militia was required to leave the city.

What one has to keep in mind, when looking at militias, is that they are not a new post-revolution phenomenon. The scale of their power is definitely new; but they were around in the 1990s, after the imposition of sanctions on the country.[30] In addition, the Muslim Brotherhood—as well as the jihadi Salafists—appeared as early as the Afghan war in the early 1980s.[31] Gaddafi was quite successful in clamping down on Islamist terrorists; he jailed most of them and dissolved the terror groups such as the Libyan Islamic Fighting Group (LIFG). Yet, even before his fall, he released LIFG members and prominent Muslim Brotherhood leaders, for unclear reasons. Interestingly, many of these

---

[26]*L'Express*, "Libye: conflit autour de l'or noir," September 5, 2013, available at: http://www.lexpress.fr/actualite/monde/proche-moyen-orient/libye-conflit-autour-de-l-or-noir_1278661.html.

[27]BBC, "Guide to key Libyan militias and other armed groups," November 28, 2013, available at: http://www.bbc.co.uk/news/world-middle-east-19744533.

[28]Ibid.

[29]BBC, "Libya clashes: Misrata militia ordered out of Tripoli," November 18, 2013, available at: http://www.bbc.co.uk/news/world-africa-24982399.

[30]Skandrani, G. (2013) "Un an après la mort de Kadhafi: la Libye n'a plus d'Etat," *La Voix De La Libye*, January 28, available at: http://lavoixdelalibye.com/?p=7248.

[31]Ibid.

men—who were veterans of the Afghan war and/or al-Qaeda (AQ) members—joined the militias that overthrew Gaddafi.[32]

On a hopeful note, the Libyans are determined to get rid of the militias ruling the country.[33] So, for example, militias surrounded buildings of the Ministry of Justice and Foreign Affairs,[34] [35] on 30 April 2013. On 10 May 2013, though, pro-democracy protesters supporting the government drove them out.[36] Local authorities also called for a three-day general strike and civil disobedience in Tripoli, to start on 17 November 2013.

The Libyan central power has been trying to confront the difficulty of establishing security forces for two years now. After the attack against the U.S. embassy in Benghazi that killed the U.S. ambassador in September 2012, the government has been attempting to control the armed groups that were formed during the uprising against Gaddafi.[37] Interestingly enough, the government has legitimized some of those militias and has declared others illegal. Even though the militias have been denounced countless times (and for good reasons), they still keep a certain legitimacy because of their fighting during the revolution.

But the real problem lies more in the weakness of the state, rather than the power of the militias. Gaddafi really intended for himself and his cronies to be in charge of the country, and so neglected to build

---

[32]*Le Parisien*, "Extrémistes en Libye et Al-Qaïda: des affinités mais pas d'affiliation," October 8, 2013, available at: http://www.leparisien.fr/flash-actualite-monde/extremistes-en-libye-et-al-qaida-des-affinites-mais-pas-d-affiliation-08-10-2013-3206927.php.

[33]Tigrine, M. (2013) "Grève générale et appels a la désobéissance civile a Tripoli: Les Libyens détermines a se débarrasser des milices," *Liberté Algérie*, November 18, available at: http://www.liberte-algerie.com/international/les-libyens-determines-a-se-debarrasser-des-milices-greve-generale-et-appels-a-la-desobeissance-civile-a-tripoli-210572.

[34]BBC, "Libya gunmen surround justice ministry in Tripoli," April 30, 2013, available at: http://www.bbc.co.uk/news/world-africa-22352530.

[35]DW, "Militias again surround ministry buildings in Libya," April 30, 2013, available at: http://www.dw.de/militias-again-surround-ministry-buildings-in-libya/a-16780981.

[36]Eljali, A. and Fornaji, H. (2013) "Protestors force out Ministry militiamen," *Libya Herald*, May 10, available at: http://www.libyaherald.com/2013/05/10/protestors-force-out-ministry-militiamen/#axzz2sea2uNXM.

[37]Gouëset, C. (2013) "Libye: "Les enlèvements illustrent la faiblesse de l'Etat," *L'Express*, October 10, available at: http://www.lexpress.fr/actualite/monde/afrique/libye-l-enlevement-du-premier-ministre-illustre-la-faiblesse-de-l-etat_1289945.html.

any institutions that could have been helpful in the post-revolution environment.

The militias know how to use their leverage in order to reach their goals; so, for instance, when they seized the oil fields over the summer of 2013, it was more a matter of pressuring the government than actually receiving some of the oil revenues.[38] The militias have also obtained the removal of several Defence and Interior ministers who were not particularly favorable to them.

Tribal Violence

Unfortunately, the violence is not limited to the militias and terror groups; tribal conflicts could be a ticking time bomb as well. There are several of them in Libya, with the most potentially dangerous being between the tribes of Misrata and Warfallas (the latter being the largest tribe in Libya, located all over the country).[39] The Misratis accuse the Warfallas of assassinating Omar Mukhtar, the hero of Libyan resistance against Italian colonialism for 20 years;[40] but it is widely believed that Italian forces captured and hanged him in 1931.[41] In addition, the Warfallas' stronghold in Beni Walid was the last pro-Gaddafi bastion standing, thus further increasing the tension between the two tribes. The fighting between the two has resulted in the deaths of hundreds. For the moment, the conflict seems to be limited to Beni Walid; yet it could possibly spread.

The tribal animosity is not just confined to large cities, or to one particular region, or to Arab groups alone: for example, ethnic Tebu militias largely oversee Tuareg districts, and have suffered from the ire

---

[38]Mandraud, I. (2013) "Libye, un Etat en morceaux," *Le Monde*, December 3, available at: http://www.lemonde.fr/libye/article/2013/12/03/libye-un-etat-en-morceaux_3524722_1496980.html.

[39]Skandrani, *op. cit.*

[40]*The Milli Gazette*, "The Italian occupation and the Libyan resistance," n.d., available at: http://www.milligazette.com/Archives/15122001/1512200105.htm, accessed on: January 30, 2014.

[41]Ibid.; See also: "History of Omar Mokhtar and Libya," *Home of Islam—Muslim Unity*, available at: http://www.freewebs.com/islamic-site/warrior/omar.html, accessed on: January 30, 2014.

of Arab militias that have long viewed them with suspicion.[42] In January 2014, 88 people were killed and 130 injured during fighting between the two tribes. Back in 2012, infighting killed 150 people.[43]

This just adds to the already extremely volatile situation that pushed the government to declare a state of emergency on January 19, 2014.[44]

Hanan Salah, a researcher for *Human Rights Watch* in Tripoli, perfectly describes the untenable chaos that is reigning over the country: "In Libya it has become fully acceptable to use force as a means to achieve certain objectives [...] It has become an everyday thing. You don't like something? Kidnap the prime minister for a few hours. Kidnap the son of the defence minister. Whether willingly or unwillingly, the government has put itself in this position."[45]

Al-Qaeda

The militias are not the only ones instilling terror; AQ is actually very active in the country. Some of the Libyan AQ operatives came back to Libya during the insurrection against Gaddafi in 2011.[46] Their involvement with the Libyan rebels allowed them to be recognised, to obtain military weapons, and to form militias that have had particular influence in the east of the country. They also established some training camps—especially in the south, where they recruit young men to send them to Syria.

AQ has progressively established itself in Libya, taking advantage of the chaos and the power vacuum after Gaddafi's fall and the lack of a capable army. It has actually thrived after the French intervention in Mali that pushed a number of hard-core jihadists such as Mokhtar

---

[42]Daragahi, B. (2013) "Libya: Rule of the gun," *Financial Times*, November 19, available at: http://www.ft.com/cms/s/0/a8f8a2e2-5107-11e3-9651-00144feabdc0.html#axzz2sTRlHnyf.

[43]*Jeune Afrique*, "Heurts dans le sud libyen : au moins 88 morts en deux semaines," January 25, 2014, available at: http://www.jeuneafrique.com/Article/DEPAFP20140125162657/.

[44]Daragahi, B. (2014) "Tripoli declares state of emergency in Libya's south," *Financial Times*, January 19, available at: http://www.ft.com/cms/s/0/0c672536-8102-11e3-b3d5-00144feab7 de.html#axzz2sTRlHnyf.

[45]Daraghi (2013), *op. cit.*

[46]Skandrani, *op. cit.*

Belmokhtar to settle in southern Libya, where no one really controls the territory.

Former Libyan Prime Minister Ali Zeidan has conceded that government investigations have turned up Tunisians, Algerians, Sudanese, and Nigerians undergoing training in Benghazi.[47] Yet, despite the regular arrival and departure of fighters undergoing training, Zeidan has said that "there are no permanent camps."[48] Instead, he thought that most fighters stayed only one or two days. This is highly unlikely, and it seems that this is purely a damage-control statement.

Indeed, large swaths of Libyan territory are under jihadist control, and the training camps are very much of a reality.[49]

Libya has porous borders, with al-Qaeda in the Islamic Maghreb (AQIM) cells established in Derna and Benghazi. The In Amenas attack in neighbouring Algeria also occurred close to the porous desert border with Libya.

The most active terror group within the country is the AQ-affiliated Ansar al-Sharia (AAS)—which attacked an army's patrol near Benghazi, on 25 November 2013.[50] This group was also responsible for the attack on the U.S. consulate in Benghazi in September 2012,[51] although it denied its involvement.[52] AAS took advantage of the secu-

---

[47]Youssef, N. (2013) "Benghazi, Libya, has become training hub for Islamist fighters," *Miami Herald*, December 12, available at: http://www.miamiherald.com/2013/12/12/3814687/benghazi-libya-has-become-training.html.

[48]Ibid. See also: Tilouine, J. (2013) "Mohamed Abdelaziz: 'La Libye risque de devenir un État failli,'" *Jeune Afrique*, December 5, available at: http://www.jeuneafrique.com/Articles/Dossier/ARTJAWEB20131205174501/onu-developpement-securite-aqmimohamed-abdelaziz-la-libye-risque-de-devenir-un-tat-failli.html.

[49]Lasserre, I. (2013) "Guerre contre Kadhafi, une victoire tactique mais un échec stratégique," *Le Figaro*, October 10, available at: http://www.lefigaro.fr/international/2013/10/10/01003-20131010ARTFIG00568-guerre-contre-kadhafi-une-victoire-tactique-mais-un-echec-strategique.php.

[50]Tigrine, M. (2013) "Affrontements meurtriers entre les salafistes et l'armée à Benghazi: La menace djihadiste prend forme en Libye," *Liberté Algérie*, November 12, available at: http://www.liberte-algerie.com/international/la-menace-djihadiste-prend-forme-en-libye-affrontements-meurtriers-entre-les-salafistes-et-l-armee-a-benghazi-211058.

[51]Mandraud, I. (2013) "En Libye, les Islamistes très présents mais en ordre dispersé," *Le Monde*, December 3, available at: http://www.lemonde.fr/libye/article/2013/12/03/en-libye-les-islamistes-tres-presents-mais-en-ordre-disperse_3524724_1496980.html.

[52]Ibid.

rity void and now controls some territories in the east and in some districts of Benghazi, Sirte, and Derna.[53]

Since the fall of Gaddafi, major public and visible targets have been hit by terror groups: the U.S. consulate in Benghazi, on 11 September 2012; the French embassy, in March 2013; the Ministry of Interior, in July 2013; and the kidnapping of Prime Minister Zeidan, in October 2013. Abou Anas al-Libi, one of America's most wanted terrorists, was captured in October 2013, by U.S. Special Forces, in a raid in Tripoli.

While Islamist groups such as the Muslim Brotherhood and other Salafi outfits refuse to be affiliated with AQ (and prefer acting under an independent leadership), some still share an ideological affinity with AQ that should not be underplayed. According to several experts on Libya, some of these Islamist groups have become so powerful that they have refused to become part of AQ's network, as they would rather act independently under their own emir.[54]

The West's Future Role

The West should very much try to solve the ever-thorny issue of the loose weapons. It is not just all about the light weaponry, but more seriously of the roughly 4,000 surface-to-air missiles and 6,400 barrels of "yellowcake" (uranium ready to be enriched, which could come into the hands of AQ).[55] According to Bharuddin Midhoun Arifi, a military commander in the city of Sabha, AQ has offered one million dollars in exchange for the leftover weapons from the Gaddafi era, which includes uranium "yellowcakes" and surface-to-air missiles. Also, as sheer numbers go, MI6 estimates that the amount of weapons in Libya is more than the entire British arsenal.[56]

---

[53]Ibid.

[54]*Le Parisien*, "Extrémistes en Libye et Al Qaida: des affinités mais pas d'"affiliations," October 8, 2013.

[55]Colomès, M. (2013) "Libye—La poudrière nucléaire du capitaine Arifi," *Le Point*, October 27, available at: http://www.lepoint.fr/editos-du-point/michel-colomes/libye-la-poudriere-nucleaire-du-capitaine-arifi-27-10-2013-1748388_55.php.

[56]Drury, I. (2013) "Don't turn Syria into a 'Tesco for terrorists' like Libya, generals tell Cameron," *Daily Mail*, June 17, available at: http://www.dailymail.co.uk/news/article-2342917/Dont-turn-Syria-Tesco-terrorists-like-Libya-generals-tell-Cameron.html.

The situation is so dire that calls for international military have been heard very recently. So, for example, Niger has been very vocal in advocating Western military action[57] underlining that the countries that helped unseat Gaddafi needed to provide the "after sales service." But at least France publically said through its Foreign Minister Laurent Fabius that an intervention was not in the works.[58]

Even former Prime Minister Zeidan had warned or maybe bluffed back in November 2013 that the "international community cannot tolerate a state in the middle of the Mediterranean that is a source of violence, terrorism and killings."[59]

Even though full military intervention has been ruled out by Western countries, undercover and sporadic operations by various countries have been taking place in the south. Even the Algerians have reportedly been active in dismantling jihadist training camps.[60] Le Figaro recently revealed that U.S. Special Forces are actually conducting military operations against the jihadists in the south with the blessing of Libyan authorities.[61] Indeed since late 2013, U.S. Delta forces disguised as nomads, supported by drones, are supervising a group of Libyan Special Forces fighting off al-Qaeda in the south. According to a French military source, "The United States estimate that the threat of a disintegration of Southern Libya is such that it cannot just use aerial means to ha ndle this threat." It is also likely that French and British forces might join the Americans in such operations. French Admiral Edouard Guillaud, the just outgoing Chief of Defense Staff, recently stated "The ideal would be to mount an international operation with the blessing of Libyan authorities in the south

---

[57]Champeaux, N. (2014) "Le Sud de la Libye, nouveau sanctuaire des jihadistes," *RFI*, February 5, available at: http://www.rfi.fr/afrique/20140205sud-libye-nouveau-sanctuaire-jihadistes-terrorisme-hassoumi/.

[58]Cherfaoui, Z, (2014) "Intervention militaire occidentale dans le sud de la Libye," *El Watan*, February 11, available at: http://www.elwatan.com/international/les-francais-disent-non-a-niamey-11-02-2014-245357_112.php.

[59]Bouatta, D. (2014) "Face au chaos généralisé de la Libye," *Liberté Algérie*, February 27, available at: http://www.liberte-algerie.com/international/des-occidentaux-pensent-qu-une-nouvelle-guerre-est-necessaire-face-au-chaos-generalise-de-la-libye-216560.

[60]Ibid.

[61]Champeaux, *op. cit.*

of the country."[62] Adding to that, French Defense Minister Jean-Yves Le Drian, said "Libya is a first-rate challenge" and "we will be obliged to help the neighbouring countries to defend themselves against the Libyan chaos."[63]

Conclusion

The socio-economic and political issues that led people to revolt against the Gaddafi regime have mostly survived the transition and are potentially threatening the "democratic" rule. The risks remaining are associated with a revival of civil unrest and the creation of a societal hierarchy, plus a territorial division that could lead to what Abdul Alhakim al-Feitouri calls the "Balkanisation of Libya."[64]

The country has been hit with a perfect storm: first, militias controlling every aspect of the daily life of people; second, al-Qaeda (AQ) and its affiliates very present in the south, and potentially launching terror attacks; third, a very weak state. Libya has turned into a virtual failed state, where most of the socio-economic and political issues that contributed to Gaddafi's ousting are still very much alive and threaten the "democratic" rule.

In many aspects, "Libya 2014" is much worse than "Libya 2011." Human security remains the biggest problem, and, until it is tackled properly, Libya has no shining prospects. Of all the Arab Spring countries, Libya is actually the one that has fared the worst, while having the best potential. The problems facing the country are daunting, and it is very difficult to see a way out. Nonetheless, the resources and, hence, the financial interests at stake in Libya make it clear that the international community will one day, sooner rather than later, have to tackle these issues head-on.

---

[62]Duteil, M. (2014) "Toubous contre djihadistes: la pétaudière du Sud libyen," *Le Point*, February 3, available at: http://www.lepoint.fr/editos-du-point/mireille-duteil/toubous-contre-djihadistes-la-petaudiere-du-sud-libyen-03-02-2014-1787235_239.php.

[63]Ibid.

[64]El-Katiri., *op. cit.*, p. 29.

Chapter Six

The Arab Spring and Egypt's Open Season against Women

Emily Dyer

On January 25, 2011, the Egyptian revolution brought a dramatic end to President Hosni Mubarak's three decades in power. While this date is celebrated throughout Egypt as the first step towards achieving "bread, freedom and social justice," for millions of Egyptian women, it marks the day that their lives were thrown into turmoil.

What followed was an attack on women's rights and roles in society throughout various transitions of political power. Having faced years of discrimination and oppression under former President Hosni Mubarak's autocratic rule, women were further marginalised and abused under the four and a half month rule of the Supreme Council of the Armed Forces (SCAF), followed by the rule of the Muslim Brotherhood's Freedom and Justice Party (FJP) and now the military-led interim government.

The revolution's three-year anniversary marks the next phase of Egypt's political transition—parliamentary and presidential elections in 2014. Yet, Egypt's open season of appalling discrimination and violence against women has shown no signs of coming to an end. Several months ago, female activists were rounded up[1] off the streets, sexually abused by the police and dumped in the desert outside Cairo. A recent UN report[2] revealed that 99.3 percent of women in Egypt have been sexually harassed, and countless women attending large protests have been gang raped and tortured with sharp instruments. And, unsurprisingly, Egypt was named the worst place to live for women in the Arab

---

[1]"Egyptian Police Beat Women and Abandon Them in Desert," *The Times*, November 28, 2013, available at: http://www.thetimes.co.uk/tto/news/world/middleeast/article3933844.ece

[2]"Sexual Harassment in Egypt... The Causes and Confrontation Methods," *UN* Women, April 2013, available at http://www.un.org.eg/Publications.aspx?pageID=43

world in a recent poll.[3] As many ask what lies ahead for Egypt in 2014, the women question should be at the forefront of our attention.

Women's Roles, Reversed

Regardless of the crucial role that women played in the revolution, they soon faced exclusion, discrimination, and violence in the years that followed. Women have broadly been excluded from political participation, both at high-level parliamentary representation (decreasing from 10 percent in 2010, to 3 percent in 2012) and through the ability of NGOs and activists to create change through civil society.[4] Furthermore, the varied roles played by women in revolution and creating social change in broader society has been severely undermined.

Egyptian women have been and are still often portrayed as the supporters of men, rather than acting as political agents themselves. During and following the revolution, women were referred to as "the daughters, mothers, sisters and wives" of revolutionaries and their contribution to the uprising was described as "unconditionally supporting their other halves" in ousting Hosni Mubarak.[5] Many Egyptian women felt as though they were being portrayed as "the sandwich-makers and the Florence Nightingales of the revolution; by which, all we did was we went and gave food to the male revolutionists and stitched them up when they were hurt."[6] In some cases, the Muslim Brotherhood attempted to discourage women from taking part in protests all together, claiming that it is "more dignified for women to stay at home and let their brothers and fathers protest for them."[7]

---

[3]"Egypt is worst Arab State for Women, Comoros Best: Survey," *Reuters*, November 12, 2013, available at: http://www.reuters.com/article/2013/11/12/us-arab-women-idU.S.BRE9AB008 20131112.

[4]Dyer, E., "Marginalising Egyptian Women," The Henry Jackson Society (October 2013), available at: http://henryjacksonsociety.org/wp-content/uploads/2013/12/Marginalising-Egyptian-Women.pdf.

[5]"MB female activitists [sic] demonstrate what won't kill you will make you stronger," *IkhwanWeb*, April 4, 2011, available at: http://www.ikhwanweb.com/article.php?id=28338.

[6]Interview with Mona Eltahawy, June 4, 2013.

[7]Ibid.

In fact, women played a central role in all aspects of the revolution: working in field hospitals and checkpoints in Tahrir Square and the more supportive roles were shared between men *and* women.[8] According to eyewitnesses, women "were everywhere": from looking after injured demonstrators, to standing "on the frontline" of the protests,[9] "throwing stones with the men."[10] As a result, they were forced to pay the highest price for taking part in the revolution: "we got broken, we got sexually assaulted."[11] The Brotherhood's "revisionist version" of women having a purely supportive,[12] more "feminine" role in creating revolutionary change suggests an attempt to deny their political agency in creating social change.

As well as having their role as grassroots revolutionaries undermined, Egyptian women have long been excluded from the top levels of political power and influence. While the Freedom and Justice Party (FJP) claimed to be working hard to consolidate "the right of women to [...] representation in important positions in the state,"[13] it was actually heavily marginalising them from government institutions—including the lower and upper houses of parliament—the House of Representatives (formerly known as the People's Assembly) and *Shura* Council respectively—and, the Constituent Assembly (the committee responsible for amending the constitution). In fact, female representation in high-level positions was lower under Egypt's first elected government than under the previous regime, despite women showing an increased appetite for political participation following the 2011 revolution.[14]

---

[8]Ibid. See also: Interview with Dalia Abd el-Hameed, Gender and Women's Rights Officer at the Egyptian Initiative for Personal Rights, June 4, 2013.

[9]Ibid.

[10]Interview with Dr Nawla Darwiche, Director of the New Woman Foundation, June 5, 2013.

[11]Interview with Mona Eltahawy, June 4, 2013.

[12]Ibid.

[13]"Dr. Omaima Kamel: New Constitution Will Safeguard Women's Rights in Full," *Ikhwan-Web*, July 27, 2012, available at: http://www.ikhwanweb.com/article.php?id=30211.

[14]El-Naggar, T., "TNS: 43 Percent of Women Believe their Situation has Become Worse," *Zawya*, March 26, 2013, available at: http://www.zawya.com/story/TNS_43_of_Women_Believe_their_Situation_has_Become_Worse-ZAWYA20130326101923/.

The Battle for Civil Society

The crackdown on women in the public sphere spread from the streets and the corridors of the Shura Council to women's rights NGOs and wider civil society. Immediately following the revolution, the state carried out a crackdown on human rights groups. In February 2011, the Hesham Mubarak Center for Law was raided, followed by a series of raids against Egyptian and international NGO offices, in December 2011. In early June 2013, the state convicted 43 NGO workers, giving them prison sentences of up to five years.[15] The crackdown on NGOs continued and, in some cases, worsened under Muslim Brotherhood rule, from late June 2012.

Shortly before President Morsi was ousted from power in mid-2013, his government proposed a draft NGO law to further empower the authorities' ability to restrict the activities and funding of human-rights NGOs.[16] Moreover, human-rights NGOs, particularly women's-rights groups, were heavily stigmatised by the Muslim Brotherhood; its political wing, the Freedom and Justice Party (FJP); and wider society. Human-rights organisations were often branded as being "lackeys of the West,"[17] due to their work in international forums.[18]

Likewise, groups supportive of international conventions were labeled as being part of an "international agenda" (and, therefore, unrepresentative of "the inherent pure values of the Egyptian people").[19] The National Council for Women (NCW) was criticised and ignored for working with foreign organisations: accused of aligning itself too closely with the West, on the basis that this directly contradicts the "Islamic identity" of the Egyptian woman. For instance, the NCW's position regarding the UN declaration on the status of women

[15]"Egyptian Court Convicts 43 NGO Employees," *BBC News*, June 4, 2013, available at: http://www.bbc.co.uk/news/world-africa-22765161.

[16]Morayef, H., "Why Egypt's New Law Regulating NGOs is Still Criminal," *Human Rights Watch*, June 11, 2013, available at: http://www.hrw.org/news/2013/06/11/why-egypts-new-law-regulating-ngos-still-criminal.

[17]Interview with Dr Hania Sholkamy, June 6, 2013.

[18]Interview with Dalia Abd el-Hameed, Gender and Women's Rights Officer at the Egyptian Initiative for Personal Rights, June 4, 2013.

[19]"Election Program: The Freedom and Justice Party," The Freedom and Justice Party, 2011, available at: http://www.fjponline.com/view.php?pid=80.

was censured by Essam al-Erian, head of the FJP's parliamentary com-mittee.[20] Given the fact that the NCW acted as a buffer between the state and women's rights NGOs, this heavily undermined the ability of NGOs to have an influence on policies affecting women.[21]

Separate Yet Not Equal

Alongside political marginalization, the state played a key role in restricting women's roles in the public sphere, through segregation. Sexual segregation in public spaces increased following the 2011 revo-lution, particularly in February 2013, during the Muslim Brother-hood's time in power. Segregated train carriages were introduced on several popular transport routes, and segregation was introduced in several schools and hotels. While the state claimed that segregation was a solution to help prevent sexual harassment, it was widely viewed as part of the problem, rather than the solution, in widening the gap in understanding between men and women.[22] Understanding and com-munication between men and women has weakened, to the extent that the narrators of the YouTube video joked about 90 percent of Egyp-tians having become "sexually illiterate." This, combined with the restrictions on sexual satisfaction has led to mass-sexual frustration and a toxic environment on the streets, whereby women dread having to use public transport or even walk down a busy street.

In the long term, those fighting for women's rights are likely to find it harder and harder to create change in a society that is increasingly divided by sex. Dr. Hania Sholkamy explained that the state-led segrega-tion of women "casts a very dark shadow over gender relations in general [and] pervades every aspect of people's lives"—in that the state's control of women's bodies is likely to lead to similar power dynamics between men and women in the private domain, leading to "domestic-violence

[20]Dakroury, N., "Shura Council Criticises the National Council for Women," *Daily News Egypt*, June 11, 2013, available at: http://www.dailynewsegypt.com/2013/06/11/shura-coun-cil-criticises-the-national-council-for-women/.

[21]Interview with Dr Hania Sholkamy, June 6, 2013.

[22]Dyer, E., "Marginalising Egyptian Women," The Henry Jackson Society (October 2013), available at: http://henryjacksonsociety.org/wp-content/uploads/2013/12/Marginalising-Egyptian-Women.pdf.

transgressions."[23] Therefore, while providing an instant and short-term solution to treating the symptoms of harassment, segregation does not cure the societal disease itself; it worsens it. As a result, Egypt's new government would be best served targeting the root causes of sexual harassment, and undo previous steps towards public gendered segregation.

Sexual Violence

Though sexual harassment has long been a serious problem in Egypt, sexual attacks against women are widely thought to have increased in both severity and frequency following the revolution, including mob attacks (many with sharp instruments) during large-scale protests. By late 2013, 99.3 percent of women reported having experienced some form of sexual harassment.[24] Images of women being violently harassed and beaten (most iconically, the "blue bra" girl, who was beaten by the police) became commonplace online and in the Western media, throughout 2011 and 2012. Furthermore, while it is impossible to collect accurate information regarding the number of sexual-harassment and rape cases (due to the lack of women who go on a report the incident), the Interior Ministry claimed that reported rapes had increased from 119 in 2011, to 129 in 2012.[25] Given the restrictions on sexual freedom in Egypt, serious questions need to be asked about what impact they are having on the streets.

Women's sexuality has not just been attempted to be shielded from men, but destroyed all together. While FGM in Egypt was officially made illegal in 2008, the problem has remained widespread following the revolution.[26, 27] Despite the absence of recent statistics, the rate of

---

[23]Interview with Dr Hania Sholkamy, June 6, 2013.

[24]"Sexual Harassment in Egypt... The Causes and Confrontation Methods," *UN Women*, April 2013, available at http://www.un.org.eg/Publications.aspx?pageID=43

[25]"Raped Egypt Women Wish Death Over Life as Crimes Ignored," *Bloomberg*, March 7, 2013, available at: http://www.bloomberg.com/news/2013-03-07/raped-egypt-women-wish-death-over-life-as-crimes-ignored.html.

[26]"Law No. 126 of 2008 Amending the Law on Children (No. 12 of 1996)," *The UN Secretary-General's Database on Violence Against Women*, July 21, 2009, available at: http://sgdatabase.unwomen.org/searchDetail.action?measureId=25149&baseHREF=country&baseHREFId=465.

[27]*Female Genital Mutilation/Cutting: A Statistical Overview and Exploration of the Dynamics of Change*, UNICEF (2012), available at: http://www.unicef.org/media/files/FGCM_ Lo_res.pdf.

operations carried out is thought—by women's rights activists—to have increased following the revolution.[28]

The fact that approximately 90 percent of Egyptian women have suffered the torture of Female Genital Mutilation (FGM) is a largely unknown fact—particularly in the West. FGM is a form of torture used to de-sexualise women by removing the clitoris and often mutilating other parts of the vagina (in part to ensure virginity before marriage). FGM is widely regarded to be a cultural practise whereby the external female genitalia are partially or totally removed "for non-medical reasons,"[29] as a way of "de-sexualizing women, and repressing sexual desire."[30] Women and girls who experience FGM are put at serious risk of infection and death throughout and following the procedure, and are often left with life-long pain and suffering as a result of the physical and emotional damage inflicted.[31]

As a result of FGM, the sexual pleasure and equality within a relationship belongs to the man alone, whereas the woman is forced to endure crippling pain, infection, and depression (to name a few of the consequences of FGM) throughout her entire adult life. Nevertheless, the FJP, the Muslim Brotherhood, and other leading strands of Egypt's Islamist movement have repeatedly attempted to justify and legitimise FGM through various religious; medical; and legal channels. During its time in power, the FJP claimed th at it was "working on [...] promulgating a law criminalizing all forms of violence against women and girls."[32]

However, despite often claiming to oppose FGM, the FJP attempted to lift state control over the practice by portraying FGM as

---

[28]Khojji, Z., "A Crime Against Women," *The Majalla*, July 16, 2013, available at: http://www.majalla.com/eng/2013/07/article55243392.

[29]"Definition of Female Genital Mutilation—Female Genital Mutilation Legal Guidance," The Crown Prosecution Service, available at: http://www.cps.gov.uk/legal/d_to_g/female_genital_mutilation/#definition.

[30]Ibid.

[31]*How Does FGM/FGC Affect Women's Health?—Promoting Gender Equality*, United Nations Population Fund, available at: http://www.unfpa.org/gender/practices2.htm#15.

[32]Statement by H.E. Dr. Pakinam Al Sharkawi, Deputy Prime Minister & Special Assistant of the President for Political Affairs, Arab Republic of Egypt, Before the 57th Session of the Commission on the Status of Women, The Permanent Mission of Egypt to the United Nations New York, March 2013, available at: http://www.un.org/womenwatch/daw/csw/csw57/generaldiscussion/memberstates/egypt.pdf.

a private family issue. Mohamed Morsi stated that FGM is a private issue between mothers and daughters, adding that families—not the state—should decide on whether to carry out the ritual.[33] However, the decision to undergo FGM is rarely one that the daughter is capable of making or consenting to, due to her young age; rather, it is solely decided upon by the mother or guardian of the child. Therefore, the Egyptian state's attempt to portray FGM as a choice was both false and misleading.

By promoting and/or failing to prevent FGM, the Egyptian government has breached its legal obligation to protect the rights of women and, even more seriously, girls. Firstly, FGM must be treated as child abuse, due to its ability to harm one's health and infringe upon one's physical; mental; spiritual; and social growth.[34] Secondly, UNICEF's Convention on the Rights of the Child (CRC)—ratified by Egypt—states in Article 19 that children have the right of protection from all forms of mental and physical violence.[35] The Article also indicates that the role of the government is to "ensure that children are properly cared for and protect[ed...] from violence, abuse and neglect by their parents, or anyone else who looks after them."[36]

Moreover, the fact that FGM may lead to death through blood loss and/or disease, means that the practice directly threatens the right of women and girls to live, as well as the right to a body free of disease or mutilation. Therefore, despite promising to criminalise all forms of violence against women, the FJP—through its opposition to, and in some cases promotion of, FGM—stood in direct violation of its legal obligation to "take all effective and appropriate measures with a view to abolishing traditional practices prejudicial to the health of children."[37] In this case, the "traditional practice" is arguably the most

---

[33]Allam, A., "Egypt: A Toxic Mix of Tradition and Religion," *The Financial Times*, July 7, 2012, available at: http://www.ft.com/cms/s/0/8185dd5c-c5c0-11e1-a5d5-00144feabdc 0.html.

[34]"Promoting Gender Equality," United Nations Population Fund, available at: http://www.unfpa.org/gender/practices2.htm.

[35]*Fact Sheet: A Summary of the Rights under the Convention on the Rights of the Child*, UNICEF, available at: http://www.unicef.org/crc/files/Rights_overview.pdf.

[36]Ibid.

[37]*Convention on the Rights of the Child*, United Nations Human Rights, Office of the High Commissioner for Human Rights, available at: http://www.ohchr.org/en/professionalinterest/pages/crc.aspx.

serious form of violence against women. FGM is (and was) therefore used by the state, to control what it regarded as its biggest threat: women's bodies and sexual freedom.[38]

Conclusion

The 2011 revolution against 30 years of oppression under Mubarak's regime profoundly altered the fabric of Egyptian society. Many issues facing women that had previously gone undiscussed and ignored were brought out onto the street and spoken about in public space. Egypt is now a fundamentally revolutionary place, with weekly protests and paintings of the hundreds who lost their lives during the revolution lining the streets of Cairo. However, the significance of these arguably irreversible changes to society was hugely taken for granted by those who took power, who proceeded to attack the very electoral promises and democratic freedoms used to win office.

Women were one of the greatest forces within the 2011 revolution, yet proved to be the cheapest bargaining chip during the Muslim Brotherhood's year in power (from June 2012 to July 2013). Many of the long-standing issues facing women became worse, and women's rights and roles in society were undermined by the state in the name of reclaiming Islamic identity against the West and the *filul* (the former regime).

The ousting of the FJP, and the subsequent demise of the Muslim Brotherhood, was fundamentally due to its attempts to survive as a legitimate leading democratic party whilst imposing an Islamist ideology upon the Egyptian people. Despite minor improvements under the rule of Adly Mansour's interim government, women's rights groups have so far been left disappointed yet again. While it remains to be seen what will come of the planned parliamentary and presidential elections of early 2014, it is likely that—without fundamental and immediate changes—the plight of women in Egypt will continue.

---

[38]Interview with Dr. Nawla Darwiche, Director of the New Woman Foundation, June 5, 2013.

Part III

Comparative Transitions:
The Arab Spring in Local and
International Context

Chapter Seven

Looking for Lessons: What Transitions from across the Mediterranean and the Atlantic Can Offer the Middle East

Edward P. Joseph

There are good reasons to be skeptical about transplanting lessons from the Balkans, or any part of the world for that matter, to the tumult in the Middle East once known as "the Arab Spring." Indeed, comparing the countries of the Maghreb or Levant with their neighbors across the Mediterranean and along the Adriatic seems mainly to bring yawning differences into sharper relief. Whether Albanian or Serb, Bosniak (Muslim) or Croat (Catholic), Macedonian or Montenegrin, the core outlook and cultural fundament in the Balkan region is, in contrast to the Arab world, decidedly European.[1] Despite their bloody wars in the 1990s and continuing mutual suspicions, the vast majority of the feuding Balkan peoples at least share a common "destination"—becoming a modern European country with functioning markets, in which individual rights are respected, rule of law prevails, and religion is largely separated from the state. In sharp contrast with the Middle East, the ethno-religious tussle in the Balkans is largely over the question of who will control the levers of state power, but not (with a few exceptions) over the fundamental character of that power.

From Syria to Iraq, Bahrain, Saudi Arabia and Lebanon, however, sectarian tensions are freighted not only by the question of "who rules?" but stretch to deeper questions over the character of the state, the role of religion, the degree of tolerance for individual rights and women's rights, education and more. The same holds true in Egypt, Tunisia and Libya, where deep differences in fundamental outlook animate divisions that may also have a tribal or competitive "who rules?" component. In short, the bitter conflicts in the Balkans may

---

[1]Turkey, which has widely invoked as a model for the Middle East, is not part of this discussion of the Western Balkans.

run deep, but they are usually not very wide; while the Middle East is riven by a vast gulf of differences over the fundamental questions about the character of the state, as well as by deep mutual suspicions.

Another reason for skepticism is that the Arab Uprisings, which began in Tunisia, have already had more influence on the Balkans and elsewhere than vice-versa. From Tahrir Square to Taksim Square to Sarajevo's Bosnia-Herzegovina Square, citizens have drawn inspiration from the outpouring of protests (and the clever use of social media) that brought down Ben Ali and Mubarak—despite the chaos in Egypt, the horrific violence in Syria, and the instability in Libya that has ensued. The "Occupy" movement that began in the U.S. also has had a major influence on Balkan protests—but it was the Arab Spring that served as the original inspiration for "Occupy."

Moreover, this year's angry protests in Bosnia have called into question more than the misrule spawned by an unwieldy governing structure and an array of elected, but unaccountable, politicians. The international community and even representative democracy itself have become the targets of protester ire, as Bosnians, like so many in Europe, voice their disillusionment over established, nominally democratic institutions and ineffective prescriptions. The great irony is that while protesters in the Middle East were (at the outset of the Arab Spring) expressing long-suppressed discontent with authoritarian rule and demanding democratic reforms, established democracy itself has taken a major hit in Europe, with perceived corruption, endless austerity amidst economic stagnation and, as in the Middle East, a sense of dwindling opportunity. Developments in countries like Hungary, whose leader has rolled back on a range of democratic protections, have called into question the value of the ballyhooed EU accession process.

So, as disappointment over the Arab Spring is matched by disillusionment with conventional democracy in Europe, now is a good time not just to impart lessons from the Balkans to the Middle East, but perhaps to exchange them in both directions. Angry Bosnians infused by radical left-wing ideology might do well to reflect on the mass dissatisfaction of Egyptians who, after only a year of misrule by the ideologically driven Muslim Brotherhood, eagerly embraced a decidedly non-democratic regime simply because it promised an end to chaos. The failed Egyptian experiment with a radical shift in ideological direction should be a reminder to Bosnians that, in the end, the government must meet the basic needs of the people. Embracing tried-and-true EU reforms, however tedious and imperfect, to build up the country's existing, conventional institutions will have a better chance of meeting those needs than a radical, ideologically driven agenda that might, as in Egypt, end up in disaster if actually attempted.

As for lessons that the Middle East could learn, clearly the most significant one—if the most difficult to apply—is the value of having national consensus on the country's strategic orientation. The best example of this from the Balkans is in Serbia and Kosovo, which last year managed to put their longstanding conflict into a new perspective by agreeing to "normalize relations." This breakthrough was wholly driven by the shared interest among most Serbs and Kosovars to join the European Union. While some in each country can criticize the normalization deal, few challenge the core incentive for compromise: advancing the country's relationship with the EU. In turn, this reinforced national consensus has already helped stem the dangerous attraction of "Greater Albania" in Kosovo, and the flirtation that some Serbs have had with Russia as a potential alternative to the EU. Both of these dubious trends, which promised only internal divisiveness, are now marginalized. The emerging consensus on joining the EU has managed to narrow political differences, from broad ideological battles to more productive discussions over how to develop institutions, fight corruption and grow the economy. Croatia, which joined the EU last year, exemplifies the transformative power of the EU. Foreign Minister Vesna Pusic, herself a former civil society activist, credits the "mundane tasks" associated with the EU accession process with reframing charged, polarizing debate.[2]

Unfortunately, the countries of the Middle East cannot join the EU or NATO, or any other supra-national organization that might have such a channeling effect on debate, but that should not stop civil society or political leaders from the search for a national project on which national consensus could be built. Cleaning up the environment, for example, is a subject that is not intrinsically divisive. While struggling to come to terms over intensely sensitive questions over religious

---

[2]Foreign Minister Vesna Pusic speaking at Johns Hopkins School of Advanced International Studies in Washington, DC on February, 28, 2014.

rights, the rights of women, or other issues that come up when writing a Constitution, civil society and political leaders could actively explore ways to work across the sectarian and religious divide and forge national consensus on unifying issues like the environment. By opening up space for, say in Egypt, the most conservative Islamist voices to join with young civil society activists and officials in a structured conversation over environmental laws, the possibility for the beginning of dialogue on other, more sensitive matters might emerge.

Imparting another lesson from the Balkans, dialogue is an area where the international community could, in principle, be of active assistance. Nearly every international organization, as well as a battery of international NGOs, has endeavored for years to foster some kind of dialogue, if not full reconciliation, in the Balkans. One of the most striking efforts in this regard has occurred in Kosovo—not between feuding Serbs and Albanians, but actually within the divided Serb community itself. Spearheaded by U.S.-based NGO activists, the initiative has brought those Serbs in the south who actively cooperate with the Albanian-led government in Kosovo together with those in the north who see such cooperation as traitorous. While divisions remain, the effort has diminished the demonization which had plagued the divided Serb community. Transplanting such experiences to a place like Egypt is complicated by the hostility shown toward the work of international NGOs so far, but indigenous Egyptian civil society groups do not face the same barriers and could, as the U.S.-group working in Kosovo did, identify real opportunities to serve as catalysts for much-needed dialogue.

However, Bosnia offers another less encouraging lesson on the limits of dialogue that might keep expectations in check for countries like Syria and Iraq that are torn by sectarian violence. There has been no fighting in Bosnia since the war ended nearly two decades ago, but despite outside dialogue interventions that began literally in the earliest days after the peace agreement was signed, ethnic communities remain deeply polarized. Even though there is full freedom of movement in the country, a common language, and as noted above a shared European orientation, suspicion, not trust, still pervades. The lesson here is that even the best-designed dialogue interventions will hit hard limits if not matched by larger progress on the political questions which divide communities. Bosnians may have stopped fighting a long time ago, but some leaders have openly proclaimed their opposition to the country's common institutions and, especially at election time, made naked appeals to the narrow ethnic interest.

Dialogue can help attenuate the slide towards polarization, but will fall far short of the goal of true reconciliation if not matched by real progress on larger political questions. If Iraq's government continues to play such a polarizing role, no one should expect NGO or other efforts to bridge dialogue to achieve widespread results. Failing to accept the predominance of political dynamics is to set unrealistic expectations for ground-up dialogue.

Experience in the Balkans teaches us that there is really no substitute for a viable, well-constructed peace agreement when it comes to managing ethno-sectarian violence. For example, theorists have for years been touting trade and economic growth as the panacea for continuing divisions in Bosnia. Unfortunately, rather than improve relations, external trade has actually exacerbated the country's division. This is because the deeply flawed Dayton peace accord attained peace by splitting the country into two asymmetrical entities. The more cohesive, largely mono-ethnic Serb entity of Republika Srpska has the ability to set its own trade and economic policies, and even engage directly with EU institutions independently from its counterpart entity, the Bosniak-Croat "Federation." So, the ability of the RS to progress economically while the split, unwieldy Federation remains mired in wasteful administration and political division, has only further inclined Serbs to want even less to do with the country's central government in Sarajevo. The RS President, Milorad Dodik, has even proposed outright separation of his entity from Bosnia—a step that would bring the country into serious conflict, while opening up the Pandora's Box of revanchist claims and nationalist projects around the region. Meanwhile, internal trade between the two entities, abetted by freedom of movement, has done little to knit the communities together.

By contrast, Macedonia is another deeply challenged and divided Balkan country, whose economic growth has not been a cause for more fracturing. This is because its peace accord, the Ohrid Agreement, did not rest on the ethno-territorial model applied in Bosnia. Instead, the country's vying parties—ethnic Albanians and ethnic Macedonians—agreed to terms wholly without reference to territory.

Instead, the Albanians (who, were they given compact territory, might well emulate the Bosnian Serbs in their optimal desire to separate from Macedonia), accepted a deal which increases their rights within the country's existing territorial structure. This "Ohrid Agreement" created no new territorial units, not even cantons or new municipalities. Instead, power was substantially shifted from the central state to existing municipal units—a step that benefitted predominantly Macedonian municipalities as well as Albanian ones. Additionally, "Ohrid" simultaneously boosted Albanian powers and representation at the level of the central government, increasing their incentive to actively participate in state-level institutions. This means that the group with the greatest incentive to secede—the Albanians—has no foundation on which to build a proto-state (like the RS has in Bosnia), and has very good reason to participate in the country's central institutions (unlike the Bosnian Serbs who see development of the central government in Sarajevo as a threat to their entity). The fact that tensions still exist between Macedonians and Albanians only reinforces the value of their agreement; they like and trust each other no more than do Bosnia's Serbs, Croats and Bosniaks, but they act in ways that keep the state functioning.[3]

These lessons might yet be of value to Syrians, if the day ever comes when the parties there engage in serious peace talks. There's no doubt that Alawites and Kurds will both demand some form of defined territory within the new Syrian state. Applying the lessons from Bosnia and Macedonia, peacemakers must make every effort to provide the state that emerges with integrative characteristics. As in Macedonia, a well-designed balance of local rights and centralized powers can create incentives for productive inter-action, avoiding the pitfall of highly autonomous regions that serve only to perpetuate centrifugal dynamics, and therefore, conflict.

At the other extreme, given the perpetuation of sectarian strife in Iraq today, clearly that country might have benefitted from a modicum of federalization along the lines created for Bosnia, not just with respect to the existing Kurdistan regional government, but between

---

[3]Tensions between ethnic Albanians and ethnic Macedonians would be markedly lessened if the country could Greece would relent and allow the country to proceed into NATO membership and full EU candidacy.

the two most implacable groups, the minority Sunnis and the majority Shiites whose leadership seems intent on exploiting Baghdad's central-ized powers for maximum sectarian advantage. In other words, there are benefits from the ethno-territorial solution in terms of providing group security—as well as risks in going too far by putting the ethnic sub-unit into antagonism with the central government.

Lebanon's lasting, but less-than-stable inter-confessional arrange-ment no doubt also offers some lessons that might be applied—or avoided—in an eventual Syrian peace agreement. Though this system was the end-product of French occupation, Lebanon, Syria, Bosnia, Kosovo and Macedonia all share a common Ottoman heritage. In tackling the pernicious challenge of tribal and ethno-sectarian vio-lence in the Middle East, it might be useful, as a starting point of analysis, to distinguish all areas which were under longstanding Ottoman rule from those in the Maghreb that developed independ-ently from the Sublime Porte in Istanbul. The legacy of the millet sys-tem and the overall Ottoman approach to managing ethno-religious tensions is present across the former empire, from the Balkans through the Levant. There should be no surprise that additional simi-larities emerge between countries like Iraq and Bosnia, each of which has three dominant groups and whose Ottoman foundation was even-tually succeeded by a form of socialism.

In sum, the Balkans share an Ottoman legacy and ethno-religious strife with large swathes of the Middle East—but do *not* share their pronounced, uniformly European orientation nor the possibility for every Balkan country to join Euro-Atlantic institutions. So, in the search for lessons, it makes sense to cast the net wider to another part of the world which has also produced notable transition success stories.

Latin America has seen a remarkable transformation almost throughout the continent from extremist right- and left-wing dicta-torships to mostly functioning democracies. Unlike the Balkans, how-ever, democratic progress was not achieved in a burst after the end of the Cold War with a headlong plunge to NATO and the EU, but rather as a slow, largely home-grown effort with multi-party elections the last—not first—step in the transition.

Mexico and Chile stand out as particularly notable examples. In each case, the catalyst for reform came from within as the ruling elements, PRI (in Mexico) and Pinochet regime (in Chile), felt the pressure for reform from within the middle class and business community that saw the benefits of integrating with—and fitting in with—the world economy. The PRI and Pinochet began to liberalize in the belief that small reforms would increase the longevity of their rule. Indeed, much of the 1980s saw their continuity at the top of Mexico and Chile, respectively. But what began as small openings eventually yielded highly significant, incipient change from the bottom as opposition political parties, civil society, human rights groups and the media all began, step-by-step, to take advantage of openings.

In this approach, elections were the crowning piece of a bottom-up process of cultivating both democratic institutions and democratic values. Indeed, Vicente Fox, the first opposition figure to win the Presidency in modern Mexican history, was not elected until the year 2000. But unlike Egypt, Mexico has steadily progressed on the democratic path after its election milestone. Despite the challenge of drug-related violence which, like terrorism, might have justified a return toward general authoritarianism, democracy remains ever more rooted in Mexico. And unlike Hungary, which has backslid on its EU-mandated reforms, Chile has as well made remarkable, continuous democratic and economic strides after jettisoning its authoritarian regime.

It is not too late for even Egypt, not to mention the far more encouraging Tunisia, to learn from the Mexican and Chilean experiences. Bereft of the unifying force and tutelage of the European Union, Egypt, Tunisia, Libya and other countries of the Middle East could emulate the slow-and-steady approach to democracy in Latin America, gradually liberalizing while inculcating the values of pluralism, tolerance, accountability and rule of law that infuse democratic institutions and undergird even the most enlightened Constitutions. Indeed, Middle Eastern monarchies like Jordan and Morocco seem to be moving down this tortoise-not-the-hare path towards democracy. When the time comes for transition to full democratic rule, the prospects could be improved for moderate forces—and society at large—to be prepared.

Latin America also offers an encouraging example in the struggle that the Middle East faces in dealing with the other bane of democratic development: Islamist extremism. In Latin America, Communism served for decades as a useful foil for the region's authoritarian regimes, justifying crackdowns which, in turn, only increased the appeal of revolutionary socialism practiced in Cuba. Even before the fall of the Berlin Wall, however, the luster of Castro-ism began to fade. Those countries, like Mexico and Chile, that began the hard work of developing the foundations for democratic rule were poised to eventually take advantage when Communism was further discredited. In unreformed Venezuela and, to a lesser degree, Bolivia, no such alternatives were in place, creating the opening for a collectivist dictatorship in Venezuela and a crusading left-wing government in Bolivia. In Peru, however, the recent return of an avowedly left-wing president has not fundamentally altered the country's democratic and market oriented direction. Democratic values and institutions have progressed enough in Peru for antagonists (the government and the business community) to forge compromise instead of resorting to extremism and polarization.

Unfortunately, as long as Iran remains a theocracy, the Middle East may lack its "Cuba," i.e., a failed ideologically-based regime whose collapse discredits not just the regime, but the ideology as well. The collapse of Muhammed Morsi's winner-take-all approach to governance has surely discredited the Muslim Brotherhood, but it remains to be seen if that antipathy extends to the appeal of heavy-handed "political Islam" or its authoritarian expression in a non-Arab country like Iran. It may take time and enlightenment not yet in evidence, but proud Egypt, once the beacon of the entire Islamic world, might one day become a model for the region to follow if its leaders embrace the examples of the most successful Latin American democracies and allow openings for real democratization. Tunisia, the launching pad for the then-called Arab Spring, might also fulfill this exemplary role if it builds on its successful, nearly two-plus-year Constitution-writing exercise with a continued effort to inculcate the values of pluralism, civility, tolerance, and rule of law in a way in which otherwise opposed elements of society can find their place. While one must be realistic about the prospects for such strife-torn countries as Syria and Iraq, one can at least hope for the day when countries like Tunisia or even Libya and Egypt will themselves be examined as the source of positive lessons for aspiring democracies.

Chapter Eight

Lebanon's Arab Spring: The Cedar Revolution Nine Years On

Rupert Sutton

With the anniversaries of many of the major events seen during the Arab Spring passing in early 2014, much of the optimism of the time has long since faded. Increased economic volatility, political instability, and street violence have been features of the upheaval, while in Syria an ongoing civil war has killed over 120,000 people and is driving sectarian violence in Iraq and Lebanon.[1] Despite this pessimistic outlook, though, it is still too early to predict the failures of the revolutions in the Arab Spring countries. The economic, political and security developments of an earlier uprising in the region instead suggest that, given time, instability can be overcome and a country can begin to recover.

This uprising, the Intifadat al-Istiqlal, or Cedar Revolution, in Lebanon bears many similarities to those that took place across the region in 2010–2011. Demonstrations following the February 14, 2005 assassination of the former Prime Minister, Rafic Hariri, brought hundreds of thousands onto the streets and resulted in the resignation of Prime Minister Omar Karami; the formation of a new government, following free elections; and the withdrawal of Syrian troops from Lebanon.

Despite being followed by economic decline, political polarisation, and increased violence—as currently experienced by those countries that saw Arab Spring revolutions—Lebanon's economy was able to recover, while an agreement reached in Doha in May 2008 ended open street fighting between political factions and enabled a deeply divided political system to function again with relative stability. By 2011, the overt influence of Damascus had faded and the country had seen four years of significant GDP growth, suggesting that—with

---

[1] "Death Toll in Syria Likely as High as 120,000: Group," *Reuters*, May 14, 2013, available at: http://uk.reuters.com/article/2013/05/14/us-syria-crisis-deaths-idU.S.BRE94D 0L420130514.

time—the upheaval of revolutions across North Africa may be replaced with stability, under more accountable government.

This optimism is tempered however by the fact that, today, Lebanon is once again facing economic malaise, political paralysis and paramilitary violence, all driven by the conflict in Syria. This threatens the fragile progress made since 2008, and suggests that the political polarisation exacerbated by the Cedar Revolution has left Lebanon more vulnerable to division. If this is the case then it may be that, even if Lebanon's uprising shows stability can be achieved, the Arab Spring countries will exhibit a similar susceptibility to political unrest in the future.

The Cedar Revolution and the Arab Spring

On 14 February 2005, a massive car bomb exploded on Beirut's Rue Minet el Hos'n, killing former Lebanese Prime Minister Rafic Hariri and 22 other people. In the week following the bombing, up to 20,000 people marched from the scene of his death to Beirut's Martyrs' Square,[2] chanting slogans blaming the Damascus government for the assassination, and calling for a withdrawal of Syrian troops from the country.[3] Protests continued in the days following this, regularly drawing over 20,000 people, while a tent city called "Camp Freedom" was set up in Martyrs' Square.[4] Demonstrators also called for the resignation of the pro-Syrian government led by Omar Karami, and criticised the pro-Syrian President Emile Lahoud (whose term had been extended by three years just months before, following pressure from Damascus).[5]

Prime Minister Karami resigned on February 28 (though he was reappointed by President Lahoud, to form a unity government, on March 10).[6] By this time, the under-pressure Syrian President, Bashar

---

[2] "The Cedar Revolution," *NOW*, available at: https://now.mmedia.me/lb/en/archive/The-Cedar-Revolution169.

[3] "Beirut protesters denounce Syria," *BBC News*, February 21, 2005, available at: http://news.bbc.co.uk/1/hi/world/middle_east/4283543.stm.

[4] "The Cedar Revolution,", *op. cit.* (footnote 3).

[5] "Lebanon—2005," *Freedom House*, available at: http://www.freedomhouse.org/report/freedom-world/2005/lebanon#.Us_ekfRdVQg.

[6] "Pro-Syrian Lebanese PM re-appointed," *The Guardian*, March 10, 2005, available at: http://www.theguardian.com/world/2005/mar/10/syria.jamessturcke.

al-Assad, had announced that all Syrian troops would withdraw from Lebanon by the end of April 2005.[7] Despite counter-demonstrations in support of Damascus, when up to 500,000 people gathered to watch Hezbollah's Hassan Nasrallah speak,[8] opposition to Karami continued and, on March 14, over 800,000 people marched on Martyrs' Square.[9] A month later, with protests continuing and politicians failing to agree on the formation of a unity government, Karami resigned for a second time, before the elections on May 31. These elections, declared by the UN Security Council to be "fair and credible," began on 29 May and concluded on 19 June in a clear victory for an anti-Syrian coalition between Hariri's son, Saad's Future Movement and the Progressive Socialist Party (PSP), which formed a government under Prime Minister Fouad Siniora.[10]

While the Arab Spring protests of 2011 may have focused on oppressive domestic regimes, and particularly individuals such as Muammar Gaddafi and Hosni Mubarak, a parallel between these and the Lebanese uprising can immediately be drawn. In the development of tented protest communities, like "Camp Freedom," and the vast numbers of often secular middle-class protesters who occupied the streets, the protests of the Cedar Revolution mirrored and arguably inspired those seen in Tahrir Square. Similarly, the call for the resignation of unpopular leaders Lahoud and Karami were no different to the slogans shouted in Tunis and Cairo. The mass protest of those supportive of the ruling government was also seen—though it did not turn violent in 2005, as some later did during the Arab Spring. In addition to these factors, the fall of the Karami government within two months of the protests beginning and the establishment of an opposition government through democratic means, were similar to the processes which saw the Muslim Brotherhood parties, Ennahda

---

[7]"Assad pledges Lebanon withdrawal," *BBC News*, March 2, 2005, available at: http://news.bbc.co.uk/1/hi/world/middle_east/4310699.stm.

[8]"Syria Supporters Rally in Lebanon," *The Washington Post*, March 9, 2005, available at: http://www.washingtonpost.com/wp-dyn/articles/A16165-2005Mar8.html.

[9]"'Record' Protest Held in Beirut," *BBC News*, March 14, 2005, available at: http://news.bbc.co.uk/1/hi/world/middle_east/4346613.stm.

[10]See: Annan, K., "Letter dated 26 October 2005 from the Secretary-General addressed to the President of the Security Council," United Nations Security Council (2005), p. 3, p. 7, available at: http://www.un.org/en/ga/search/view_doc.asp?symbol=S/2005/673.

and the Freedom and Justice Party (FJP), elected in Tunisia and Egypt, respectively.

The Aftermath of Revolution

These were not the only similarities though, and in the months following Hariri's assassination, despite the relatively auspicious beginnings of the Cedar Revolution, Lebanon soon began to experience many of those problems now facing countries like Tunisia, Libya, and Egypt. These included the damaging economic impact, political polarisation and security concerns that can be seen today in all of these countries.

As with the Arab Spring nations, the repercussions of the Cedar Revolution saw Lebanon's economy suffer. Unlike Libya and Yemen, however, Lebanon did not see its economy shrink during the years following the revolution, with GDP growth maintained.[11] However, the revolution still had a detrimental effect, with GDP-growth figures of 7.4 percent in 2004 falling to 1 percent in 2005 and just 0.6 percent in 2006.[12] During the same period, consumer-price inflation, shrinking by 0.7 percent in 2005, grew to 5.6 percent in 2006, before hitting 10 percent in 2008,[13] while the country's debt-to-GDP ratio rose fast: from 167 percent at the end of 2004, to 182 percent in 2006.[14]

---

[11] This is compared to Yemen, which saw GDP growth of 7.7 percent in January 2011 replaced with a 10.5 percent decrease in January 2012. See: "Yemen GDP Annual Growth Rate," *Trading Economics*, available at: http://www.tradingeconomics.com/yemen/gdp-growth-annual, and Libya, where GDP growth had fallen by 60 percent in January 2012. See: "Libya GDP Annual Growth Rate," *Trading Economics*, available at: http://www.tradingeconomics.com/libya/gdp-growth-annual.

[12] "Lebanon—World Development Indicators," The World Bank Group, available at: http://data.worldbank.org/country/lebanon.

[13] "Inflation, average consumer prices," International Monetary Fund, available at: https://www.imf.org/external/pubs/ft/weo/2013/02/weodata/weorept.aspx?sy=2005&ey=2018&scsm=1&ssd=1&sort=country&ds=.&br=1&pr1.x=78&pr1.y=15&c=446&s=PCPIPCH percent2CPCPIEPCH&grp=0&a=.

[14] "General Government Gross Debt," International Monetary Fund, available at: https://www.imf.org/external/pubs/ft/weo/2013/02/weodata/weorept.aspx?pr.x=75&pr.y=8&sy=2004&ey=2018&scsm=1&ssd=1&sort=country&ds=.&br=1&c=446&s=GGXWDN_NGDP percent2CGGXWDG_NGDP&grp=0&a=.

The uprising also had a negative effect on the Lebanese tourism industry, one of the country's most important economic sectors. A favorite holiday destination for visitors from the Gulf, the country had seen visitor numbers increase year-on-year between 1997 and 2004. However, from 1,278,000 visitors in 2004, the number of incoming tourists fell to 1,017,000 in 2007: a drop of 20.5 percent, which coincided with the worst of the instability brought on by the Cedar Revolution.[15] In December 2006, following political unrest caused by multiple ministerial resignations and the assassination of Pierre Gemayel,[16] the head of the Lebanese Hotel Association claimed that hotel occupancy was at just 25 percent during a period of the year when the country was expecting up to 400,000 visitors.[17] At the same time, international-tourism receipts as a percentage of exports fell from 45.1 percent in 2004, to just 28.5 percent in 2008.[18]

The damage that the Cedar Revolution caused the country's tourism industry was also reflected elsewhere in the wider economy, as strikes called by the Hezbollah-led opposition, political deadlock and violence all damaged business confidence. The manufacturing sector's growth, which had shown a steady rise since 2001, fell from 8.3 percent in 2004, to -0.1 percent in 2005 and -6.7 percent in 2006. Aside from 7.2 percent growth in 2007, likely caused by reconstruction work following the war between Israel and Hezbollah in 2006, the industry continued to shrink following this: contracting by 6.3 percent in 2008, and 4.2 percent in 2009.[19] This was accompanied by a fall in energy production: from 240.5 kiloton equivalent (kte) in 2004, to 177.3kte in 2008—though it is likely that a proportion of this was also caused by damage to facilities during the 2006 conflict.[20] One knock-on effect of this can be seen in the unemployment figures (with those out of work

---

[15] "International Tourism, Number of Arrivals: Lebanon," The World Bank Group, available at: http://data.worldbank.org/indicator/ST.INT.ARVL?page=1.

[16] "Lebanese Christian Leader Killed," *BBC News,* November 21, 2006, available at: http://news.bbc.co.uk/1/hi/world/middle_east/6169606.stm.

[17] "Protests Blow to Beirut Economy," *BBC News,* December 8, 2006, available at: http://news.bbc.co.uk/1/hi/world/middle_east/6162941.stm.

[18] "Lebanon—World Development Indicators," The World Bank Group, available at: http://data.worldbank.org/country/lebanon.

[19] Ibid.

[20] Ibid.

rising from 7.9 percent of the population in 2004, to 8.9 percent in 2007).[21]

The similarity between the economic troubles experienced by the Arab Spring countries and Lebanon following the Cedar Revolution is also mirrored in the political polarisation that followed the uprising. Echoing the ongoing divide between Islamist and secular groups in Egypt, Libya, and Tunisia, this dispute had its roots in pre-existing political fault lines, yet had been exacerbated by the 2005 uprising. Support or opposition to Syrian influence in Lebanon, the ideological focus point of both the Cedar Revolution and of Lebanese politics after the civil war, still existed; yet, the revolution had made power-sharing politics a more zero-sum game. When the anti-Syrian parties, known as the "March 14 Coalition," had come to power following the Cedar Revolution, they had allowed the pro-Syrian March 8 Coalition opposition few Ministers in the cabinet. This had left Christians in the Free Patriotic Movement, Phalange, Baath and Syrian Social Nationalist parties on the sidelines,[22] and in a situation in which a significant proportion of the population now felt underrepresented. As such, despite the election victory won by the Future Movement and its supporters in 2005, the opposition continued to call for a unity government in which it would have a veto,[23] undermining political stability and ensuring ongoing unrest.

This political divide was further exacerbated by the creation of the UN Special Tribunal investigating Hariri's assassination, which was strongly opposed by Hezbollah and the Syrian government.[24] Similar to the political disputes over the religious extent of the new constitution in Tunisia, or the conflict between the Muslim Brotherhood and the judiciary or armed forces in Egypt, opponents of the process were willing to collapse the Lebanese government (with all five Shia minis-

---

[21]Ibid.

[22] "Security Tops New Cabinet's To-Do List," *The Daily Star*, July 21, 2005, available at: http://www.dailystar.com.lb/News/Lebanon-News/2005/Jul-21/5090-security-tops-new-cabinets-to-do-list.ashx#axzz2qMmjWG1H.

[23] "Hezbollah's Leader Calls for Street Protests," *The New York Times*, November 20, 2006, available at: http://www.nytimes.com/2006/11/20/world/middleeast/20lebanon.html?_r=0.

[24] "U.S. Issues Lebanon 'Plot' Warning," *BBC News*, November 1, 2006, available at: http://news.bbc.co.uk/1/hi/world/americas/6107224.stm.

ters resigning in November 2006 to try and prevent the passage of the tribunal draft bill).[25] Driven by political difference rather than confessional fault lines, as demonstrated by the presence of the pro-Syrian Christian Free Patriotic Movement siding with Hezbollah, the polarisation that these issues caused was deeply destabilising. When President Lahoud's extended term of office ended in November 2007, no consensus candidate could be found to replace him, and Siniora's cabinet was forced to take on Presidential powers.[26] After nearly 18 months of paralysing demonstrations, heavy fighting eventually broke out in May 2008, before agreement in Doha saw the opposing factions begin to compromise.

These street battles were the culmination of an increase in political violence which had accompanied the economic and political decline evident since Hariri's assassination, and which can be compared with those experienced by the Arab Spring countries. From June 2005 to December 2007, the country saw a number of political assassinations of Syria's opponents,[27] comparable to the assassinations of Chokri Belaid and Mohamed Brahmi in Tunisia in 2013.[28] Between June 2005 and September 2007, six prominent Lebanese political figures or journalists opposed to the Syrian regime were killed in bomb or gun attacks and a further two escaped assassination attempts.[29] Just two months after Syrian troops were withdrawn, journalist Samir Qasir

---

[25] "Hezbollah Ministers Quit Cabinet," *BBC News*, November 12, 2006, available at: http://news.bbc.co.uk/1/hi/world/middle_east/6139730.stm.

[26] "Siniora Says Cabinet Assumes Presidential Powers," *Gulf News*, November 24, 2007, available at: http://m.gulfnews.com/siniora-says-cabinet-assumes-presidential-powers-1.213778.

[27] A bomb attack in July 2005 targeted the pro-Syrian Defence Minister, Elias Murr, leaving him with minor injuries. See: "Murr Escapes Deadly Car Bomb Attack," *The Daily Star*, July 13, 2005, available at: http://www.dailystar.com.lb/News/Lebanon-News/2005/Jul-13/9074-murr-escapes-deadly-car-bomb-attack.ashx#axzz2q1B89K35.

[28] See: "Tunisia Shocked by Assassinations: Opposition Leaders Mohamed Brahmi and Chokri Belaid Killed with the Same Gun," *The Independent*, July 26, 2013, available at: http://www.independent.co.uk/news/world/africa/tunisia-shocked-by-assassinations-opposition-leaders-mohamed-brahmi-and-chokri-belaid-killed-with-the-same-gun-8733972.html.

[29] Journalists Ali Ramez Tohme, who escaped a car bomb attack on September 15, 2005, and May Chidiac, who was seriously injured in a similar attack on her car on September 25, 2005. See: "Third Attack Against Press in Four Months," *Committee to Protect Journalists*, September 26, 2005, available at: https://cpj.org/2005/09/third-attack-against-press-in-four-months.php).

was killed when a car bomb exploded outside his home;[30] this was followed on June 21 by the killing of Communist Party leader George
Hawi with a car bomb.[31] On December 12 Gebran Tueni, described
by UN Secretary-General Kofi Annan as "a tireless advocate of a sovereign Lebanon and free press," was killed in a car bombing[32] and in
December 2006 gunmen shot dead anti-Syrian MP Pierre Gemayel.[33]
The following year, Sunni MP Walid Eido was killed in a car-bomb
attack on Beirut's waterfront on June 13[34] and Christian MP Antoine
Ghanem was killed in a car bombing in east Beirut.[35]

In addition, a spate of bombings throughout 2005 targeted Christian areas, with at least eight attacks from March 19 to September 17
striking towns and neighbourhoods including New Jdeideh, Jounieh
and Ashrafiyeh, killing five and wounding at least 60.[36] Likely carried

---

[30] "Hundreds Mourn Beirut Journalist," *BBC News*, June 4, 2005, available at:
http://news.bbc.co.uk/1/hi/world/middle_east/4609329.stm.

[31] "Fierce Critic of Syria Killed in Beirut Blast," *The Telegraph*, June 22, 2005, available at:
http://www.telegraph.co.uk/news/worldnews/middleeast/lebanon/1492580/Fierce-critic-of-
Syria-killed-in-Beirut-blast.html.

[32] "Security Council Receives Mehlis Report; Annan Condemns New Assassination in
Lebanon," *United Nations News Centre*, December 12, 2005, available at: http://www.un.org/
apps/news/story.asp?NewsID=16905&Cr=middle&Cr1=leban#.Us7EVPRdVQg.

[33] "Lebanese Christian leader killed,", *op. cit.* (footnote 17).

[34] "Lebanese MP Dies in Beirut Blast," *BBC News*, June 14, 2007, available at: http://news.
bbc.co.uk/1/hi/world/middle_east/6749663.stm.

[35] "MP Antoine Ghanem Assassinated," *The Daily Star*, September 20, 2007, available at:
http://www.dailystar.com.lb/News/Lebanon-News/2007/Sep-20/47135-mp-antoine-
ghanem-assassinated.ashx#axzz1zUoMKoRi.

[36] See: "Car Bomb Rocks Beirut," *The Guardian*, March 19, 2005, available at: http://www.
theguardian.com/world/2005/mar/19/syria.lebanon. See also: "Fresh Lebanon Bombing
Kills Three," *BBC News*, 23 March 2005, available at: http://news.bbc.co.uk/
1/hi/world/middle_east/4374111.stm. See also: "Bomb Hits Beirut's Christian Area," *BBC
News*, 27 March 2005, available at: http://news.bbc.co.uk/1/hi/world/middle_east/
4385265.stm. See also: "Bomb Damages Christian Town Near Beirut," *The Washington Post*,
April 2, 2005, available at: http://www.washingtonpost.com/wp-dyn/articles/A19372-
2005Apr1.html. See also: "Bomb Kills One, Wounds 6 in the Port City of Jounieh," *The
Daily Star*, May 6, 2005, available at: http://www.dailystar.com.lb/News/Lebanon-News/
2005/May-06/5307-bomb-kills-one-wounds-6-in-the-port-city-of-jounieh.ashx#
axzz2q1B89K35. See also: Sadler, B., "Explosion Hits Beirut," *CNN*, July 22, 2005, available
at: http://edition.cnn.com/2005/WORLD/meast/07/22/lebanon.explosion/index.html. See
also: "Car Bomb Explodes in Beirut: One Dead and 30 Wounded," *Asia News*, September
17, 2005, available at: http://www.asianews.it/news-en/Car-bomb-explodes-in-Beirut:-one-

out by Syrian supporters attempting to undermine security, the attacks were comparable to those striking the Coptic Christian community in Egypt following the Arab Spring.[37] However, the fighting of May 2008, when the discovery of Hezbollah-controlled hidden cameras at Rafic Hariri International Airport led to government accusations that the group was planning an attack, was the most serious.[38] By this point, the relationship between Siniora's government and the Hezbollah-led opposition had deteriorated substantially. The declaration on May 6, according to which Hezbollah's telecommunications network would be dismantled, unleashed six days of fighting across Lebanon, during which Hezbollah was able to take control of large areas of West Beirut and killed at least 61 people.[39]

Recovery

With these developments in mind, it is likely that observers looking at Lebanon in spring 2008 could well have come to the same conclusions about the fate of the Cedar Revolution as many have about the Arab Spring. However, the shoots of recovery after the uprising had been apparent since late 2007 and the following years would see Lebanon begin to regain the ground lost following the assassination of Hariri.

The Lebanese economy was the first to show these signs, with GDP growth measured at 7.5 percent in the closing months of 2007, and then showing strong growth in 2008, 2009 and 2010.[40] Inflation also fell from the high point reached in 2008 back to a low of 1.2 per-

---

dead-and-30-wounded-4136.html. See also: "Powerful Explosion Near Beirut Hotel Injures at Least 3," *The New York Times*, August 23, 2005, available at: http://www.nytimes.com/2005/08/23/international/middleeast/23lebanon.html?adxnnl=1&adxnnlx=1124802094-t3xMNr3qz+TfiO6F3gWUkQ&_r=2&.

[37] "Egypt Police Boost Security at Churches Ahead of Coptic Christmas," *Reuters*, January 6, 2014, available at: http://www.reuters.com/article/2014/01/06/us-egypt-copts-idU.S.BREA050HA20140106.

[38] "Hezbollah in Airport Spying Row," *BBC News*, May 3, 2008, available at: http://news.bbc.co.uk/1/hi/world/middle_east/7382289.stm.

[39] "Lebanon Army Gives Gunmen Deadline to Disarm," *Al Arabiya News*, May 12, 2008, available at: http://www.alarabiya.net/articles/2008/05/12/49725.html.

[40] "Lebanon—World Development Indicators,", *op. cit.* (footnote 13).

cent in 2009 and 4.5 percent in 2010,[41] while government debt fell to 142 percent of GDP by 2010.[42] Following the signing of the Doha Agreement, the Lebanese tourism industry also began to recover significantly (with 2008 the first year to see visitor numbers rise since 2004, and 2010 seeing more than 2 million visitors).[43] Meanwhile, in January 2010, Lebanon's tourism chief Nada Sardouk claimed that the country's hotels had seen "80 percent to 90 percent hotel occupancy this year [2009],"[44] suggesting that these visitors were staying in the country rather than travelling onwards. International tourism receipts as a percentage of exports also rose, to reach 39.2 percent in 2010, while a return to sustained growth was also present in the manufacturing sector between 2010 and 2012. All this was likely to have contributed to an accompanying fall in unemployment: down from 9 percent in 2008, to 5.8 percent in 2011.[45]

As well as this, the country's divisive and confrontational political environment, while still apparent in the positions taken on the UN Special Tribunal's investigation into the assassination of Rafic Hariri,[46] ceased to have such a damaging effect. This was, in part, due to the fact that the March 8 Coalition had returned to power as part of a unity government following the Doha Agreement[47] and was then able to gain 10 seats out of 30 in a similar cabinet under Saad Hariri following the 2009 elections.[48] Following the fall, in January 2011, of Saad Hariri's government over the tribunal issue, Najib Mikati was able to form a new cabinet—dominated by March 8 ministers—within six months and still maintain Lebanese involvement in the process,

---

[41] "Inflation, Average Consumer Prices," *op. cit.* (footnote 14).

[42] "General Government Gross Debt," op cit. (footnote 15).

[43] "International Tourism, Number of Arrivals: Lebanon," *op. cit.* (footnote 16).

[44] Stoddart, V., "Beirut is Reborn as a Glitzy Playground for Tourists," *USA Today*, January 22, 2010, available at: http://usatoday30.usatoday.com/travel/destinations/2010-01-21-beirut-bounces-back_N.htm.

[45] "Lebanon—World Development Indicators," *op. cit.* (footnote 19).

[46] "Hezbollah and Allies Topple Lebanese Unity Government," *BBC News*, January 12, 2011, available at: http://www.bbc.co.uk/news/world-middle-east-12170608.

[47] "Lebanon—2009," *Freedom House*, available at: http://www.freedomhouse.org/report/freedom-world/2009/lebanon#.UtUQ2vRdVQg.

[48] "Lebanon's National-Unity Cabinet Formed," *NOW*, November 9, 2009, available at: https://now.mmedia.me/lb/en/nownews/lebanons_national-unity_cabinet_formed.

with the transitional period punctuated by only minor civil unrest.[49] This suggests that, unlike the period immediately following the uprising, co-operation was preferred to conflict by Lebanon's opposing political groups—something that may be beginning to be seen in Tunisia.[50]

A significant improvement in political and civil rights was also evident in the years that followed the Cedar Revolution and was exemplified by *Freedom House* changing the country's rating from "Not Free" in 2005 to "Partly Free" in 2006, something that Lebanon has maintained to 2013. The "Freedom Rating" awarded by the NGO also changed significantly in the years following the Cedar Revolution: improving from 5.5 in 2005 to 4.0 in 2011.[51] This was accompanied by movements to end arbitrary detention and torture, with Freedom House declaring in 2011 that the "security forces' practice of arbitrary detention has declined since 2005, though isolated incidents still occur," and that "the government has made some progress toward ending torture since 2007."[52]

Meanwhile, as with the improvements in economic and political instability, political violence and assassinations became less frequent. The assassination of the pro-Syrian Druze politician Saleh Aridi, in September 2008[53] was the only high-profile political killing until the death of the Internal Security Forces (ISF) intelligence chief Wissam al-Hassan in October 2012.[54] Additionally, September 2008 saw a reconciliation agreement signed between warring Sunni and Alawite

---

[49] "Lebanon's Mikati Forms New Cabinet With Hezbollah Support," *Bloomberg*, June 13, 2011, available at: http://www.bloomberg.com/news/2011-06-13/lebanon-s-mikati-forms-new-cabinet-with-hezbollah-support.html.

[50] "Tunisia's NCA Agrees New Constitution," *BBC News*, January 24, 2014, available at: http://www.bbc.co.uk/news/world-africa-25878534.

[51] See: "Lebanon—2005," *op. cit.* (footnote 6) and "Lebanon—2011," *Freedom House*, available at: http://www.freedomhouse.org/report/freedom-world/2011/lebanon#.UtAOh_RdVQg. (N.B.: *Freedom House* ranks countries between "1" and "7," with "7" being awarded to the most repressive regimes.)

[52] "Lebanon—2011," *op. cit.* (footnote 52).

[53] "Lebanese Politician Sheik Saleh Aridi Killed In Car Bombing," *The Guardian*, September 11, 2008, available at: http://www.theguardian.com/world/2008/sep/11/lebanon.syria.

[54] "Wissam Al-Hasan Assassinated in Ashrafiyeh Bomb Blast," *Naharnet*, October 19, 2012, available at: http://www.naharnet.com/stories/en/57713.

militias in the northern city of Tripoli after sectarian fighting linked to political disagreements in Beirut had killed at least 22 people.[55] While 2008 did see two significant bomb attacks in Tripoli, one of which killed at least 15 people, these were not believed to have been linked to the political violence generated by the Cedar Revolution and were, instead, likely to have been carried out by al-Qaeda-inspired Islamist terrorists.[56] The same was true of significant violence in the Nahr al-Bared refugee camp during the summer of 2007 (sparked when the Islamist terrorist group Fatah al-Islam attacked Lebanese Army positions, in retaliation for the arrest of its members).[57]

The Road from Damascus

Despite this recovery, the progress made has since stalled in the face of unrest generated by the ongoing civil war across the border in Syria. The malign effect Bashar al-Assad's regime had on Lebanon prior to 2005 has returned since late 2011 and has left the country struggling to deal with increasing economic, political and security problems once again.

As with the years following the Cedar Revolution, the knock-on effect of the conflict in Syria has been mostly felt by the Lebanese economy and GDP growth in particular has slowed dramatically. While the economy is yet to experience negative growth, the figures have fallen from 7 percent growth in 2010, to 3 percent in 2011 and just 1.3 percent in 2012.[58] Inflation also appears to be rising again, reaching 6.3 percent in 2013.[59] The tourism industry has also suffered, as members of the Gulf Cooperation Council (GCC) have warned their citizens against travel to Lebanon and, in some cases, have

---

[55] "Sunni, Alawite Leaders Sign Truce Deal in Tripoli," *The Daily Star*, September 9, 2008, available at: http://www.dailystar.com.lb/News/Lebanon-News/2008/Sep-09/50899-sunni-alawite-leaders-sign-truce-deal-in-tripoli.ashx#axzz2qH7D5TJT.

[56] See: "Lebanon Bomb Kills 15 In Attack on Army," *Reuters*, August 13, 2008, available at: http://www.reuters.com/article/2008/08/13/us-lebanon-blast-idU.S.LD6575120080813.

[57] "Three-Month Battle Ends as Army Takes over Refugee Camp," *The Guardian*, September 3, 2007, available at: http://www.theguardian.com/world/2007/sep/03/syria.lebanon.

[58] "Lebanon—World Development Indicators," *op. cit.*

[59] "Inflation, Average Consumer Prices," *op. cit.*

advised those present there to leave.[60] Figures for the number of visitors entering the country, as well as for international-tourism receipts as a percentage of exports, are not available for 2012-2013; yet, by the end of 2011, both had also fallen significantly from the previous year. In June 2013, Lebanon's Tourism Minister stated the president of Lebanon's Syndicate of Hotel Owners claimed that hotel occupancy was down 30 percent from the previous year.[61]

The outbreak of the civil war has also had an enormously damaging influence on Lebanon's political structures, with its legislative and executive bodies left hopelessly paralysed as opposing coalitions support different sides in Syria. The resignation of Prime Minister Najib Mikati in March 2013[62] left Lebanon with a caretaker government for nearly a year, with Prime Minister-designate Tammam Salam simply unable to form a replacement government.[63] The country's Parliament meetings have also been boycotted by a number of major parties, failing to reach quorum eight times in the past year and meeting for the first time since May 2013 on March 19, 2014.[64] In addition to this, parliamentary elections due for May 2013 have been postponed to November 2014, while—despite the increase in political rights logged by *Freedom House*, following the Cedar Revolution—Lebanon's "Freedom Rating" has declined to 4.5 in 2013.[65]

---

[60] See: "GCC States Issue Lebanon Travel Warning," *Al Arabiya News*, June 6, 2013, available at: http://english.alarabiya.net/en/News/middle-east/2013/06/06/GCC-states-issue-Lebanon-travel-warning-.html. See also: "Saudi Arabia Urges Citizens to Leave Lebanon," *The Daily Star*, November 21, 2013, available at: http://www.dailystar.com.lb/News/Lebanon-News/2013/Nov-21/238559-saudi-arabia-calls-on-citizens-to-leave-lebanon.ashx#axzz2qMmjWG1H.

[61] "Syrian Bombs Empty Lebanese Tables as Conflict Hits Tourism," *Bloomberg*, June 6, 2013, available at: http://www.bloomberg.com/news/2013-06-05/syrian-bombs-empty-lebanese-tables-as-war-hits-tourism-mainstay.html.

[62] "Lebanese Prime Minister Najib Mikati Resigns," *Reuters*, March 22, 2013, available at: http://uk.reuters.com/article/2013/03/22/us-lebanon-mikati-idU.S.BRE92L0TG20130322.

[63] "Cabinet Formation Still at Impasse, Salam Says," *The Daily Star*, October 1, 2013, available at: http://www.dailystar.com.lb/News/Lebanon-News/2013/Oct-01/233151-cabinet-formation-still-at-impasse-salam-says.ashx#axzz2qMmjWG1H.

[64] "Parliament Fails to Convene Once More," *The Daily Star*, December 18, 2013, available at: http://www.dailystar.com.lb/News/Lebanon-News/2013/Dec-18/241522-parliament-fails-to-convene-once-more.ashx#axzz2qH7D5TJT.

[65] "Lebanon—2013," *Freedom House*, available at: http://www.freedomhouse.org/report/freedom-world/2013/lebanon#.UtAPEvRdVQg.

Significant political violence has also returned to the country and has been seen in Beirut, Tripoli and Sidon, as well as across the Bekaa Valley. The assassination of ISF Intelligence Chief Wissam al-Hassan was the first major car-bomb attack in Beirut since 2008,[66] yet since then, there have been a number of large bomb attacks in the capital, with recent explosions killing the former Finance Minister, Mohamad Chatah (a persistent critic of the Syrian regime) and striking the Shia district of Haret Hreik.[67] In November 2013 the Iranian Embassy was struck by a double suicide bombing[68] and two large car bombs targeted Hezbollah strongholds in South Beirut in July and August 2013.[69] Street fighting and sniping at sectarian interfaces in Tripoli has continued since August 2012, with the most recent round continuing sporadically since November 2013 and killing dozens.[70] In addition, in May 2013, Islamist gunmen clashed with the Lebanese Armed Forces in Sidon, leaving over 40 people dead.[71] Rocket fire from Syrian rebel forces regularly strikes border towns such as Hermel and Arsal in the Bekaa Valley[72] and Shia towns seen as Hezbollah strongholds in East Lebanon have been targeted by jihadists with a number of suicide car-

---

[66] "Wissam Al-Hasan Assassinated in Ashrafiyeh Bomb Blast," *op. cit.*

[67] "Beirut Blast Kills Sunni Ex-Minister Mohamad Chatah," *BBC News*, December 27, 2013, available at: http://www.bbc.co.uk/news/world-middle-east-25524729. See also: "Car Bomb in Beirut Kills Four, Wounds 77," *The Daily Star*, January 2, 2014, available at: http://www.dailystar.com.lb/News/Lebanon-News/2014/Jan-02/242913-huge-explosion-rocks-beiruts-southern-suburbs.ashx#axzz2qH7D5TJT.

[68] "Lebanon Blasts Hit Iran's Embassy in Beirut," *BBC News*, November 19, 2013, available at: http://www.bbc.co.uk/news/world-middle-east-24997876.

[69] "Car Bomb Kills 21 in Beirut Southern Suburb," *The Daily Star*, August 15, 2013, available at: http://www.dailystar.com.lb/News/Lebanon-News/2013/Aug-15/227505-explosion-in-southern-suburb-of-beirut-witnesses.ashx#axzz2qH7D5TJT. See also: "Over 50 Hurt As Car Bomb Hits Hezbollah Beirut Stronghold," *Reuters*, July 9, 2013, available at: http://www.reuters.com/article/2013/07/09/us-lebanon-explosion-idU.S.BRE96807Z20130709.

[70] "Sniper Fire Kills One As Clashes Flare in Lebanon's Tripoli," *Reuters*, January 5, 2014, available at: http://www.reuters.com/article/2014/01/05/us-syria-crisis-lebanon-idU.S.BRE A040AA20140105.

[71] "Lebanese Army Storms Assir Complex, Preacher Flees," *The Daily Star*, June 24, 2013, available at: http://www.dailystar.com.lb/News/Local-News/2013/Jun-24/221395-fierce-clashes-rock-south-lebanon-city-for-second-day.ashx#ixzz2X9bBrhZD.

[72] "Rocket Attack Kills 8 In Arsal, Stokes Tensions," *The Daily Star*, January 18, 2014, available at: http://www.dailystar.com.lb/News/Lebanon-News/2014/Jan-18/244451-rocket-attack-kills-8-in-arsal-stokes-tensions.ashx#axzz2rDvgPnS6.

bomb attacks.[73] As the war in Syria has continued, the violence in Lebanon has worsened and is currently at a much more serious state than at any time during the Cedar Revolution (other than May 2008).

Conclusion

In the three years following the Cedar Revolution, Lebanon experienced similar societal problems to those currently being felt by the Arab Spring countries across the Middle East and North Africa. Despite these difficulties, the three indicators of economy, politics and security show that, after several years of immediate instability following the uprising in 2005, Lebanon was able to overcome these issues and begin to develop successfully once more. However, the significant instability manifesting in the country, as a result of the violence in Syria, has since reversed much of progress made since the second half of 2008, with the political polarization and accompanying violence which followed the Cedar Revolution becoming particularly apparent once more.

Taking this into account, it is possible to suggest that, given time, those states currently facing political instability post-Arab Spring will be able to follow Lebanon's example and challenge their economic, political and military problems post-revolution. The key variables as to whether this will happen depend on the extent to which the economies, political environment and security situation of these countries have been damaged by their revolutions and how severe the political fragility, which is likely to affect these states for some time, is. Despite this, the fact that the measure of economic and political cohesion regained by Lebanon before the outbreak of violence in Syria has since been reversed suggests that even if the level of damage caused by revolution is lower than expected, states may still be vulnerable. In that case, it is worth noting that even those states which are able to recover from upheaval may continue to be ill-equipped to deal with further political turmoil for many years to come.

---

[73] "Suicide Car Bomb Kills At Least Four in Lebanon's Hermel," *The Daily Star*, February 1, 2014, available at http://www.dailystar.com.lb/News/Lebanon-News/2014/Feb-01/246080-sound-of-explosion-in-lebanons-hermel-al-manar.ashx#axzz2wbSJQz7E and "Suicide Bomber Kills Three in E. Lebanon," *The Daily Star*, February 22, 2014, available at http://www.dailystar.com.lb/News/Lebanon-News/2014/Feb-22/248183-suicide-bomber-kills-two-soldiers-in-e-Lebanon.ashx#axzz2u4YS3Zq7.

Part IV

Migration and Diaspora

Chapter Nine

Europe's "Rio Grande:" (Im)mobility in the Mediterranean

Leila Hadj-Abdou

Those who cross its surface are often hardly typical of the societies from which they come (if the word "typical" has any meaning anyway). If they are not outsiders, in some sense decentered, when they are set out, they are likely to become so when they enter different societies across the water, whether as traders, slaves, or pilgrims. But their presence can have a transforming effect on these different societies, introducing something of the culture of one continent into the outer edges, at least, of another.

David Abulafia (2011)[1] about the Mediterranean
in historical perspective

Mobility, including human mobility, change, permeability and diversity, defines the very essence of the Mediterranean. The Mediterranean has witnessed the circulation of ideas, people and goods across its shores throughout human history. The unity of the Mediterranean history thus "lies paradoxically, in its swirling changeability, in the diasporas of merchants and exiles [...]," as the historian David Abulafia[2] notes. Nowadays, the Mediterranean represents more than ever a space of mobility, a space in constant flux. Globalization and international migration since the 1950s has further strengthened its fluctuating nature. Capturing this essence of the Mediterranean, the renowned writer Amin Maalouf[3] has been inclined to define the region's identity as "less tribal, less exclusive, less limited, less a prisoner of the selecting myths, more open to the others and to the realities to the future world."

Maalouf's description of the Mediterranean identity conveys an image of societies which have the potential not to be imprisoned by

---

[1]Abulafia, David (2011) "Mediterranean History as Global History." *History and Theory* 50.

[2]Ibid., p. 228.

[3]Maalouf, Amin (2010) "The Challenges of Interculturality in the Mediterranean," *Quaderns de la Mediterrània* 14, p. 80.

the idea of a single nation, religion or ethnicity, but enriched by and conscious of multiple allegiances and affiliations. Observing the current events that followed what has been commonly called the "Arab Spring," however, distort this image. In many places, divides and conflicting interests among people in the Mediterranean seemed to have deepened instead of alleviated. One of these dividing lines is centered on the movement of people across the Mediterranean to Europe. The Arab Spring has provoked not exclusively support for democracy, but also anxiety about the arrival of refugees and immigrants to the EU and its member states, in particular at its southern edges. Small islands in the Mediterranean, such as Italy's Lampedusa, have become symbols of both this anxiety and the hardships of those that reach out for a life in Europe by crossing the sea line that marks one of the greatest regional wealth differences in the world. At the height of the Arab Spring in 2011, the United Nations High Council for Refugees (UNHCR)[4] called the Mediterranean the most deadly stretch of water for asylum seekers and migrants. Comparing the 2011 numbers of those who died in the Mediterranean while trying to cross it with those who arrived alive in Italy and Malta, Philippe Fargues[5] concluded that the probability of dying while travelling from Libya to Europe is as high as 6.5 percent. In 2013, 45,000 people chose the Mediterranean sea-route to come to Europe.[6]

In light of these developments, the aim of this chapter is to give an overview on contemporary human mobility across the Mediterranean, and to understand its dynamics. Questions that will be tackled are: How have patterns of immigration to (and within) Europe evolved over time? How has Europe dealt after and before the Arab Spring with refugees and immigrants landing on its Mediterranean shores?

In order to address these questions, the chapter is divided into two parts. It first offers an overview of the evolution of immigration patterns

---

[4]UNHCR (2012) "Mediterranean Takes Record As Most Deadly Stretch of Water for Refugees and Migrants in 2011." UNHCR, press release, January 31, 2012.

[5]Fargues, Philippe (2012) "Demography, Migration, and Revolt in the Southern Mediterranean." In Merlini, Cesare and Roy, Olivier (eds.), *Arab Society in Revolt. The West's Mediterranean Challenge*, Brookings Institution Press. Washington D.C., p. 40.

[6]IOM (2014) "International Organization for Migration. Migrants risking lives in Mediterranean topped 45,000 in 2013."

and major policy trends in the past decades up to today. It secondly explores the politics of the European Union and its Southern Mediterranean member states in response to the movement of people, focusing in particular on their cooperation on migration control as a major element of Europe's external relations in the Mediterranean Basin.

Migration Trends in the Mediterranean Since the 1950s

Oh where are you going?/Eventually you must come back./How many ignorant people have regretted this before you and me?[7] "

Ya Rayah, popular Algerian Chaabi song about the immigrant, 1970s

The Mediterranean Basin is a sending, receiving as well as transit region of immigration. The development of post-war migration patterns in the region has evolved in several distinct phases[8].

Immediate Post-War Immigration

The immediate post-Second World War period was characterized by large south-to-north flows within Europe from northern Mediterranean countries (Greece, Italy, Portugal and Spain). Western European countries, in particular Belgium, Britain, France, Germany and Switzerland, received significant numbers of labor immigrants from Europe's South.

Southern European immigrants at that time were often depicted in public discourse—in a similar way as North African immigrants at a later stage—as fundamentally culturally distinct compared with the native population in the West and the North of Europe, and hence were portrayed as facing problems adapting to their "host" countries, which reinforced discrimination and stigmatization of these groups.[9]

---

[7]Original: Ya rayah win msafar trouh taaya wa twali. Chhal nadmou laabad el ghaflin qablak ou qabli Ya rayah win msafar trouh taaya wa twali. Chhal nadmou laabad el ghaflin qablak ou qabli.

[8]Cf. De Haas, Hein (2011) "Mediterranean Migration Futures: Patterns, Drivers and Scenarios," *Global Environmental Change* 21S.

[9]Lindo describes that, for instance, Italians in the Netherlands have been portrayed as "warm-blooded, easily excitable idlers." They were said to speak too loudly in public places, and to steal native, young women from Dutch men. As a result, in some places Mediterranean guest-workers were prevented from entering venues, such as dance clubs. Especially

In addition to international migration, there were also large-scale internal migration movements within Europe's Mediterranean countries[10]. Italy in particular exhibited a large number of internal migrants, who furthermore were to a great extent classified as irregular: A law from 1939 (abolished in 1961) sought to curb urbanization, but had the effect that many of the hundreds of thousands of people that moved from the rural south to the northern cities of Italy in the 1950s fell into the category of "illegality."[11]

While Southern European immigration fuelled post-war reconstruction in Europe initially to a significant degree, most migration in Southern Mediterranean countries was internal, and few migrated to Europe[12].

From the 1960s Onwards: Southern Mediterranean Guest Workers

In the 1960s, labor immigration from the new North African nation states (Tunisia, Morocco, Algeria) that had recently gained independence,[13] as well from Turkey to Europe gradually started to increase. After the Northern Mediterranean source for human labor began to ebb, many European states signed bilateral labor agreements with Southern Mediterranean governments. Germany signed an agreement with Turkey in 1961, followed by Austria, Belgium, France and the Netherlands in 1964. France additionally signed agreements with Morocco in 1963 and with Tunisia in 1964.[14]

While guest worker regimes were essential to Western Europe's postwar economic boom, they also significantly benefitted sending

---

people from the south of the northern Mediterranean countries were perceived as adapting poorly to the 'customs' of their host countries. With the later arrival of large groups of Turks and Moroccans, the attention would slowly shift away from Southern Europeans. Lindo, Flip (2000) "The social advancement of Southern European labour migrants in the Netherlands" In: Vermeulen, Hans and Penninx, Rinus (eds.): *Immigrant Integration. The Dutch Case.* Het Spinhuis. Amsterdam, p.127 ff.

[10]Geddes, Andrew (2003), *The Politics of Migration and Immigration in Europe*, Sage: London, p. 155.

[11]Ibid.

[12]de Haas (2011), *op. cit.*, p. 61.

[13]Tunisia and Morocco gained independence in 1956, while Algeria did in 1962.

[14]OECD (2004) "Migration for Employment. Bilateral Agreements at a Crossroads," Paris, p. 222 ff.

countries in reducing unemployment by exporting their surplus of labor power, as well as individual workers who could often earn significantly more abroad than they would in their home countries. These policies, however, also came with an ethical "disadvantage" as is underlined by the oft-quoted remark by the Swiss author Max Frisch that "we called workers, but got humans instead." Guest workers were recruited on a temporarily basis, and their settlement and their social and political integration in the receiving European countries was neither stipulated nor desired. Political philosophers since Michael Walzer[15] have hence identified guest worker regimes as deeply problematic in the framework of liberal democratic societies as a point of justice. Guest workers constituted, as Walzer[16] observed, a "disenfranchised class," who were often exploited, in part because they were disenfranchised and lacked effective representation of their interests.

The 1973 Oil Crisis Reshapes Migration Patterns

During the 1970s, many of the temporary "guests" actually turned into permanent settlers, which made the democratic dilemma of not granting them political representation more severe. Their settlement was an unintended result of restricted immigration control in the 1970s, which put an end to the previous circular migration. To put it more bluntly, this development was an early example of policy failure as regards immigration control in Europe. Policymakers have often viewed immigration as something that can be turned on and off like a tap, as Castles[17] has framed it, but history has repeatedly proven this assumption as wrong.

Following the first Arab oil embargo in 1973 and the subsequent economic downturn in Europe, labor recruitment came to an official end. Western European governments closed their borders in order to stop immigration. However, this had the effect that those immigrants who were already in Europe decided to stay out of fear of not being allowed to reenter Europe. Instead of moving back and forth, they

---

[15]Walzer, Michael (1983), *Spheres of Justice. A Defense of Pluralism and Equality*, Basic Books: New York.

[16]Ibid., p. 59.

[17]Castles, Stephen (2002) "Migration and Community Formation under Conditions of Globalization," *International Migration Review* 36(4), p. 1145.

used their right of family reunification and brought their family members to stay with them. Hence, as Fargues[18] put it, "Immigration was no longer driven by the economic logic of labor markets but the sociological stimulus of families and networks." European governments, including France and Germany, introduced programs to make immigrants leave. However, European courts protected and enforced immigrant rights to family reunification and residence, often against the will of national governments.[19]

New Reconfiguration in the 1980s and 1990s

Another turning point was the transformation of the former emigration nations in the Northern Mediterranean into immigrant nations. Greece, Portugal, and especially Italy and Spain became relevant receivers of immigration from the 1980s onwards. The steady growth of the Southern European economies made these countries, in combination with increasingly stricter admission rules in (post-1989) Western Europe, an attractive destination for Southern and Eastern Mediterranean immigrants. The response in Southern Europe to immigration, however, differed to a certain extent to the one in Western Europe. Southern European governments did not anticipate the arrival of large numbers of immigrants, and many immigrants went through phases of irregularity. For instance, neither Italy nor Spain provided a legal way of entering the country for work purposes until their first immigration laws of 1985 and 1986; and after legal regulations were eventually in place, they proved rather rigid and inappropriate for the real demand for foreign labor.[20] The low annual migration quotas established by the governments resulted in combination with the relatively large informal economies of these states in an irregular status for many immigrant workers.[21] In response, Italy and Spain repeatedly used "amnesties" to regulate immigration. Starting in 1986,

---

[18]Fargues (2012) *op. cit.*, p. 31.

[19]Castles, Stephen (2006) "Back to the Future? Can Europe meet its Labour Needs through Temporary Migration?" International Migration Institute. University of Oxford. Working paper 01/2006, p. 4.

[20]Barbulescu, Roxanna (2012) "The Politics of Immigrant Integration in Post-Enlargement Europe Migrants, Co-ethnics and European Citizens in Italy and Spain" EUI PhD thesis. Florence, p. 58.

[21]Ibid.

Italy has implemented five regularization programs so far, which have legalized almost 1.5 million people,[22] and in Spain 1.1 million immigrants have benefitted from five waves of regularizations.[23] Although in both countries they are not the major groups of unauthorized immigrants, laborers from Mediterranean North African states represent a large number of irregular migrants in both countries. Notwithstanding the political implications, studies have shown, though, that irregular immigrant labor has had a positive economic impact, at least in the short term, on Southern European countries.[24]

The New Millennium

During the 2000s, immigration from North African countries to Southern Europe continued. Additionally, immigration from Egypt to Europe started to become more significant.

It has to be noted, however, that in terms of immigration patterns until today there is a striking divide between the Mashrek[25] and the Maghreb[26] (for an overview see table 1). The majority of immigrants from the Mashrek still tend to go to the oil-exporting neighboring Arab countries, while Maghreb immigrants predominantly choose to come to the European Union.[27]

At the same time, the Maghreb became itself increasingly a destination and transit country of immigration.[28] Partly as a result of Gaddafi's pan-African orientation in the wake of the embargo imposed on Libya by the EU, the UN and the U.S., which stipulated open-door policies towards Sub-Saharan African countries,[29] immigrants

---

[22]Clandestino (2009) "Final Project Report. Undocumented Migration: Counting the Uncountable. Data and Trends Across Europe," p. 69.

[23]Ibid., p. 77.

[24]Triandafyllidou, Anna, Gropas, Ruby and Vogel, Dita (2007), "Introduction," in *European Immigration. A Sourcebook*, Aldershot: Ashgate, p. 5.

[25]Egypt, Jordan, Lebanon, Palestine, Syria.

[26]Algeria, Morocco, Tunisia, Libya.

[27]Fargues, Philippe (2013a), "International Migration and the Nation State in Arab Countries," *Middle East Law and Governance* 5, p. 13.

[28]de Haas (2011) *op.cit.*, p. 61.

[29]Cuttita, Paolo (2010) "Readmission in the Relations between Italy and North African Mediterranean Countries." In Cassarino, Jean-Pierre (ed.), *Unbalanced Reciprocities: Coopera-*

Table 1. Emigration & Immigration in EU from selected Mediterranean countries (2013 stocks)[a]

Country	Emigration (to EU in brackets)	Immigration
Algeria	961,850 (877,398)	95,000
Libya	100,656 (66,344)	768,372
Morocco	3,371,979 (3,056,109)	77,798
Tunisia	466,595 (414,077)	35,192
Maghreb total	4, 901, 080 (4,413, 928)	976, 362
Egypt	4,464,963 (224,122)	184,070
Jordan	339,755 (33,066)	191,307
Lebanon	602,280 (148,717)	302,315
Syria	1,643,747 (131,108)	102,396
Mashrek total (excl. Palestine)[b]	7, 050,745 (537,013)	780,088
Turkey	3,765,100 (1,629,400)	1,278,671

[a]EU Neighbourhood Migration Report 2013 (eds. by Fargues, Philippe), 6
[b]For Palestine no total emigration numbers exist, according to the *EU Neighbourhood Migration Report 2013* the numbers for the EU are 14,627.

from this region increasingly settled in North African countries, as well as joined North African immigrants in trying to get to Europe via the Mediterranean sea route.

The 2000s were eventually also a period of restriction of border controls in Southern Europe,[30] as well as an extension of Europe's efforts to control immigration across the Mediterranean (see section three). These measures, however, did not lead to a halt of immigration; instead it reshaped immigration routes, which now span almost the entire Mediterranean region[31].

Immigration to Europe's South did not stop entirely during the recent economic recession, although Europe's Mediterranean countries were hit hard. But the recession definitely slowed immigration down, and also revived emigration trends from Southern European countries to Western Europe.

---

tion on Readmission in the Euro-Mediterranean Area. Washington: Middle East Institute, p.45.

[30]The sealing of borders and restriction of entry in this region is indeed a relatively recent phenomenon, before the 1990s there were no visas for North Africans to come to the South of Europe.

[31]Cf. de Haas (2011), *op. cit.*, p. 61.

Migration in the Aftermath of the Arab Spring

Siamo multo preoccupati per il rischio di una guerra civile e per i rischi di un' immigrazione verso l'Unione Europe di dimensioni epocali[32]

Italian Interior Minister Franco Frattini, *Corriere della Serra*, 2/22/2011

The revolts in the Arab world starting in 2011 triggered ideas of unprecedented migration movements to Europe. Italy's government, for instance, predicted an "epochal" migratory influx of "biblical" proportions, with potentially hundreds of thousands of displaced persons ready to land on European shores.[33]

In retrospect, this scenario did not become reality. The Arab Spring had much more implications for migration and mobility in the region itself than it had for Europe. The violent conflicts in Libya and Syria have indeed generated large flows of refugees. The overwhelming majority, however, were received by neighboring Arab countries. From the 1,128,985 persons that fled Libya during spring and summer 2011, only 27,465 (i.e., 2.4 percent) came to Italy or Malta, the two EU countries affected most by the revolts.[34] In the wake of the conflict in Syria, seven million people were displaced, of which 2.5 million have so far sought refuge abroad. The neighboring countries, with the exception of Israel,[35] who kept its borders closed, Lebanon (900,000), Turkey and Jordan (600,000 each), as well as Iraq (220,000), took the main bulk of those people. Moreover, Egypt also hosts 135,000 Syrian refugees. Europe was, by comparison, rather hesitant to provide protection.[36]

---

[32]"We are very worried about the risk of a civil war and the risk of immigration to the European Union of epic dimensions" (translation by the author).

[33]Campesi, Giuseppe (2011) "The Arab spring and the Crisis of the European border regime. Manufacturing emergency in the Lampedusa crisis," EUI Working Papers 2011/59. Robert Schuman Centre for Advanced Studies. Florence, p.5.

[34]Fargues, Philippe and Fandrich, Christine (2012) "Migration after the Arab spring," MPC Research Report 2012/09, p.17.

[35]Israel is officially at war with Syria.

[36]According to an Amnesty International report (December 2013), only 10 member states have offered resettlement or humanitarian admission to Syrian refugees in reaction to a resettlement plan by the UNHCR. Some of them, moreover, have offered only very few places (e.g. Spain: 30).

Between March 2011 and December 2013, the European Union member states received 69,740 asylum claims from Syrian citizens and made 41,695 positive decisions.[37] This number corresponds to 2.9 percent of the overall Syrian refugee population. Two-thirds of these refugees were accepted by only two EU member states, Germany and Sweden. What is more, nearly half of those who sought asylum in Europe in 2013 were only able to reach the territory of a member state by irregular entry, putting their lives at risk at sea with traffickers, a share that more than tripled compared to 2011[38]. According to Fargues[39] this increase reflects the growing barriers that refugees face when coming to Europe, i.e. the recent sealing of land borders with Turkey by Greece[40] and Bulgaria.[41] Those who chose the sea-route were mostly trying to reach another destination than Greece,[42] as the latter is known for granting asylum to a very limited extent. Receiving 1015 claims through December 2013, Greece only approved 25 cases.[43] The European state, which has suffered most in the economic recession and is facing a dramatic rise of the extreme right, has deported a large number of Syrians back, exposing them anew to the violence in their home country.

Apart from the aforementioned groups, a further group which was hit by displacement in the framework of the Arab uprisings is migrant workers, including many Sub-Saharan Africans. Most of them have not made it to Europe. They have either returned to their home coun-

---

[37]Fargues, Philippe (2014) "Europe Must Take On its Share of the Syrian Refugee Burden. But How?" Policy brief. Robert Schuman Centre for Advanced Studies, p. 2.

[38]Ibid.

[39]Ibid.

[40]In July 2012, Greece with the assistance of FRONTEX, the European border protection agency, and the European Asylum Support Office put 1,800 border guards to the Greek-Turkey Evros border and placed 26 floating barriers along the river. More than 80 percent of Syrians crossing into Europe in the first quarter of 2012 did so through this border. Fandrich, Christine (2012) "Healing a Neighbourhood. Potential EU Responses to the Syrian Refugee Crisis," Migration Policy Center. Policy Brief July 2012. Florence, p. 4.

[41]Fargues (2014), *op. cit.*, p. 2.

[42]Under the Dublin III adopted in 2013 (no. 604) (similarly to the Dublin I and Dublin II) regulation a refugee has to seek asylum in the first EU member state it enters. Fingerprints are stored, and hence asylum cannot apply in any other EU member state (plus Norway, Iceland, Switzerland).

[43]Fargues (2014) *op.cit.*, p. 3.

tries or were forced to stay in the conflict region as a result of a lack of opportunity and resources to leave. This group is particularly vulnerable, since there is no clear institutional responsibility in the current international system either for protecting or assisting displaced migrant workers.[44]

In terms of voluntary migration, surveys demonstrated that the events in the region did not significantly alter the aspirations of people to leave their countries.[45] Consequently, the Arab revolts have not produced a major change in former trends of migration to Europe thus far.[46]

Irregular entry, however, has recently indeed peaked to some extent as suggested by the increased number of Syrian refuges, who had to rely on smugglers in order to apply for asylum in Europe.[47] As indicated before, heightened border controls, including the "outsourcing" of border controls across the Mediterranean (see section three), but also other European-wide policy measures, such as carrier sanctions,[48] whereby carriers are held liable for transporting people without valid migration documents, make it increasingly difficult to reach European territory. This partly explains why people are willing to put up with the high risks when crossing the Mediterranean Sea. It has to be noted at this point that although in public discourse they are often perceived as such, people who enter Europe by boat are not necessarily irregular migrants. The NGO Pro Asyl[49] has, for instance, documented that of all boat people who landed on Italian shores in 2008, 75 percent applied for asylum, of which in 50 percent of cases asylum was

---

[44]Koser, Khalid (2012) "Migration, Displacement and the Arab Spring. Lessons to Learn," Brookings Opinion. March 22, 2012.

[45]Abtelfattah, Dina (2011) "Impact of Arab revolts on Migration CARIM Analytic and Synthetic Notes," 2011/68. Robert Schuman Centre for Advanced Studies. Florence, p.8.

[46]Fargues et al. (2012) *op.cit.*, p. 4.

[47]A legal precondition for applying for asylum is the actual arrival at the territory of that state.

[48]Carrier liabilities and consequent carrier sanctions shifted the burden of control checks from the state to transport companies. The Schengen Agreement integrated a procedure that made carriers responsible for transporting passengers who were not entitled to access into the Schengen Area.

[49]Pro Asyl (2010) "Fatale Allianz. Zur Kooperation der Europaeischen Union mit Lybien bei der Flucht-und Migrationsverhinderung" Frankfurt am Main, p. 11.

granted. It can be assumed that these percentages are potentially even higher in the wake of the current uprisings in the region.

Moreover, as Fargues and Fandrich[50] have argued, the political instability in the Arab countries has caused rather a rerouting of existing (irregular) migration flows than it stimulated new ones.[51] They note that while the numbers of entries of refugees and migrants by boats has peaked in Italy after the Libyan uprising in 2011, they were actually accompanied by a decrease in numbers in Malta and Spain. They thus remark that if all three countries are taken together, irregular entries occurred in larger numbers in 1999, 2006 and 2009 than in 2011.[52] The decision to take the sea route to Italy was a response to an opportunity (lack of control during the height of the revolutions) more than a response to the upheavals itself.[53] At large, it is therefore accurate to say that the Arab Spring has not radically transformed migration patterns in the Mediterranean.[54]

Europe's Contemporary Response to Mobility in the Mediterranean

What the EU is effectively doing is signing a cheque to house people as far away from its shore as possible.

Nando Signa, 2013[55]

The Securitization of Immigration and the Extra-Territorialisation of Border Control

In order to understand current policy trends, it has to be taken into account that immigration is today among the main concerns of European citizens. The Eurobarometer survey published in December 2013 indicates that 12 percent of the respondents consider immigra-

---

[50]Fargues et al. (2012), *op. cit.*, p. 4.

[51]Ibid.

[52]Ibid.

[53]Ibid.

[54]De Haas, Hein and Signa, Nando (2012) "Migration and Revolution," *Forced Migration Review* 39. June 2012, p. 4.

[55]Signa, Nando (2013) "The death of migrants in the Mediterranean is a truly European tragedy."

tion one of the two most important challenges facing their country. This mirrors to some extent the fact that while previously immigration has not been a matter of public political debate to a significant extent, from the 1990s onwards political parties in Europe have extensively used the issue of immigration to mobilize potential voters. The issue of immigration has shifted from an issue debated behind gilded doors, primarily under labor market considerations, to an issue publicly contested, perceived as a threat and discussed mainly under a security perspective. Thus, the issue of migration has become the subject of a securitization process,[56] which in result has led to an increasing militarization of Europe's borders.

At the same time European integration has started to shape the policy field of immigration. The EU and its member states have increasingly extra-territorialized border control, making the issue of immigration a core of the EU's external relations. Rijpma and Cremona,[57] who have coined the term extra-territorialisation, have described this process as

> the way in which the EU and its Member States attempt not only to prevent non-Community nationals from leaving their countries of origin, but also to ensure that if they manage to do so, they remain as close to their country of origin as possible, or in any case outside EU territory. It furthermore covers measures that ensure that if individuals do manage to enter the EU, they will be repatriated or removed to "safe third countries."[58]

The Mediterranean region has been the premier site of developing and putting these policies into practice. The Barcelona Process, which was launched in 1995 by the Ministers of Foreign Affairs of the then-15 EU members and 14 Mediterranean partners, establishing a framework of bilateral and regional relations already comprised the issue of immigration. The Barcelona Declaration,[59] which formed the basis of

---

[56]Huysmans, Jef (2008), *The Politics of Insecurity: Fear, Migration and Asylum in the EU*, London: Routledge.

[57]Rijpma, Jorrit J. and Cremona, Marise (2007) "The Extra-Territorialisation of EU Migration Policies and the Rule of Law," EUI Working Papers Law 2007/01.

[58]Ibid., p. 12.

[59]Barcelona declaration (1995), adopted at the Euro-Mediterranean Conference. 27-28/11/95, p. 8.

the Euro-Mediterranean Partnership (EMP), declared that "the partners, aware of their responsibility for readmission, agree to adopt the relevant provisions and measures, by means of bilateral agreements or arrangements, in order to readmit their nationals who are in an illegal situation." Italy, for instance, signed its first agreement on both readmission and police cooperation with Tunisia in 1998, in which the North African country committed to readmit not only their own nationals but also third-country nationals (except nationals from the Arab Maghreb Union) who transited from its national territory.[60] Similar agreements with other countries followed.[61]

In the years to come, the issue of immigration gained further relevance in the EU external relations. The European Council meeting in Seville in 2002 introduced for the first time a compulsory "re-admission of illegal immigrants" clause in any future cooperation, association or equivalent agreement of the EU or the EC with third countries. When making this decision the countries of the Mediterranean basin were mentioned specifically.[62] Consequently, migration control also became a major strategic priority within the European Neighborhood Policy,[63] which was from the mid-2000s onwards the major policy framework of the European Union's partnership with the Mediterranean.

As Guild[64] observed, the development of the European Neighborhood Policy (ENP) was initially inspired by an "expansive spirit of inclusion of the neighbours in the benefits of the internal market including free movement of persons"; eventually, the approach regarding the movement of persons has changed significantly, putting instead predominantly obligations on the neighbors to act as the

---

[60]Cuttita, *op. cit.*, p. 32.

[61]Ibid., p. 34.

[62]Aubarell, Gemma, Zapata-Barrero, Ricard and Augarell, Xavier (2009) "New Directions of National Immigration Policies: The Development of the External Dimension and its Relationship with the Euro-Mediterranean Process," Euromesco paper 79, Brussels, p. 10.

[63]This prioritization of border control also manifests itself at Europe's Eastern borders. A 2009 report by the EU Court of Auditors revealed that 90 percent of all EU aid to the Neighbourhood partner countries of the Ukraine, Belarus and Moldova was spent on ' border management'. Bialasiewicz, Luiza (2012) "Off-shoring and out-sourcing the Borders of Europe. Libya and EU border work in the Mediterranean," *Geopolitics* 17 (4), p.846.

[64]Guild, Elspeth (2005) "What is a Neighbour? Examining the EU Neighbourhood Policy from the Perspective of Movement of Persons," June 10, 2005.

buffer between the EU and other third countries as regards irregular migration. In order to reach this end, according to Guild[65] a "bundle of rights and possibilities which have already been accorded in other venues and by other means are being repackaged in the ENP and presented as 'carrots' to encourage the neighbours to buy into the repressive measures."

A relevant triggering factor for the further expansion of the cooperation with the Mediterranean as regards immigration matters in the framework of the ENP were the 2005 shootings and following deportations of migrants trying to enter Europe through the Spanish North African enclaves Ceuta and Mellila. Six years earlier, wired fences were erected in these places, which, as Sudo[66] put it, "represented for centuries a focus for economic and cultural exchange" in the Mediterranean.

The Ceuta and Mellila events and their global media attention led to a revision of Europe's concept of migration control, which resulted in the proclamation of the "Global Approach to Migration" (GAM) by the EU in autumn 2005.[67] The GAM put an emphasis on legal migration, migrant rights and asylum, and the promotion of development in the sending countries.[68] However, as Cassarino[69] argues, the new shift was rather rhetorical, and at large the EU policies towards its southern neighbors remained *de facto* stable. To put it differently, the priority tended to remain on migration control, readmission and return instead of facilitating legal migration. This approach has turned to some extent into a self-feeding dynamic, in which stricter controls caused an increase in irregular migration, which in turn generated the need for more controls.[70]

---

[65]Ibid.

[66]Sudo, Pietro (2006) "Ceuta and Melilla: Security, Human Rights and Frontier Control," IEMED 2006, p. 213.

[67]Cassarino, Jean-Pierre and Lavenex, Sandra (2012), *EU-Migration Governance in the Mediterranean Region: the Promise of (a Balanced) Partnership?* IEMED 2012, p. 284.

[68]Ibid.

[69]Ibid.

[70]Eylemer, Sedef and Şemşitit, Sühal (2007) "Migration-Security Nexus in the Euro-Mediterranean relations," *Perception*, Summer/Autumn 2007, p. 61.

"Hierarchies of Priorities": Migration Control Before Human Rights

What is more, the prioritization of migration and border control has compromised the European Union's commitment to human rights and democracy.[71] The EU and its member states have reinforced cooperation with southern Mediterranean countries on border control and the readmission of migrants, regardless of whether their governments respected basic human rights of those who were returned to these countries, let alone asylum-seekers rights.[72]

One of the most problematic cases in that regard is the cooperation with Libya. Libyan authorities have been regularly reported in the past of having deported (readmitted) people directly back to their country of origin, regardless of their conditions or right to asylum.

There is also evidence that a significant number of migrants have been abandoned by officials at the southern border with Niger. Unable to reach Europe, but also unable to return home, many migrants were left at the mercy of local officials and smugglers and have been forced to work in extreme, exploitative conditions.[73] Those not deported were imprisoned in detention centers, where they had to cope with violence, forced labour, and sexual assaults by officials, as documented by the UNHCR and Amnesty International.[74] Sub-Saharan refugees who were kept in Libyan detention centres, such as Kufra, have also reported that they were sold by Libyan police forces to smugglers and were at a later point re-imprisoned and later again sold. Many migrants hence were sold as if they were a commodity and imprisoned several times.[75]

Italy and Libya signed a readmission agreement in 2004, which in addition to other factors facilitated the lifting of the European Union's embargo on the country in the same year.[76] One of the conditions of

---

[71]Cf. Tocci, Nathalie and Cassarino, Jean-Pierre (2011) "Rethinking the EU's Mediterranean Policies Post-1/11" Istituto Affari Internazionali Working Papers 11/06, March 2011.

[72]Ibid., p. 8.

[73]Bialasiewicz, *op. cit.*, p. 854.

[74]Ibid.

[75]For an excellent overview about these practices see the documentary "Like a Man on Earth" (2009), by Zalab.

[76]Cuttita, *op. cit.*, p. 46.

the EU for lifting the embargo, though, was Libya's ratification of the 1951 Convention on the Status of Refugees. The country under Gaddafi's leadership, however, never did ratify the Convention and continuously denied the existence of any refugees in the country.[77] Notwithstanding this fact, Italy financed three detention centers in Libya in the 2000s. In 2009 an Italian company[78] won the bid to construct an electronic security barrier to be erected at Libya´s southern borders. The construction was estimated to cost 300 million Euros and was agreed to be equally financed by the EU and the Italian state.[79]

One year previously (2008), Italy and Libya also signed a Treaty of Friendship, Partnership and Cooperation, which allotted Gaddafi a sum of 5 billion USD as compensation for Italy's past colonization (1911–1943) of the country. Italian Prime Minister Silvio Berlusconi promoted the agreement, declaring that "we will get more gas and oil from Libya and less irregular migration."[80]

This agreement, in addition to the earlier readmission agreement, led to numerous deportations of migrants from Italy to Libya. Moreover, from 2009 onwards, migrants intercepted in international waters by Italian coast guard vessels would be ferried to Libya directly before assessing their rights; repeated cases of boats being pushed back to Libya after having actually reached Italian shores became public.[81] In reaction, international organizations as well as the European Parliament have repeatedly urged Italy to halt mass deportations to Libya, and have emphasized the necessary compliance with the non-refoulment principle enshrined in the 1951 Geneva Convention.[82]

In late 2010, an agreement of the European Commission, which included the close cooperation with Gaddafi's Libya on border control

---

[77]Bialasiewicz, *op. cit.*, p. 858.

[78]Companies of other EU member states have also made significant profits from securitizing Libya's borders (see Bialasiewicz, op. cit.).

[79]Ibid, p. 859.

[80]Pro Asyl, *op. cit.*, p. 9.

[81]Bialasiewicz, *op. cit.*, p. 853.

[82]"No Contracting State shall expel or return ('refouler') a refugee in any manner whatsoever to the frontiers of territories where his [or her] life or freedom would be threatened on account of his [or her] race, religion,nationality, membership of a particular social group or political opinion." (Article 33).

and the fight against irregular immigration, was under negotiation, but was never signed as the civil war started to spread in early 2011.[83]

Side Effects: Facilitating Repression

In addition to creating "'off-shore' black holes where European norms, standards and regulations do not apply," as Bialasiewicz[84] has framed it, another consequence of the extra-territorialisation of border control was the reinforcement of the power of some authoritarian governments in the region to monitor and control their own population. The past government of Ben Ali in Tunisia is an illustrative example of this "side effect". As Cassarino[85] has poignantly put it, the EU-Tunisia cooperation on migration control has led to a criminalization of irregular migration, which "constituted one of the many ways to 'legally' conceal the root causes of social discontent in depressed areas and to tame, at the same time, the aspirations and behaviours of those left behind."[86] Especially the 2008 Tunisian protests give evidence that the management of emigration and cooperation with Europe was a way for the Tunisian government to repress discontent. That year, social mobilizations of the local population against the local authorities in three southwestern cities took place, which gained popularity in various other southern cities[87]. Similar to the later uprisings that would provoke Ben Ali's fall, claims for *horrya* (freedom), *aadl* (justice), and *karamat* (dignity) were spreading throughout the country.[88] The protests lasted for over six months, and led to the killing of several protestors, torture, and over 200 arrests.[89] Many Tunisians had left the country in the aftermath of the protests. To strengthen its power, the Tunisian government agreed on a new bilateral agreement with Italy on the removal of irregular Tunisian migrants, which accelerated procedures of identification in close collaboration with

---

[83]Bialasiewicz, *op. cit.*, p. 859.

[84]Ibid., p. 861.

[85]Cassarino, Jean-Pierre (2014) "Channelled Policy Transfers. EU-Tunisia. Interactions on Migration Matters," *European Journal of Migration and Law* (16).

[86]Ibid., p. 105.

[87]Ibid., p. 109–110.

[88]Ibid.

[89]Amnesty International (2009), *Behind Tunisia's Economic Miracle, Inequality, and Criminalization of Protest*, London.

Tunisian authorities;[90] a measure that raised serious concerns within human rights advocates circles, in particular about the potential readmission of those who have been involved in the protests. When deciding upon the agreement, the political elites of the time were well aware that the "reinvigorated cooperation with Italy in the field of migration and border control would foster its regime legitimacy and reliability in European political circles while deflecting political attention from resilient human rights violations in Tunisia."[91]

After the Arab Spring: Wa Horrya?[92]

Much has changed in the Mediterranean since the Tunisian street vendor Mohammed Bouazizi set himself on fire out of desperation in 2010. At the one end of the spectrum, there is Tunisia, which at the beginning of 2014 adopted a constitution that was internationally praised as outstandingly progressive and a model for the Arab world.[93] At the other end there is Syria, which is still in the midst of war, and has claimed the lives of over 140,000 people so far.[94]

One thing, however, seemed to have remained relatively stable: Europe's approach to border control. As the EU Home Affairs Commissioner Cecilia Malmström has underlined:

> In 2011, the EU missed a historic opportunity to show North African countries and the world that it was committed to defending the fundamental values upon which it was built. Instead of helping these countries and giving protection to those in need, the EU was too concerned with security matters and simply closed it borders. It's as if we said "It's wonderful that you've started a revolution and want to embrace democracy, but we have an economic crisis to deal with so we can't help."[95]

---

[90]Cassarino (2014), *op. cit.*, p. 110.

[91]Ibid.

[92]Horrya means freedom, which was one of the guiding words of the slogans of the Arab Spring (Bread, jobs, and freedom).

[93]It has still, though, provoked some criticism. See e.g. Guellali, Anna (2014) "The Problem with Tunisia's New Constitution."

[94]Solomon, Erika (2014) "Syria's Death Toll Now Exceeds 140,000: Activist Group," Reuters 2/15/2014.

[95]Malmström, Cecilia (2012) "Migration is an opportunity, not a threat" Global Hearing on

After the outbreak of the revolutions, European Union member states were aiming to re-establish cooperation to curb immigration in the Mediterranean as quick as possible. In April 2011, Italy pressed the Tunisian interim government to sign an accelerated repatriation agreement,[96] which offered 200 million Euros in aid and credit in return for Tunisia's cooperation in preventing further departures and accepting returned migrants.[97] The agreement, though, is nonbinding, and the Tunisian authorities publicly emphasized that their priorities are elsewhere, having inherited the economic and social challenges of the past regime.[98]

Two months later (June 2011), Italy obtained an agreement with the National Transitional Council of Libya for cooperation on irregular immigration, including the return of irregular migrants.[99] As a result, 13,000 migrants were returned in 2011. As Carrera, den Hertog and Parkin, stress,[100] it was not clear whether these repatriations took full account of the risks of returning individuals to post-revolutionary and post-conflict zones. The European Commission soon followed Italy's example. In a visit to Tunis in April 2011 President Barroso made clear that the EU's financial support to Tunisia of 400 million Euros had to be reciprocated by actions to counter irregular migration.[101]

However, times have changed. The Tunisia of today is less willing to be Europe's policeman than the one of yesterday, and the new political elite in Tunisia is faced with an "unprecedented degree of accountability towards its citizens, which was unconceivable under Ben Ali's regime."[102]

---

refugees and Migration Hague 5 June 2012. European Commission - SPEECH/12/417, 05/06/2012.

[96]Cassarino (2014), *op. cit.*, p. 116.

[97]Carrera, Sergio, den Hertog, Leonhard and Parkin, Joanna (2012) "EU Migration Policy in the wake of the Arab Spring. What prospects for EU-Southern Mediterranean Relation?" MEDPRO Technical Report no. 15, August 2012, p. 6.

[98]Cassarino (2014), *op. cit.*, p. 116.

[99]Ibid.

[100]Carrera et al, *op. cit.*

[101]Ibid.

[102]Cassarino, Jean-Pierre and Lavenex, Sandra (2012), *EU-Migration Governance in the Mediterranean Region: the Promise of (a Balanced) Partnership?* IEMED 2012, p. 11.

In November 2011 the EU´s programmatic document, a Global Approach to Migration and Mobility (GAMM), was adopted. From 2011 onwards there was a reinforced emphasis on the concept of mobility as a direct result of the increased attention to the Union´s extra-territorialized migration control policies in the wake of the Arab Spring. The European Commission officially promoted a vision of cooperation on migration with non-EU countries that should be "mutually beneficial," which finally resulted in the adoption of the GAMM.[103] Consequently, the Commission today defines its relations with the Southern Mediterranean countries on migration related issues as "facilitating mobility but discouraging irregular migration."[104] The GAMM is to be implemented via Migration, Mobility and Security Dialogues in which so-called Mobility Partnerships form the major policy instruments for cooperation[105]. Although Mobility Partnerships have been portrayed as a shift away from the dominant focus on security and border control, and towards opening up new venues for mobility, this is actually not the case.[106] In the framework of Migration and Mobility Dialogues, readmission and reinforced border controls have remained the guiding principles of interaction. An analysis of previous mobility partnerships with neighbors at the eastern border moreover shows that they hardly open any new avenues for legal migration.[107] The concept of mobility in the EU jargon refers predominantly to temporary movement (short-term visitors, tourists, students, researchers, business people or visiting family members), in contrast to more permanent forms of migration.[108]

So far the EU has only reached a mobility partnership with one country in the Mediterranean: The European Commission and the governments of Belgium, France, Germany, Italy, the Netherlands, Portugal, Spain, Sweden and the UK signed a mobility partnership with Morocco in summer 2013. The Commission is negotiating a partnership with Tunisia and has lately started a Dialogue on Migra-

---

[103]Carrera et al., *op. cit.*, p. 1.

[104]European Commission (2014) "Southern Mediterranean."

[105]Carrera et al., *op. cit.*, p. 1.

[106]Ibid., p. 11.

[107]Cassarino et al. (2012), *op. cit.*, p. 285.

[108]Carrera et al., *op. cit.*, p. 13.

tion, Mobility and Security with Jordan.[109] The EU has offered Egypt several times to start a Dialogue on Migration, Mobility and Security. Egyptian authorities, however, have declined the offer.

Conclusion

> *I will never forget the sight of 280 coffins today. I will bear this with me for the rest of my life and I think they express something that we need to think about in the European Union, this isn't the European Union we want.[...]*
>
> EC Commissioner Cecilia Malmström,[110] in response to the death of refugees and migrants in Lampedusa

On October 3, 2013, 366 migrants drowned when their boat sank less than a mile off the shore of the Italian island of Lampedusa. Immediately after the tragedy, then-Italian Prime Minister Enrico Letta announced that all those who died would receive Italian citizenship.[111] They were put in coffins and buried on Italian land. At the same time, the public prosecutor accused 114 rescued adults of irregular migration, which is punishable by a fine of 5000 Euros and expulsion.[112] Can irony get any more bitter than this, the renowned migration scholar Hein de Haas,[113] hitting the nail on the head, asked?

The official answer of the EU to the 2013 events in Lampedusa was EUROSUR, a new border surveillance system operated by the EU's border protection agency FRONTEX. EUROSUR will cost the European Union 196 billion USD by 2020.[114] It has been suggested that the surveillance system, in addition to control its borders more efficiently, will help Member States to track and identify vessels at sea, and therefore will save lives.[115] However, the problem with the boat that sank in Lampedusa in October 2013 was not a lack of detection.

---

[109]European Commission (2014), *op. cit.*

[110]Malmström, Cecilia (2013) "280 Coffins."

[111]de Haas (2013), *op. cit.*

[112]Ibid.

[113]de Haas (2013), *op. cit.*

[114]Taube, Friedel (2013) "Eurosur, sureveillance or protection of refugees?"

[115]See European Commission (2013) "Lampedusa follow up: concrete actions to prevent loss of life in the Mediterranean and better address migratory and asylum flows," IP/13/1199 , 04/12/2013.

The boat had been identified by the Italian Maritime Rescue Coordination Center, and several national authorities were aware that the boat was in trouble.[116]

The image of hundreds of coffins that circulated all over the world in the framework of the October 2013 event was one of the tragic highlights of the by now over two decades of "fighting a delusional migrant invasion."[117] But it is very likely that it will not be the last one.

Europe seems to remain locked into the wrong and misleading dilemma of irregular and regular migration,[118] which is embedded in a one-sided discourse of security.

I would like to end this chapter with a quotation by the European Commissioner Cecilia Malmström[119] who has argued, "Migration will always be a part of our past, present and future. It is up to us how we see and we deal with this reality." One could not agree more.

---

[116]Rooney, Celia (2013), *Exploiting a Tragedy: The Securitization of EU Borders in the Wake of Lampedusa.*

[117]de Haas (2013), *op. cit.*

[118]Cf. de Haas et. al., *op. cit.*, p. 4.

[119]Malmström (2012), *op. cit.*

Chapter Ten

The Mediterranean Diasporas' Role: Pathway to Prosperity?

Andy Mullins

In the past two decades, diasporas from Southeast Europe and North Africa have grown in size and importance. During and after the Wars of Yugoslav Succession, ex-Yugoslavs moved as refugees across the world to establish communities from Stockholm to St. Louis, following decades of employment-motivated relocation to Western Europe. In a sense, it was recognition of the ex-Yugoslav diaspora in North African countries, building and expanding the business ties established some decades ago by the Non-Aligned cooperation discussed in the introduction to this volume, that launched the Mediterranean Basin Initiative.[1] In late 2010, at the start of the Jasmine Revolution and the Arab Awakening, 10 percent of Tunisians lived and worked abroad.[2] Around the same percentage of Egyptians and Moroccans live abroad; five percent of Algerians are overseas, with the number as high as 16 percent among Libyans.[3] In the past, migration from these countries was primarily unskilled labor and/or regime opponents, and governments paid little attention to their burgeoning citizenry overseas.

But diasporas have continued to pay attention to their homelands, remaining politically connected, acting as informal cultural and economic consuls, and—increasingly importantly—returning money to their families and communities of birth. Remittances in 2013 were estimated to exceed $410 billion—four times the total development aid in the global market. As movement across borders, regular or

---

[1] Toperich, Sasha and Andy Mullins. (2012). "A New Paradigm for the Mediterranean: EU-U.S.-North Africa-Southeast Europe," in *Unfinished Business: The Western Balkans and the International Community* (Vedran Džihić and Daniel Hamilton, eds.). Washington, D.C.: Center for Transatlantic Relations, pp. 239–244.

[2] MTM i-Map migration and development layer: Tunisia. Available online at http://www.gfmd.org/files/pfp/mp/Tunisia_EN.pdf.

[3] "Overseas Libyans Started Voting Today." *Libya Herald*, July 3, 2012.

irregular, has become easier and more frequent, remittances are becoming one of the most important channels for development. Migrants can contribute to development in a number of ways— attracting traditional foreign aid or foreign direct investment, building democratic capacity, or return migration—but it is remittances that have proven most attractive to governments.

The diasporas of the Mediterranean affect the economic, political, and social pictures in their homelands in different ways, but there are common features to highlight. While there is certainly a wide range of policies exercised by Mediterranean governments with regard to their citizens abroad, the general trend has been toward more state involvement. Motivated sometimes by political expediency, sometimes by economic concerns, governments have established offices and foundations to coordinate remittances and granted voting rights. Of note after the revolutions in North Africa, many diaspora members have found their way into government, encouraging this cycle. In its 2012 report on least developed countries, the United Nations Conference on Trade and Development (UNCTAD) recommended the establishment of ministry-level institutions to coordinate diaspora policy as part of the national development strategy.[4]

As one diaspora organization leader noted, there are subtle or overt pressures to return home after the Arab Awakening, in spite of lower pay, opportunities, and experiences, because "your country needs you."[5] On the other side, concerns about the vast development potential of remittances center on their individual, family-to-family transmission, rather than the collective good. Governments are moving toward institutionalizing and coordinating diaspora relationships with the homeland.

---

[4]UNCTAD. (2012). *The Least Developed Countries Report 2012: Harnessing Remittances and Diaspora Knowledge to Build Productive Capacities*, p. 123.

[5]"Three Ways The Tunisian Diaspora Can Support the Transition." *Tunisia Live.* March 4, 2014. Available online at http://www.tunisia-live.net/2014/03/04/three-ways-the-tunisian-diaspora-can-support-the-transition/

Diaspora's Defining Features

Simply put, there is no singular definition of diaspora—i.e., in the abstract there is little to distinguish migration flows (as covered by Leila Hadj-Abdou's accomplished chapter) from diasporas. The IMF offers, "…A group of persons who have migrated and their descendants who maintain a connection to their homeland;" the U.S. Department of State includes "collective memory and myth," "the presence of the issue of return," and "consciousness and associated identity," *inter alia.*[6] All-inclusive, these definitions do not tell us much about the difference between migration and diaspora, or whether such a distinction is relevant.

As Paul Collier argues, diasporas tend to develop out of low-level migration flows, as more adventurous job-seekers establish communities and lower the costs of migration for their countrymen and women[7]—the "snowball" or "flood" often cited in opposition to reducing barriers to free movement. The developments cited in the introduction have worked in concert with this social catalyst to expand migrant communities at a much higher rate than any time in history.

Diasporas also tend to be politically active, whether in lobbying to influence their host country's policy toward the homeland or being directly involved in the homeland itself. In the 1990s, as external votes expanded around the world, newly independent Croatia was notable for directly representing the diaspora in presidential elections and in parliament, with as many as 12 delegates elected from abroad. (Playing on memories of World War II and the Independent State of Croatia, the HDZ architects of the post-Yugoslav order in Zagreb knew that nationalism would play well with "hyphenated-Croatians" and they would reap the electoral rewards.) Egyptians abroad were prohibited from voting by mail prior to the ouster of Hosni Mubarak, but made their voices heard in the referendum on the 2012 Muslim Brotherhood-designed constitution, voting overwhelmingly in support of it; with the Brotherhood's reversal of fortune following the June 2013

---

[6]Ratha, Dilip and Sonia Plaza. "Harnessing Diasporas." *Finance & Development*, September 2011, p. 48.

[7]Collier, Paul. (2013). *Exodus: How Migration is Changing Our World*. New York: Oxford University Press.

coup, these sympathizers have been barred from mail balloting once again.[8] Eighteen of the Tunisian Constituent Assembly (NCA) members were elected from abroad in 2011, and eight of Algeria's 382 parliamentarians are expatriates.

Development wisdom holds that the experience of diasporas living in democratic countries, particularly over the course of generations, might encourage democratization at home. The historical record here is mixed. As noted, Croatians in the United States, Canada, Australia, and Western Europe voted overwhelmingly for Franjo Tuđman's HDZ in the 1990s, despite his party's emphasis on the ethnic nation over minority rights and the democratic deficit that resulted.[9] In Tunisia, the Islamist party Ennahda—not the most liberal party on the scene—won 9 of the 18 seats allocated for the diaspora in the 2011 NCA elections. This included one of the two North American seats, two of the five in France, and two of the three in Italy, with only 45 percent of Tunisians in the Arab world voting in this direction. Group attitudes toward democracy among immigrant communities vary widely, so this should not be taken as indicative of diaspora attitudes toward democracy in general, but it is illustrative.

Democratic capacity-building through return migration is another possible channel for democratization, and indeed many new politicians in the post-revolutionary countries have taken this route. Gaddafi's repressive regime in Libya forced most opposition elites into exile, including the first president of the General National Congress, Mohamed Magariaf, and his Prime Minister Ali Zeidan. Diasporas can also mobilize democracy assistance in their host countries, as many communities in America have done in partnership with the U.S. Agency for International Development (USAID) and the State Department. Diaspora lobbies were instrumental in establishing the Tunisian-American Enterprise Fund and Egyptian-American Enterprise Fund, two public-private partnerships with assets valued in the

[8]"Egyptian Diaspora Vote on New Constitution." *Al Jazeera*, January 7, 2014. Available online at http://www.aljazeera.com/news/middleeast/2014/01/egyptian-diaspora-vote-new-constitution-201415502887537.html.

[9]Wayland, Sarah V. (2003). "Immigration and Transnational Political Ties: Croatians and Sri Lankan Tamils in Canada," *Canadian Ethnic Studies*, 35(2), p. 61.

tens of millions of dollars to seed and promote investments in these countries.

Governments and the Diaspora

As recommended by the International Organization for Migration (IOM), the governments of North Africa and Southeast Europe have sought ways to "engage, enable, empower, and educate" their diasporas. Initially this was pursued through direct existing avenues, such as consulates. However, ministerial level engagement is increasingly popular; Morocco, Algeria, and Tunisia all have ministers either dedicated exclusively to the diaspora community or fit this responsibility into social services or other portfolios. This is also common in Southeast Europe, where Serbia and Kosovo, among others, have or have had cabinet-level positions dedicated to the diaspora. These ministers, often working in consultation with elected or appointed expatriate councils, develop strategies to improve communication and open new opportunities for collaboration between the community abroad and the homeland.

It is difficult to evaluate whether these policies are successful from an economic standpoint. Certainly remittances are growing: Morocco received $6.8 billion last year from abroad, Tunisia received $2.17 billion, and Algeria $1.8 billion, all historic highs. Anecdotally, Tunisia's government in particular has been effective in interfacing with the diaspora community in Washington, with an attractive "start-up" brand advocated by Prime Minister Mehdi Jomaa and carried forward by partner institutions. But these policies will likely only continue to be effective if they recognize that state coordination of these resources is not a requirement for sustainable growth. In fact, there is evidence that remittances directed to or through state institutions, along with heavy doses of state-to-state development aid, may be an unforeseen reiteration of the "resource curse" observed in oil-rich states in particular that prevents democratization and social development, as these sources of income insulate governments from having to efficiently manage scare resources for welfare goods and the like.[10]

---

[10]See Ahmed, Faisal Z. (2013). "The Perils of Unearned Foreign Income: Aid, Remittances, and Government Survival," *American Political Science Review*, 106(1), pp. 146–165.

In fact, the direct nature of remittances may be their greatest benefit. Decision-making on sending remittances is generally done at the closest social level, i.e., within families, who know best the needs of the recipients and are best able to gauge the efficacy of the intervention.[11] Increasing overhead by establishing bureaucratic measures intended to pursue the common good instead of the individuals' good strengthens the state relative to individuals and encourages competition over state patronage rather than the development of a fair market, as Barry and Øverland note.[12] This is compounded by the fact that remittance providers like Western Union can charge more than ten percent for what amounts to a basic financial transaction, and such providers often have exclusive relationships with the banking and postal networks in receiving countries by agreement with the government.[13] Western Union's sponsorship of the African Diaspora Marketplace, a USAID grant competition, and its sub-program the Libya Diaspora Marketplace, highlights this feature of the remittance landscape. Mobile banking, facilitated by the explosion of mobile telephone networks throughout North Africa and the entire continent, has been one way to bypass this traditional obstacle.

Opportunities for Growth

What is clear is that migration represents the most untapped—and almost certainly most effective—channel for improving the lives of citizens of Mediterranean countries. In 2008, Gallup found that "more than 40 percent of adults in the poorest quartile of countries 'would like to move permanently to another country;'" this is not a realizable dream for many people, even as movement across borders is at unprecedented levels.[14] Research suggests that enabling easier movement—more easily facilitated by the extant diaspora communities, as outlined above—would add tens of trillions of dollars to the

---

[11]Barry, Christian and Gerhard Øverland. (2010). "Why Remittances to Poor Countries Should Not Be Taxed," *Journal of International Law and Politics*, 42(1), p. 1185.

[12]Ibid.

[13]Ratha, Dilip. (October 2009). "Dollars Without Borders." *Foreign Affairs*. Available online at http://www.foreignaffairs.com/articles/65448/dilip-ratha/dollars-without-borders.

[14]Clemens, Michael A. (2011). "Economics and Emigration: Trillion-Dollar Bills on the Sidewalk?" *Journal of Economic Perspectives*, 25(3), p. 83.

global economy.[15] Citizens in the diaspora tend to be wealthier than their compatriots at home, and enabling them to help one another in every mutually beneficial way possible should be a priority of donors.

This is why encouraging state governments to take a leading role in coordinating diaspora policy, particularly when it comes to remittances, may not be necessary. In relating to their diasporas, governments have a mixed record of playing to divisive memories for political gain; coupled with the added temptation of huge untapped economic resources, the possibility of misuse is present, and there could be better ways to achieve the possible gains. Experience from Southeast Europe shows us this potential, as in the case of Macedonia, where in 2011 diaspora voters were able to participate in parliamentary elections for the first time and reliably went for the ruling (and nationalist) VMRO-DPMNE.

Governments, of course, can be willing partners in unlocking the development potential of the diaspora. They are best able to do this by developing the rule of law at home and prioritizing individual property and political rights, or by replicating the draws of abroad to begin with. It has been shown that enabling diaspora communities to remit with the lowest possible transaction costs would have tremendous benefits for the welfare of the entire country, not just the direct recipient households, as some argue.[16] Inhibiting the political aspects of diaspora policy to the greatest extent possible and promoting a neutral, cooperative framework will help tap into this potential. Michael Collyer notes that governments face "growing recognition of the economic dependence on emigrants" in North Africa and are adapting their relationships accordingly.[17] Western governments should encourage them to move in a direction that emphasizes individual liberty, to give their citizens abroad a chance to find the most valuable ways to meet the needs of their compatriots at home.

---

[15]Ibid., 87.

[16]Barry and Øverland, *op. cit.*

[17]Collyer, Michael. (2010). "The Changing Status Of Maghrebi Emigrants: The Rise of the Diaspora." *Middle East Institute*. Available online at http://www.mei.edu/content/changing-status-maghrebi-emigrants-rise-diaspora.

Part V

Women and the Mediterranean: Opportunities and Challenges for Gender Equality

Chapter Eleven

Libyan Women: Past, Present, and Future

Intisar S. Azzuz

After World War II, Libya came under the mandate of the United Nations. With a population of about 1.5 million in a huge, mostly desert land, it was one of the most impoverished countries in the world when, in 1951, it became the first country to be granted independence by the UN. With UN supervision, a constitution was drafted, making Libya a monarchy in a federal system consisting of three states. In 1963, the constitution was amended and the federal system abolished, creating the United Kingdom of Libya.

Oil was discovered in the early 1960s and its revenue started to transform the country into a developing nation. It had an elected House of Representatives and an appointed Senate, a free and vibrant press, and an improving educational system. It was making slow but solid progress. But all of that was to change after Muammer Gaddafi and his so-called Free Officers staged a coup d'état which was to alter the face of Libya for the following four decades and beyond. Soon after taking over, Gaddafi consolidated his personal power and ruled ruthlessly, using oppression and fear, preventing any form of institutions, civil societies or free expression.

Since the revolution broke out on Feb 17, 2011, Libya has gone through three stages:

1. **The Revolutionary Struggle** from February 17, 2011 until the declaration of Liberation on October 23, 2011. This period saw the formation of the National Transitional Council (NTC), which operated from Benghazi, and an executive council, which operated from Qatar.

2. **The Post-Liberation Transition**: from liberation until the election of the General National Congress (GNC) on July 7, 2012. Until then, the National Transitional Council continued to exercise power, ceding some but not all executive power to

a transitional government and drawing a constitutional declaration to govern the post-NTC era after the election of the General National Congress (GNC).

3. **The GNC "Democratic" Stage**—and I put democratic in quotations—from the peaceful transition of power from the NTC to the 200-member elected GNC. This election was supposed to crown the achievement of the revolution and move Libya for the first time to a truly democratic system. If this happened smoothly and peacefully, it would have been a first in the history of revolutions. A so-called temporary government was approved by the GNC in November 2011.

The Status of Women, Past, Present and Future

The Past

The Kingdom Era. Prior to independence, Libya was a tribal society with an agrarian and Bedouin population dispersed mostly along the coast, with a few oases in the vast desert. In such a traditional, tribal and conservative society, women carried a large burden of caring for the family, yet worked hard in the farms. In the urban areas, women were mainly confined to their homes.

The independence constitution of 1951 gave all Libyans (including women) many human and civil rights. Article 10 reads:

> Libyans shall be equal before the law. They shall enjoy equal civil and political rights, shall have the same opportunities, and be subject to the same public duties and obligations, without distinction of religion, belief, race, language, wealth, kinship or political or social opinions.

Other articles state:

> Personal liberty shall be guaranteed and everyone shall be entitled to equal protection of the law;

> Freedom of conscience shall be absolute. The State shall respect all religions and faiths and shall ensure to foreigners residing in its territory freedom of conscience and the right freely to practice re-

ligion so long as it is not a breach of public order and is not contrary to morality;

Freedom of thought shall be guaranteed. Everyone shall have the right to express his opinion and to publish it by all means and methods. But this freedom may not be abused in any way which is contrary to public order and morality.

But this constitution had its flaws; it failed to establish a balance of powers, provide for a strong judiciary or include provisions for the management of elections. Nevertheless, during the kingdom era, women had equal opportunity for education, holding office and the right to vote.

Since independence, Libyan leaders sought to support women's rights and opportunities within the framework of religious values. Libyan women continued to assert their rights during the 1960s. They exercised the right to vote and participate in political activity. They could own and dispense with property independent of their husbands, form their own associations (as early as 1955) and had the right to hold office.

The Gaddafi Era. On September 1, 1969, Gaddafi led a coup d'état that overthrew the king and ended the kingdom era. On December 11, 1969, a constitutional proclamation was made granting women equal rights with men under the law. Women became more active in education and many other professions. However, their role in economic life remained small; three percent in the 1973 census compared to 37 percent for men, which is considerably slower than in other Arab countries. In the 1980s, women's employment was only 7 percent of the national force—a two percent increase in twenty years. However, researchers claimed that women's participation in economic life was closer to 20 percent when allowances are made for full and part time, seasonal, paid, and unpaid employment. Despite significant increases in female enrollments in the educational system, including university level, few women were employed in such traditionally male fields as medicine, engineering, and law.

During the 1970s, laws were passed regulating women's employment, including equal pay for equal work. Other laws encouraged women to continue to work even after marriage and childbirth, and allowed them to retire at age 55 with a pension. A minimum age of 18 was set for marriage, and women were given equal rights for divorce. Assets of both women and men prior to marriage were protected in case of divorce. In employment, women were overwhelmingly employed as teachers. Other vocations included nursing and clerical workers. Despite improving employment opportunities, women continued to be discriminated against in high offices and having influence in the government.

Other laws were enacted to give women the right to engage in the private business and finance sectors, and banks did not require the consent of the husband to obtain a loan. Employment for women reached 37 percent, an increase of 14 percent, between 1986 and 2006.

These gains in legislation were not without caveats. For example, while the law gave women the right to divorce, it required that women give "reasonable cause" for divorce. If a woman failed to do so, she would forgo her financial rights and custody of her children. Even if she succeeded in giving a "reasonable cause" and kept her children, she could not force her ex-husband to pay alimony if he simply claimed financial hardship. If she married again, she would automatically give up custody of her own children to her mother, and if deceased or financially incapable, to her mother-in-law.

Even though there were gains in women's rights during this era, women suffered disproportionately under the oppressive regime because Libyan women traditionally sacrifice themselves for their family. The general conditions that prevailed were those of corruption, poor health, educational, infrastructure, and legal systems - all affected the entire society, men and women, but more adversely on women who put husband and family ahead of self. The oppressive system imposed more hardship and psychological pain on women when their father, brother, husband or son was imprisoned, tortured or forced into exile.

The Present

Presently, the picture is mixed and worrisome. Libyan women played a key role in the success of the February 17 Revolution. Except for combat, they participated in every aspect of the revolution: they took part in demonstrations early on, documented human rights abuses, were active in social and other media, and supported the fighters. Women would sew flags, prepare meals for combatants, provide logistical support, help treat the injured, and even aid in smuggling ammunitions.

In the free post-liberation environment, women formed many civil society organizations. They were active in promoting and fighting for women rights. I was personally actively involved in several of these organizations.

Women made considerable gains in the first congressional elections for the General National Congress which took office on July 7, 2012. Forty-five percent of registered voters, or 1.3 million, and nearly half the candidates, 545 of 1,246, were women. Thirty-three of the 200 elected members, or 16.5 percent, were women. However, this is somewhat deceptive since only one woman was elected as an independent candidate, while the other 32 were elected under the electoral law which had a gender parity provision requiring each party to place its female candidates in an alternating pattern with male candidates on their slates to ensure that women were elected. This still compares favorably with Egypt's elections, in which less than two percent of those elected to parliament were women.

Women have experienced increasing harassment in the major cities over the past two years, combined with the general lawlessness in the country. But the roots of such harassment go back to the Gaddafi era, as recently reported by Voice of America:

> The Gaddafi family and their top officials were notorious for abducting women. Women would be summoned from their homes after they had been noticed at social events, according to a recently published book *Gaddafi's Harem* by *Le Monde* journalist Annick Cojean. That behavior spread through society, convincing men beyond the power circles that women were fair game.[1]

Recently, women's groups staged a protest called "Woman Scream" demanding that government authorities act on violations against women, whether in public or within the family, and bring to justice

---

[1]Voice of America. November 1, 2013. "Libya Women Report Increased Harassment." http://www.voanews.com/content/libya-women-report-increased-harassment/1781596.html

and punish those responsible for crimes of rape, violence and harassments. It placed the responsibility directly on the government for lack of enforcement and demanded accountability and enforcement of laws in this regard. In Libya, wife abuse is not brought into public life due to social norms. There is no concept of marital rape in Libyan law, and there are no laws outside the general penal code that protect the victim or punish the perpetrator.

Despite very active involvement by women in public life, strong presence in media, very active civil society organizations, good representation in the Congress and intensive campaigns to advocate their cause and assert their rights, they made very little progress in high positions in government where they could exert actual influence. Only two cabinet positions were given to women in the current 32-member interim government as well as the previous transitional one. Even though one position was the Minister of Health, women were generally limited to social and marginal ministries.

Even though women have taken advantage of their educational opportunities, it remains mostly limited to the major cities. In rural areas, girls are limited in getting education due to family restrictions. Even in cities, where women graduates greatly outnumber men in many major fields of study, such as medicine and architecture, they face limited advancement opportunities due to social conditions which place higher burdens on women for family obligations, lack of daycare services, poor transportation and inadequate support from husbands and family.

Another problem that has been facing women is in marriage. Libyan law specifies age 18 as the minimum age for marriage, yet it is widely violated in rural areas. Birth certificates can be forged to circumvent the law.

General poverty, lack of good-paying jobs and adequate housing has forced delay in marriage. Many young Libyan men migrated seeking better opportunities outside Libya and fleeing violent political conditions. This has compounded the problem for women of childbearing age of finding suitable marriage partners, adding to their social problems.

While gains made in the legal status of women over the past half-century remain on the books, many are now under threat due to pressure from some religious parties and their supporters. The Law No. 9 of 1993 went a long way toward limiting polygamy by requiring the written consent of the first wife and court permission. However, this law seems to be under threat. On his speech on the occasion of Liberation Day on November 23, 2011, National Transitional Council President Abduljaleel called for promoting polygamy.

Libya on May 16, 1989 became a state party to the Convention on the Elimination of All Forms of Discrimination against Women (CEDAW). The signature was not debated under the then-totalitarian regime. However, in the current atmosphere of open debate, this convention has stirred strong discussion and controversy. The Dar Alifta (which issues *fatwas*, or edicts, from its leader the Mufti) has warned the legislators (GNC) against approving the convention. The debate continued between supporters and opponents, ignoring the fact that Libya is already a state party to CEDAW. Dar Aliftaa issued a proclamation stating that the convention has "destructive and unfair articles, the least dangerous of which is blowing up the family and undermining its integrity, a call to moral decay, in addition to openly breaking the laws of the Quran and Sunnah."

The revolution of February 2011 has not brought improvement in the status of women. But neither has it brought real improvements in the political, legal or administrative infrastructure of the system. Laws still discriminate against women, such as polygamy and denying citizenship rights to children of Libyan women who marry non-Libyans. The vibrant activity in women's civil society organizations have abated, reflecting the general mood in the country that little has changed in the system since liberation. An attitude of apathy is gripping the people. One woman reflected this attitude by saying, "What good is it to talk if no one is listening? Neither Congress nor the two governments have given any indications that women will play a bigger role now than in the past. There are important and negative changes that have transported the social awareness to a backward position, one of which is the use of religion as a tool to oppress women within society."

The Future

Libya is now embarking on the huge task of drafting and adopting a new constitution. The General National Congress was elected and sworn into office on July 7, 2012. It was given 18 months, and tasked with the primary responsibility of drafting a new constitution through a 60-member Constitutional Commission which was to comprise 20 members elected from each region of the country, roughly representing the three original states formed in 1951 upon independence.

The 18-month life of the GNC was supposed to end on February 7, 2014, and the election for the Constitutional Commission occurred on February 20. The lax way the GNC acted in performing its primary duty of drafting the constitution has led to strong negative popular sentiment against it, in additions to its generally perceived poor performance. The GNC voted itself a mandate extension until December 24, 2014. This has given rise to many movements opposing the extension and alternative proposal to manage the transition.

Women's groups intensely lobbied for sizeable inclusion of women into the Constitutional Commission, whose draft of the constitution will shape the form of the Libyan political, legal and all aspects of life for decades to come. Despite a heavy campaign by women groups, only six of the sixty seats in the commission (or 10 percent) were reserved for women while their percentage in the population is over 50 percent. Judging by the experience of the GNC elections, it is unlikely that more than a few women would be elected, outside the allocated six.

Some groups, both within and outside the GNC, opposed a quota system, arguing that it would violate Article 6 of the interim Constitutional Declaration of August 3, 2011, the *de facto* constitution of the post-Gaddafi era, which states that "Libyans shall be equal before the law." However, this argument is not valid because of Libya's obligations under the international legal framework. As noted above, Libya is party to CEDAW, which states that "adoption by States Parties of temporary special measures aimed at accelerating de facto equality between men and women shall not be considered discrimination as defined in the present Convention..."[2]

Libya is also party to the Protocol of the African Charter on Human and Peoples' Rights, which states that "State Parties shall take

---

[2]Convention on the Elimination of All Forms of Discrimination against Women, Article 4, Paragraph 1.

specific positive action to promote participative governance and the equal participation of women in the political life of their countries through affirmative action, enabling national legislation and other measures to ensure that: a) women participate without discrimination in all elections; b) women are represented equally at all levels with men in all electoral processes; [...]; 2. States Parties shall ensure increased and effective representation and participation of women at all levels of decision-making."[3]

Despite gains, Libyan women face many challenges on the road ahead to improve their social and legal status guaranteed by legislative and constitutional statutes.

Some groups want to roll back women's rights, calling for a strict traditional role for Libyan women under Sharia law, segregating them in schools and places of employment, and even confining them to home and family. They promise to enact a more conservative constitution which would deprive women of gains made over the past half century. However, despite their vociferous pressure, these groups do not enjoy wide popular support, as recent polls have shown.

Obstacles to women achieving equality will continue, since Libya remains a male dominated society and religion could be used as a tool for discrimination.

A Promising Sign from Tunisia

Women's rights could be bolstered by articles in the constitution in neighboring Tunisia approved in early 2014. Article 20 was approved by the National Constituent Assembly on January 7, 2014. One article, which was approved by 159 out of 169 lawmakers, states that "all male and female citizens have the same rights and duties. They are equal before the law without discrimination." This upholds Tunisia's status as having one of the most progressive laws on women rights in the Arab world.

The ruling Tunisian Islamist Ennahda Party also accepted the lack of inclusion of articles enshrining Islamic Sharia law as well as accepted the "neutrality of mosques." In 2011, this party sparked con-

---

[3]African Charter on Human and Peoples' Rights, Article 9.

troversy when it proposed gender "complementarity," rather than equality in the constitution. The new draft constitution states that Tunisia is a secular state based on citizenship and rule of law. This decides once and for all making the Sharia one, rather than the only, source of legislation.

The struggle for women's rights in Libya's yet-to-be-drafted constitution and in society lies ahead. Women must remain vigilant and proactive to assert their rights and achieve measures of equality.

Chapter Twelve

UN Security Council Resolution 1325: "Women, Peace, and Security"

Samra Filipović-Hadžiabdić

The UN Security Council Resolution 1325 on "Women, Peace and Security" (UNSCR 1325) from 2000 is the first Security Council resolution specifically addressing the impact of war on women and children, as well as the role of women in the prevention and resolution of conflicts and contributing to sustainable peace. The resolution provides for specific actions to achieve full gender equality in the security sector. We can say that UNSCR 1325 provides the means for the introduction of gender equality, the obligation of all member states and the opportunity to provide stability and introduce long-term and sustainable change.

The UN Secretary-General issued a directive on October 29, 2008, which refers to the process of implementation and reporting in accordance with the UNSCR 1325, obligating member states to create National Action Plans (NAPs) for the implementation of UNSCR 1325 in Bosnia and Herzegovina (BiH).

It is important to emphasize that BiH is the eighth country in Europe, and 24th in the world, that has adopted a NAP for the implementation of the UNSCR 1325. BiH's methodology for the development, structure and process of the adoption of the NAP was used as a model for the development and adoption of the action plans of the other countries in the region. The experiences that we have gained were used as a foundation for the organization of a number of regional conferences and meetings on this topic. They also made our country a regional leader in the implementation of UNSCR 1325.

Before the start of the drafting of the NAP, the Gender Equality Agency of the Ministry for Human Rights and Refugees of BiH analyzed the examples of NAPs from other countries around the world. Comparative analysis was made between the action plans of Denmark, Norway, Great Britain, Spain, Sweden and Liberia. Literature of the

United Nations, the Council of Europe, the European Union, and relevant experts and non-governmental organizations was also used. The comparative analysis has enabled insight into the best practices of the world in the implementation of UNSCR 1325, which in turn has enabled us to more clearly define the specifics of our society and country.

The NAP for the implementation of UNSCR 1325 in BiH focuses on the contribution of women in strengthening and sustaining peace in post-war BiH. Through intensive regional and international cooperation, the NAP is trying to influence and strengthen the stability of the region.

The NAP includes introduction, analysis of the situation, and eight goals, which includes definitions of activities, deadlines, and the responsibilities of carriers and partners.

The goals of the NAP are:

1. increased participation of women in decision-making;

2. increased number of women in the military and police forces;

3. increased number of women in peacekeeping missions;

4. fight against human trafficking;

5. demining;

6. support for civilian war victims;

7. strengthening the capacity of civil servants in the security sector;

8. improvement of cooperation with NGOs and international organizations.

The Gender Equality Agency of BiH led the process of preparing the NAP for the implementation of UNSCR 1325 during 2009 in cooperation with all relevant state and entity-level institutions, as well as civil society organizations. In order to facilitate the implementation and monitoring of the NAP and make it more efficient, a 20-member Coordination Board was formed in 2011 by decision of the Council of Ministers, which includes representatives of 12 state and entity level institutions. Members of the Coordination Board participated in and contributed actively to the development, implementation and promotion of the NAP, both within the institutions, in the general public and at the international level.

Most of the relevant institutions included the activities and commitments found under the NAP in their work plans. So far the Council of Ministers and the Parliamentary Assembly of BiH have adopted two Reports on the implementation of the NAP.

A website for monitoring the implementation of the NAP was established. This website gathers information on all activities related to the implementation of UNSCR 1325. The website provides all interested parties access and insight into the activities surrounding the implementation of the NAP.

The NAP expired at the end of July 2013. In preparation for the creation of a new plan, an independent evaluation of the current implementation of NAP was conducted, with a special focus on the evaluation of the:

- structure of the NAP (objectives, activities);

- roles and contributions of the Gender Equality Agency of BiH and the Coordination Board in the implementation process;

- results of the conducted activities of NAP in the relevant institutions of BiH and the entities;

- cooperation with non-governmental sector and international organizations in achieving the objectives of the NAP.

This assessment was conducted by established international and domestic experts. It pointed out the successes, difficulties and challenges in the implementation and made recommendations for improvements of the new NAP for the period 2014–2017.

The assessment found that the NAP of BiH in many ways can represent a model for the global implementation of the UNSCR 1325. The goals and activities of the plan are fully compatible with the existing mandates of the relevant institutions and key actors responsible for security policy.

For the realization of eight ambitious goals, the cooperation between the representatives of government, NGOs and the international community was crucial. All the stakeholders were given the opportunity to provide appropriate contributions that were consistent with their expertise, existing obligations and commitments tasks.

Relevant stakeholders have accepted the NAP more as an integrating national strategy rather than an obligation imposed by international organizations. The Gender Equality Agency of BiH was recognized as a model of leadership in public policy. The Gender Equality Agency is a key player who has contributed to the success of the NAP. During the last three years, the Gender Equality Agency has consistently provided professional support to institutions in the implementation of the NAP, and has contributed to the provision of an institutional approach to these issues in various government departments. The success of BiH's NAP is even more important if we take into account the complex political system of post-Dayton BiH, and the present traditional norms that dictate relations between the sexes. There are thus still established stereotypes present in the world when it comes to the inclusion of women in peace and security issues.

The Gender Equality Agency of BiH has managed to bring these activities closer and provide a practical approach to the implementation of the NAP. Various workshops and educational materials are not only focused on UNSCR 1325 and the NAP, but are represented as integral materials that are aligned with other national strategies. This approach increased the sense of local ownership and the support for implementation among the key stakeholders.

The Coordination Board is a positive example of a common, coordinated approach and support for the implementation process. Guided by the leadership of the Gender Equality Agency of BiH, the Coordination Board is a key player in mobilizing the relevant institutions and individuals for the implementation of the NAP in BiH.

Cohesion and coordination among members of the Board is considered one of the main reasons for the success of this process and can serve as an example of the remarkable cooperation between the relevant government institutions. Most members of the Coordination Board have used their institutional authority to personally promote the objectives of the NAP.

The NAP of BiH is evaluated as a platform for achieving results, among others the following:

- Progress has been made in aligning internal regulations, rules and procedures with the objectives of the NAP, in order to improve the position of women in the security structures;

- A network of female police officers was established in both entities;

- The Ministry of Defense appointed contact persons for gender issues with the task of integrating the objectives of the NAP in the work of the Ministry and the Armed Forces;

- All institutions organized educational and promotional events related to the implementation of the NAP. For example, according to data from the Ministry of Defense, such educational activities during the last three years covered more than 4,000 people;

- Ministries of Internal Affairs have initiated the introduction of gender issues in the curricula of police academies in both entities;

- The Ministry of Security has successfully included objectives of the NAP in the work of the Peace Support Operations Training Center—PSOTC (Butmir, Sarajevo), adding training courses on human rights issues and gender equality;

- Trainings, workshops and activities run by civil society organizations contributed to the maximum use of technical expertise and strengthening of coordination and cooperation between NGOs and institutions;

- In cooperation with non-government and international organizations and with the support of the FIGAP[1] program, specific projects targeting the localization of the NAP through the prism of "human security" are being implemented.

This initiative to implement the NAP identifies local priorities and obstacles to the safety of women in local communities and the environment. Because of the way that the message of UNSCR 1325 reaches down to the local level of government, BiH is an innovative example at the global level.

---

[1]Financial Instrument for Implementation of Gender Action Plan in Bosnia and Herzegovina.

These examples of success brought international recognition of BiH, which is not typically recognized as an efficient system of public administration.

Like any public strategy or policy, the implementation of the NAP has encountered certain difficulties. To cite just a few:

• Lack of harmonization between laws in the field of security and the Law on Gender Equality, which is a prerequisite for the institutionalization of gender issues and system solutions;

• Lack of technical capacity in institutions for the introduction of standards and policies to achieve gender equality in the work of institutions;

• Inadequate monitoring and evaluation system;

• Inadequate financial resources.

The current system of monitoring and evaluation is not an efficient model for full monitoring of achievement of expected results. There is an excessive number of indicators which prevents effective data analysis and tracking of real progress.

The lack of funds for effective implementation of the NAP is more than evident, because the goals and activities of the NAP have not been identified as priorities within the institutional strategies or work plans. Also, there is a problem of introducing gender-sensitive budgeting in various institutions, which is one of preconditions for implementation of strategies in this field.

The Evaluation Report about the implementation of the NAP contains recommendations on which activities that should be kept and which ones that need to be improved in order to achieve better results in the future.

Basic Recommendations

1. Additional support to the Coordination Board is required with clearly defined duties and responsibilities;

2. Improve the structure of the NAP; clearly define and refine the goals and activities within the three pillars: equal participation, prevention and protection;

3. Improve the monitoring and evaluation system;

4. Significantly reduce the number of indicators;

5. Make a special plan for the monitoring and evaluation of the NAP;

6. Provide and increase resources for the effective implementation of activities under the NAP (as from FIGAP, and other sources of funding), and initiate allocations from the budgets of the institutions;

7. Keep the effective role of the Gender Equality Agency of BiH, as it proved to be a remarkable example of coordination of all stakeholders in the implementation;

8. Keep a high level of stakeholder's ownership in the development and implementation of the new NAP. This involves increasing the contribution of civil servants and enhanced support of management of relevant institutions.

The new NAP (2014–2017) was developed through the cooperation between the Gender Equality Agency and the institutions represented in the Coordination Board for monitoring NAP implementation, as well as in consultations with NGOs. Professional and technical support for the preparation of the NAP was provided by the Institute for Inclusive Security, within the "Resolution to Act" program, and UN Women in BiH.

And finally, it is important to note that we recently received the Recommendations of the CEDAW Committee, which will be integrated into specific targets, such as the NAP objectives relating to equal participation in decision-making and support to women who have become war-time victims of sexual abuse and victims of human trafficking.

Chapter Thirteen

Women's Entrepreneurship in North Africa: Looking into the Western Balkans' Experience

Dajana Džindo

Three years after the start of the Arab Spring, the economic outlook for North African countries remains uncertain and awaits sustainable solutions. Numerous challenges, including high unemployment, significant dependence on unvaried industries, and an ample public sector led to increased recognition of entrepreneurship as a possible key driver of economic growth and greater competitiveness. Nevertheless, women's participation in this economic process remains rather neglected as a phenomenon and as a favorable source of advancement, in despite of the growth of women entrepreneurs' numbers and the accretionary research interest that marked the last decade.

Envisioned as a contribution to the discourse calling for change, and to serve as an attempt to induce greater interest for women's entrepreneurship in five Mediterranean North African countries (Algeria, Egypt, Libya, Morocco and Tunisia), this chapter draws upon information pertinent to women's entrepreneurship in the region and offers action-oriented recommendations based on the experience of the Western Balkan former Yugoslav countries: Bosnia and Herzegovina, Croatia, Macedonia, Montenegro and Serbia.

The rationale behind this combination lies in the fact that the post-authoritarian Western Balkan countries have gained broad and diverse transitional experience that could be beneficial for North Africa. While reflecting different socio-political contexts, this experience highlights the same constraints that women entrepreneurs face in similar unpropitious business environments of North Africa today. Looking into these similarities found in the Western Balkans in order to avoid deadlocks and to apply certain good practices, while responding to the specific regional challenges, could be the shortest path to accommodating women in entrepreneurship processes and improving the overall economic performance of North Africa.

Women's Entrepreneurship in Context

With regard to women's entrepreneurship, the Western Balkans is possibly North Africa's most similar region. Similarities are reflected in the demo-economic characteristics, gender-specific barriers to starting and growing ventures, features of women-owned businesses, as well as in an urgent need to generate immediate social and economic benefits through job creation and advancement of the private sector.

Women in Algeria, Egypt, Libya, Morocco and Tunisia, as in the Western Balkan countries, make up about half the population. Yet in 2012, as noted by national statistical entities, 75 percent of them did not join the labor force compared to 25 percent of men.[1] In the same year in the Western Balkan countries,[2] an average of 61 percent of the female population was considered economically inactive.[3] In addition to that worrisome data, high female unemployment in North Africa and the Western Balkans in 2012, ranging from 17 percent in Algeria to 45.7 percent in Montenegro,[4] depicts the magnitude of failure to take into account women as contributors to economic prosperity in both regions.

Although these issues are not unique to these respective regions, reasons for unpromising statistics ranking below the average of developing countries might be found in inappropriate policies directed towards women, downgrading social norms, and a generally unfavorable cultural attitude.

---

[1]Presented results are calculated as an average percentage of statistics acquired by national statistical offices: the Algerian National Statistical Office (85 percent), Egypt's State Information Service and Central Agency for Public Mobilization and Statistics (75 percent), Libya's National Corporation for Information and Documentation (71 percent), Moroccan Haut Commissariat au Plan (73 percent), and Tunisian National Institute of Statistics (72 percent).

[2]Presented result is calculated as an average percentage of statistics acquired through Labor Force Surveys conducted in 2012 by: Agency for Statistic of Bosnia and Herzegovina (62,4 percent), Croatian Bureau for Statistics (59,1 percent), Statistical Office of the Republic of Serbia (61,7 percent), Statistical Office of Montenegro (57,9 percent) and State Statistical Office of Macedonia (64 percent).

[3]For comparison, the percentage of economically inactive women in 2012 in the EU was 34 percent, according to the EU Labor Force Survey.

[4]Websites of respective national statistical offices.

Certainly, women in North African and Western Balkan countries, as in many parts of the world, struggle with restrictive norms in various life areas. Though blatant discrimination is considered to be part of the past, and constitutions as well as other statutory regulations guarantee gender equality, women in both regions most often face limitations of local culture that favor women to play the role of "housewife" and/or "mother." This cultural code emanates from the traditional views and interpretations of religion as well as from the patriarchal social system in general.

In addition, women face various barriers that impede their economic participation and in particular entrepreneurial activities. Cross-examination of the literature shows that these barriers in both regions include:

- Limited access to quality education

- Weak chances of acquiring finances

- Lack of opportunities to gain the business skills and experiences required to start and manage a business

- Limited or nonexistent access to formal and informal business networks

- Lack of relevant business information

- Gender-insensitive laws and regulations

- Limited access to formal structures and institutions

- Weak social safety nets for women

- Corruption and interference from elites

Furthermore, analysis also reveals gender differences in how women and men perceive their entrepreneurial abilities. According to MENA and national GEM reports,[5] adult women in North Africa have a lower perception that they have the skills required to start a business, express higher fear of failure, and fewer intend to open up and run an enterprise in the near future compared to men. In fact, according to these

---

[5]IDRC (2010), GEM-MENA Regional Report 2009, IDRC, Cairo; Abedou, Bouyacoub, Kherbachi (2013), GEM Algeria 2011, Algeria; Hattab (2013), GEM Egypt 2012, Egypt; Belkacem, Mansouri (2013), GEM Tunisia 2012, Tunisia.

reports, men are twice as likely to start a business in the next three years, although entrepreneurship is in general perceived as a good career choice by both genders. Similarly, women in Western Balkan countries also show a lower level of self-confidence with regard to their abilities and belief in profitability of their business ideas and ventures.

In spite of these gloomy perceptions, women do comprise a large proportion of nascent entrepreneurs in the North African region, compared with established firm owners, suggesting that women are now more involved than in previous years.[6] Women in this region tend to start smaller entities (micro- or small enterprises), usually have a lower level of capitalization, and are less likely to have paid employees or to be engaged in exporting.[7] Women-run enterprises are also more frequently driven by necessity than opportunity, which prevents the majority from crossing the spectrum from micro to high growth.

The same characteristics are visible in analysis of entrepreneurship reports from the Western Balkan region, with a special accent on constant gradual growth of women's involvement in entrepreneurial processes. For instance, a Croatian GEM report for the period from 2002 to 2011 shows that female entrepreneurial activity, measured by the female TEA index,[8] marked a gradual increase from 1.83 in 2002 to 4.71 in 2011, which coincides with the period of enhanced policy commitment. The only spotted difference related to features of women-owned businesses is the level of sophistication, which is found to be higher in the Western Balkan region.

Commonalities of these two regions are also to be found in sectors in which women-owned businesses tend to concentrate. Women in both regions most frequently operate businesses in extractive sectors such as agriculture, or the services and retail industry, while a significant percent of these businesses in North Africa operate informally. It is considered that the informal sector in general comprises up to half of all economic

---

[6]OECD (2013), *New Entrepreneurs and High Performance Enterprises in the Middle East and North Africa*, IDRC, Canada.

[7]OECD (2012), *Women in Business: Policies to Support Women's Entrepreneurship Development in the MENA Region*, OECD Publishing.

[8]TEA index is an indicator that assesses the percent of working age population both about to start an entrepreneurial activity, and that have started one from a maximum of three and a half years.

activities in North African countries, which could be explained by the unfavorable business and regulatory environment. The Western Balkan region, in contrast, records a significantly lower level of informality.

Women entrepreneurs themselves, according to GEM reports,[9] in both regions are typically aged between 25 and 45, hold secondary school certificates, and are in more than 50 percent of cases married. Recent trends suggest, though, that the female entrepreneurial demography is changing slowly in respect to education, and is including a higher (although still unsatisfactory) number of female graduates.

Learning Lessons from the Western Balkans: Toward a Culture of Innovation

The fall of the communist regime in the 1990s and the transition from a socialist economic system to a market system demonstrated that Western Balkan countries desperately need a vibrant private sector that will create jobs and increase economic opportunities. Much of the early transition efforts, decelerated by political and social hindrances, focused on adoption of national frameworks for entrepreneurship development that did not incorporate a female dimension. Following steps that expanded on targeted interventions also didn't envision women's role in the economy. Only a decade after, policies and strategies that considered women's entrepreneurship started taking shape, followed by strategically unaligned activities. Arguably, if those efforts were enforced earlier as a part of the private sector development agenda, the Western Balkan region would be witnessing a significantly lower gender gap and better performing economy today.

What is evident from the Western Balkans' experience is the fact that governments have to play the main role in enabling women's entrepreneurship growth and economy modernization, and therefore should not wait upon or rely on international organizations and non-governmental actors to carry the burden of transition and women's entrepreneurship development. This doesn't imply that other stake-

---

[9]Global Entrepreneurship Monitor (GEM) is a unique international research project launched in 1999 by world experts on entrepreneurship for the purpose of analyzing the relationship between entrepreneurship and economic growth. National reports for most countries are issued on an annual basis.

holders should be excluded from the process, but rather that only governments can ultimately improve the business environment.

Understanding that no single policy can effectuate women's entrepreneurship in transitional countries is another lesson that could be drawn from the Western Balkans' experience. After years of feeling in the dark based on the principle of trial and error, Western Balkan countries recently realized that the web of issues that influence female entrepreneurship cannot be parted or simplified, and that they need an integrated policy approach that will target innovation primarily. Countries that recognized this earlier and started applying this approach (such as Croatia and Serbia) are already noticing modest but enviable results.

Although just at the beginning of their transitional process, North African countries can't afford to waste time or opportunities as the Western Balkans did, and hence should draw upon the experience of this region and embrace an entrepreneurial development paradigm (while acknowledging women's role in it) as soon as possible.

The current underdeveloped state and obstacles in North Africa could be overcome by recognizing the value of women as human capital and by playing a proactive role in promoting their participation through development of a more dynamic and inclusive environment while mobilizing the spectrum of domestic resources. In the long term, integrative efforts to synergize women, ideas, institutions and capital would lead to sustainable social changes and economic growth.

At the same time, the willingness to develop a culture of innovation, to support diversification and women's participation in nontraditional sectors, and to make use of men's broad experiential base and assistance should have positive results on utilizing women's potential.

In that sense it can be argued that innovation, diversification, gender dialogue and development effectiveness based on integrated policy approach are the key elements for change, while the creation of higher value-added economies is set as the ultimate goal.

Taking these elements into account, while bearing in mind that each country is unique and needs customized solutions, the following recommendations (that strive to be considered just as a part of multifaceted process through which the region needs to go) along with some examples of good practices are offered.

Recommendations

North African countries made a strong commitment to gender equality through their constitutions, numerous pieces of national legislation and ratification of UN's Convention on the Elimination of All Forms of Discrimination against Women—CEDAW. But when this commitment is compared to the level of economic opportunity, it appears to be rather declarative, since all North African countries tackled the question of women's entrepreneurship development on a policy level by superficial incorporation of the female dimension in the formulation of SME-related policies, which they started passing in the 2000s (led by Morocco in 2000 and Algeria in 2001).

In order to live up to their countries' commitments, one of the foremost recommended actions to support women entrepreneurship is for governments to adopt gender-targeted policies. They should be generated as a set of context-driven policies delivered at multiple levels (national, regional and local), since policies formulated in such a manner are more conducive to entrepreneurship than single-issue policies.[10] They should furthermore be designed in consultation with the key stakeholders, based on gender-disaggregated data along with markets' specificities, and should recognize women entrepreneurs as a heterogeneous group in need of different types of support.

Adoption of these policies would signal to existing and potential women entrepreneurs that governments are serious about including the private sector in realizing their economic growth potential, hence raising the interest of potential entrepreneurs with relevant knowledge and experience to engage in entrepreneurial activities.[11]

A strategy framework designed in light of policy principles should be an accompanying step intended to utilize all resources and efforts made by various actors.

By being the first country in the Western Balkan region to launch the "Strategy for Women Entrepreneurship Development" in 2009

---

[10]Minniti M, (2009), "Gender Issues in Entrepreneurship," *Foundations and Trends in Entrepreneurship*, Vol. 5, pp. 497–621

[11]OECD (2013), *New Entrepreneurs and High Performance Enterprises in the Middle East and North Africa*, IDRC, Canada.

(for the period from 2010 to 2013), Croatia sets a good example to other countries highlighted by this paper. The strategy serves as a framework for different initiatives and institutions that attempt to increase the number of women entrepreneurs and to foster the growth of existing women-owned ventures. Under the Ministry of Entrepreneurship and Crafts, Croatia also developed and started implementing an action plan based on this strategy, thus demonstrating its commitment on an even higher level.

While holistic and consistent policy commitment to women entrepreneurship undoubtedly yields its systematic development, an appropriate institutional framework, including the establishment of focal government body with corresponding human and financial resources in disposal, should be high on the agenda.

A government agency, directorate, or council for women's entrepreneurship on the state level with supporting offices is recommended to be formed in all countries covered by this paper, although most of them have some form of body dealing with general women empowerment under responsible ministries (e.g. National Council for Women and Family under the Ministry for Family and the Status of Women in Algeria; Agency for Gender Equality under the Ministry of Human Rights and Refugees in Bosnia and Herzegovina; or General Department for Women's Affairs under the Ministry of Social Affairs in Egypt) and/or have SME agencies partially targeting women (National Agency for SMEs in Morocco or Directorate for Development of SME in Montenegro). The existence of a focal governmental unit for women's enterprise development proves to be a highly effective measure in good practice countries identified by the AfDB/ILO team of international experts, since it facilitates development, coordination and implementation of policies and programs targeting women, and allows outreach to a larger number of women.[12]

With set foundations, reflected in policy, strategy and the institutional framework, preconditions to improve the situation in categories that are seen as the most important factors facing women's entrepreneurship should already exist. These categories include: *startup regula-*

---

[12]AfDB/ILO (2007), *Assessing the Enabling Environment for Women in Growth Enterprises: An AfDB/ILO Integrated Framework Assessment Guide*, International Labour Organization, Geneva.

tions, financial resources, entrepreneurial education, and *business development services.*

Startup Regulations

For some time now, while changing their role from providers to regulators, North African countries are facing the imperative to enhance the regulatory business environment by eliminating existing barriers that prevent both men and women entrepreneurs from starting and/or growing their businesses.

According to the World Bank's Doing Business Index[13] developed to assess the degree to which a regulatory environment is conducive to starting and operating local ventures, North African countries rank very differently. From 189 countries included in the ranking in 2013, Libya ranked 187th as the worst in the region when looking at the overall ease of doing business, while Tunisia ranked as the best by taking 51st place. Specifically, with regard to ease of starting business, Libya ranked as 171st, Algeria 164th, Tunisia 70th, Egypt 50th and Morocco 39th.

According to the OECD, the cumbersome process of business registration is perceived as the biggest regulatory barrier for women starting up ventures, and it is likely one of the key reasons why a significant number of women stay in the informal sector and thus are prevented from growing their enterprises further. That process in the region includes on average 6 to 15 procedures, lasts from seven days up to one month, costs from 5 to 15 percent of income per capita, and may be influenced by a number of challenges such as reduced transparency, corruption or political instability. In addition, certain gender-related factors may make this process even more difficult for women in this region. For instance, if the registration offices are not located in the woman entrepreneur's town or village of residency, mobility restrictions can make it difficult to travel to initiate the process.[14]

Although North African countries did make slight improvements in reforming start-up regulations since 2008, still many more efforts lie

---

[13]Doing Business 2013 http://www.doingbusiness.org/rankings.

[14]OECD (2012), *Women in Business: Policies to Support Women's Entrepreneurship Development in the MENA Region*, OECD Publishing.

ahead of institutions responsible for making these processes less bureaucratic and more accessible for women. Designing and implementing a long-term strategy, which would include inventory and review of procedures, their simplification, e-governance and elements of promotions, can benefit all entrepreneurs but particularly help women.

Results of such an approach can be illustrated by the case of Macedonia, which embraced systematic reforms in the mid-2000s. In 2006, company registration in this country was changed from a judicial process to an administrative one, and a one-stop shop combined company, tax and statistics registration. Additionally, the publication requirement in the official gazette was replaced with automatic registration on the registrar's website. In the year following these first changes, new business registrations increased by about 20 percent.[15] Furthermore, as a part of reforms, Macedonia also implemented the project "Regulatory Guillotine," consequently simplifying hundreds of laws and bylaws in order to decrease red tape and corruption in state institutions, and amended the existing laws with the rule "silence means approval," which applied pressure on the administration to respond to requests within the prescribed deadline.[16]As a result of these reforms, Macedonia in 2013 became the seventh-easiest place in the world to start a business. This overall improvement showed to be especially important for women, who previously found themselves disproportionately disadvantaged when dealing with complex and time consuming procedures.

Access to Financial Resources

Access to financial resources in many parts of the world presents one of the biggest constraints to development of women's entrepreneurship. But more than in other parts of world, women in North Africa, like their male counterparts, finance their business activities through personal savings or family members and friends. The underdeveloped financial markets in this region limit options for male and

---

[15]IFC (2010), *Doing Business 2011*, The World Bank and the International Finance Corporation.

[16]MEDF (2008), *GEM Entrepreneurship in Macedonia 2008*, Macedonian Enterprise Development Foundation (MEDF).

female entrepreneurs alike, but women entrepreneurs also confront gender-specific obstacles such as insufficient collateral, limited financial literacy, or a lack of funding for women-led businesses that have moved beyond the micro-financing stage.[17] In addition, data show that terms of borrowing loans tend to be less favorable for women (including higher interest rates and shorter-term loans) since their businesses are *perceived* to be riskier, higher in costs and lower in return.[18]

The public sector, along with financial institutions, is particularly liable to change this situation. Public institutions should include a gender dimension in various financial programs (especially those targeting SMEs) and administer programs specially tailored to support growth of women enterprises. A combination of programs that were shown to be successful in Western Balkan countries could be considered as a way to start facilitating change:

Grants: Since 2004, the Ministry for Development of Entrepreneurship and Crafts of the Federation of Bosnia and Herzegovina has granted annual funds to about 60 women business owners in this entity. Though modest in size, these resources, because of their non-repayable nature, are acknowledged by women entrepreneurs as a significant and positive incentive that helped them reinforce and grow their businesses.

Co-funding programs: The Croatian Ministry of Economy, Labor and Entrepreneurship implemented in 2009 a co-funding program which, in addition to subsidizing a company's registration costs and purchase of equipment and inventory, included also the partial payment of costs for child care (75 percent of kindergarten price or 75 percent of extended stay in school program costs) for a period of one year. This proved to be one of the gender-sensitive measures that generated good results and was included in the Action Plan for Women's Entrepreneurship Development 2010–2013 as a consequence.

Guarantees to banks: The Guarantee Fund of the Autonomous Province of Vojvodina, Serbia's northern region, was established to

---

[17]OECD (2012), *Women in Business: Policies to Support Women's Entrepreneurship Development in the MENA Region*, OECD Publishing.

[18]IFC (2011), Strengthening Access to Finance for Women-Owned SMEs in Developing Countries.

provide more favorable credit terms for women entrepreneurs. The fund issues guarantees to banks as a mean of securing the orderly repayment of loans. Women have six years to repay loans, and during that period receive free business development and promotional services from the Guarantee Fund and regional development agencies. In the period from 2007 to 2012, the fund had granted 184 guarantees for women entrepreneurs that led to the opening of 718 new jobs.[19]

The public sector should furthermore spearhead the financial infrastructure building process, especially focusing on the credit bureaus development. Inability to build successful credit history caused by the lack of traditional banking relationships is a common issue preventing women from accessing finances. Including microfinance credit history, small loans history or even women's creditworthiness outside the banking system (e.g., with a utilities payment history) into bureaus' databases could alleviate this common problem.

On the other side, financial institutions and commercial banks should be encouraged to initiate specially-tailored credit programs for women, as well as to reach out to women entrepreneurs through familiar channels such as businesswomen's associations, since it is recognized that conversance with clients decreases cultural biases and increases women's chances to receive loans.[20]

Complementary pragmatic measures could be applied in addition by private and non-governmental sector to secure easier access to financial resources for women. These could include promotion of usage of venture capital, angel networks or crowd-funding; encouragement of business formalization; promotion of microcredit programs establishment based on a group guarantee model; provision of gender sensitivity training for bank officials; identification of best practices in the region; collection of gender disaggregated data and conduction of relevant researches, etc.

Entrepreneurial Education

Numerous studies confirm that a positive link between education and entrepreneurial performance exists. They revealed that better-

---

[19]Guarantee Fund of Vojvodina: http://www.garfondapv.org.rs.
[20]IFC (2011).

educated entrepreneurs have higher survival probabilities, grow faster, have a higher productivity rate, and are more likely to innovate in order to upgrade their general position on the market.[21] Therefore, providing access to education and skill trainings should be considered a top priority in supporting women's entrepreneurship.

Although by law men and women in North African countries have the same rights with regard to access to formal education, women tend to have lower educational attainment or stay illiterate. That trend started changing during the last decade, thereby significantly increasing the total number of women going all the way through high education; nevertheless, the problem lies in the fact that the majority of those enrolled in formal education don't gain relevant knowledge and skills.

Croatia was one of the first countries in the Western Balkan region that started addressing this problem systematically. In addition to adopting the Strategy for Entrepreneurial Learning 2010–2014, as for formal education, the Croatian government also adopted a National Framework Curriculum for Preschool Education, General Compulsory and Secondary Education in 2010, which could serve as an example for North African countries for how to systematically encourage entrepreneurial spirit. The main idea behind it is to integrate entrepreneurship competencies among eight basic competencies and skills to acquire in the education system throughout the official education curriculum—from preschool to graduate-level, which was a request from the private sector for a long time.[22]

The stated deficiency of activities aimed at developing entrepreneurial knowledge and skills in the formal educational system in North African countries led to an increased offering of these programs through informal education as a consequence. Cross-examination of existing programs shows that they tend to concentrate on administrative, management, finance-related, and marketing skills. Common issues related to them are seen in a lack of recognition that women

---

[21]Koellinger, Philipp (2008), "Why are Some Entrepreneurs More Innovative than Others?" *Small Business Economics* 31(1), pp. 21–37.

[22]Nevenka Cuckovic (2012), "Skills Matching in the Croatian SME Sector and Competence-Based Education and Training: Progress and Prospects," *Labour Market and Skills in the Western Balkans*, Ed. Arandarenko Mihail, Bartlett Will.

entrepreneurs form a heterogeneous group, thus requiring different approaches or levels of education (different programs for startups, women's businesses with high growth potential, women with disabilities, women with other specific needs, etc.); they are not designed to meet the needs of women in the sense of scheduling and duration (many women attending programs are mothers and housewives, and therefore chose instead to participate in one- or two-day trainings, though these produce poorer results); they don't encourage women to diversify and participate in sectors lacking female businesses; and finally they are not directing women toward higher-value-added and innovative businesses.

Therefore, when providing capacity building programs, public and non-governmental stakeholders should consider offering specially-tailored skill-building trainings as fragments of integrated programs organized on a more engaging, ongoing basis (achieving a balance between longer periods and shorter hours) and focusing on diverse skills such as internet literacy, customer development skills, language skills etc. An integrated internship element would add to the value of programs, which should furthermore support the creation of modern self-sustaining businesses through sector-specific education in higher value markets in traditional (tourism) or new sectors (e-commerce and IT businesses).

Offering training programs to women who are traditionally not seen as the "fit" target group for entrepreneurship, such as women victims of domestic violence, presents a good way of addressing several issues that women might face. While domestic violence remains an important issue in North African countries, good experience from Macedonia could offer some stimulus to initiate similar programs.

As referenced in the 2012 Policy on Gender Equality Publication,[23] the Macedonian government launched the Program for Economic Empowerment of Women Victims of Domestic Violence in 2010, covering five pilot municipalities, which was continued in 2011 extending nationwide. In addition to psychosocial therapy for all women, measures for employment were undertaken within the program, including

---

[23]Macedonian Women's Lobby (2012), *Policy on Gender Equality—Perception of Efficiency and Transparency*, Skopje.

training for career building for all program participants in 2011. The purpose of these trainings was to provide new skills to women victims of domestic violence through various exercises, thereby increasing their competitiveness in the labor market and in the long term assuring economic independence. Results from 2010 and 2011 show that 78.57 percent of women who, in addition to training participation, applied for participation in the self-employment measure have successfully completed the program and registered their own businesses. This program represents an innovative approach to the needs of women victims of domestic violence and it can be applied as a model for working with other vulnerable groups of women entering the labor market and starting their own businesses as assessed by the Macedonian Women's Lobby.

Business Development Services

After education, business development services represent the second most important factor that contributes to positive performance of women's businesses, but these services are largely underdeveloped in the MENA region and entrepreneurs make little use of them for advice and counseling.[24] Instead, entrepreneurs tend to rely on advice from people in their immediate environment. For instance, 51 percent of Tunisian entrepreneurs consult widely their spouses, family members and friends, while only 4 percent take advice from colleagues and people experienced in business.[25]

In addition, the majority of business development services in North Africa are provided by businesswomen's organizations and other non-governmental stakeholders, and are usually not coordinated, which leads often to an overlap in supply of certain types of services, or over-targeting of some groups while others remain underserved.[26]

In order to establish a supportive climate for business development, non-governmental and public BDS providers in the North African countries are therefore foremost advised to increase their visibility

---

[24]Stevenson, Lois (2010), *Private Sector and Enterprise Development: Fostering Growth in the Middle East and North Africa*, IDRC, Cheltenham.

[25]Belkacem, Mansouri (2013), GEM Tunisia 2012, Tunisia.

[26]OECD (2012) *op. cit.*

among women and to join forces in realization of programs which are underdeveloped or in nascent phases but highly demanded by women in the region. These programs should include dissemination of business information to women entrepreneurs, networking and mentoring, access to markets and access to premises.

Dissemination of business information enhances chances for women's businesses to grow and expand in markets. While developed countries use the internet (one-stop information) as the easiest way to reach out to a large number of women, lower internet penetration in rural and underdeveloped areas in North Africa requires additional activities. Using existing local facilities for frequent distribution of economic, training, legislative or regulatory information could be an efficient complementary measure facilitated through cooperation of the public and non-governmental sectors, as seen in some smaller municipalities in Montenegro and Bosnia and Herzegovina.

Mentoring and networking programs present great opportunities for women to share information, learn from other's experience, exchange contacts and enter strategic partnerships. Although these programs are frequently organized by businesswomen's organizations in North Africa (and some are even specialized just for this type of activity, like the Moroccan Women Mentoring/Networking Association established in 2011), altering certain aspects could contribute to their greater effectiveness.

For instance, mentoring programs for women entrepreneurs in North Africa typically match successful businesswomen and protégés with the rationale that only women can provide advice about gender-specific issues that novices might face. In that case, men's broader experiential base and better developed business networks in this region remain unutilized. Therefore, it is suggested to include both successful men and women in mentoring programs so they could address different business and personal challenges.

The same issue occurs when networking patterns in North Africa are analyzed, so BDS providers are advised to extend networking activities beyond efforts to primarily form interconnections among women. Also, successful networking could assist in reducing the fear of failure, which is as referenced by GEM reports, quite high among (potential) women entrepreneurs in this region.

An innovative way to do so might be accomplished through organization of "fail gatherings" such as the Fail Conference held in Zagreb, Croatia in January 2014. The goal of such events is to bring local and international successful entrepreneurs who could share stories about bad decisions they made and pivoting that ultimately led them to success, showcasing that in fact failing can be beneficial. These kinds of events are no less affordable than traditional networking meetings, but appear to be more engaging and inspiring for the entrepreneurial community.

Access to markets represents a massive hurdle for women-owned businesses in North Africa, especially for those with significant growth potential aiming to leverage online possibilities. The need to effectively place products on local markets or to access more distant markets in many regions as in North Africa is not recognized as an issue where women need extensive support.

Existing practices, including organization of comprehensive export programs (e.g. Tunisian participation in the Access Program for Women Entrepreneurs in Africa or Women Export Club run by the Moroccan AFEM), B2B and international networking events (e.g., U.S.-Moroccan Business Development Conference) and trade fairs and exhibition (e.g., artisan exhibitions in all North African countries), altogether do not satisfy the high demand expressed by women and should be strategically scaled up on the national and regional level.

Therefore, in addition to information about market features and market opportunities, women should be assisted with higher market exposure, export readiness programs, licensing and franchising programs, development of business clusters and access to procurement opportunities. Ultimately, when implemented, all of these programs lead to growth of existing women businesses but also to further integration in regional and global markets.

Without suitable premises, women tend to face additional risks that might influence the outcome of their business performance. Their *access to safe, secure and suitable business premises* may be restricted for a variety of socio-cultural and economic reasons, but the main obstacle that usually stands out is high cost.[27] Local governments should there-

---

[27]AfDB/ILO (2007) *op. cit.*

fore be encouraged to allocate and set aside premises, land or brown-fields that could be used by women entrepreneurs under certain miti-gated conditions. Another option in assisting women-owned busi-nesses is the establishment of business incubators, which, in addition to free premises and infrastructure, ensure business assistance, techni-cal services and monitoring as equally important components. Although dozens of business incubators in the Western Balkan coun-tries operate on a gender equality basis and could serve as a good example, the real champion in this area is to be found in Morocco.

The Association of Women Entrepreneurs of Morocco (AFEM) made headway by launching the first business incubator for women in North Africa in 2006 in Casablanca. The goal was to help create a favorable environment for women entrepreneurs through a two-year incubation period. Women who were selected by committee benefited from career mentoring, legal, commercial, and management service, specialized trainings and networking opportunities. After initial suc-cess in Casablanca, AFEM launched additional incubators in Rabat in 2009, El Jadida in 2011, Fez in 2012 and Tangier in 2014. The incuba-tion period was shortened to 18 months and as a result, about 60 women created their businesses. Based on this extensive experience, AFEM also developed an operational guide for launching a business incubator for women, which is publically available and can serve as a manual for stakeholders working with women entrepreneurs both in North Africa and the Western Balkans.

Conclusion

The origins of the uprising that expanded across much of the Arab world in 2011, including some North African countries, were eco-nomic in nature and are still an omnipresent concern that places eco-nomic growth and job creation at the center of political discourse. Efforts to mitigate this concern and to reform multifarious North African economies are just in their infancy, portending many chal-lenges ahead. There is no way of knowing where this transformation will take the region, but it is clear that it promises an opportunity to reassess existing economic patterns, including underestimation of women's role in economy.

Along with recognition of entrepreneurship as a key driver of change, North African countries should endorse women as important contributors to economic growth through greater engagement of relevant stakeholders and genuine political commitment.

In that process, the experience of the Western Balkans could be found as valuable. Although clearly not the epitome of a highly supportive environment where women's entrepreneurship blossoms, this experientially diverse region could provide North African countries with examples of best practices and could help the region avoid processes that don't yield desired results. In essence, Western Balkan countries could serve as a palpable example that illustrates how only the strategic reduction of challenges laying ahead of women entrepreneurs can be the way forward.

Women in North Africa are aware of this fact but are willing, even in an unfavorable environment, to begin an unpredictable journey by making the first step. The question is whether the North African governments and societies are willing to do so as well.

Chapter Fourteen

Is the Development of Women's Entrepreneurship in the Nordic States an Inspiration for Women in North Africa?

Marianne Aringberg Laanatza and Camilla af Hällström

The Nordic states are known to be prominent in questions relating to equality between women and men. The Nordic states top statistics on equality measurements and are praised for integrating women into work life. Entrepreneurial activities in general are also on the rise in these countries. In the MENA region, voices have begun to call out for a more equal society. Naturally, women's entrepreneurship is one way to achieve a more equal society.

This article will examine whether Nordic experiences—and especially Swedish experiences—with the integration of women are applicable to the MENA region and whether Nordic policies on this matter could serve as an inspiration for women's entrepreneurship in the MENA region. In order to answer our question whether the development of women's entrepreneurship in the Nordic countries can inspire women in the MENA region, it is necessary to present the characteristics of both the overall conditions and experience for women in the Nordic states and, in particular, the profile of women's entrepreneurship in the Nordic region. Furthermore, it is necessary to do the same regarding the MENA region, the role of women in society, as well as the profile of women's entrepreneurship in the MENA region.

The Position of Women in General in the Nordic Countries

In Nordic political thinking, the development of political rights for women within a democratic political system has been considered as the most efficient way and necessary to improve the position of women's rights not only from a political, but also from social and economic points of view.

The integration of women in political life began early on in the Nordic countries. Women obtained the rights to participate in the elections and candidate for seats in the parliament, both on the regional and municipality level, first in Finland (1906), then in Norway (1913), in Denmark and Iceland[1] (1915) and finally in Sweden (1919). The expectation was that women were going to vote for other women when they got political rights to vote for parliament, as well as to regional bodies and on the municipality level.

However, during the first decades after the emergence of equal political rights for women, the percentage of women in the parliaments respectively, as well as in other political bodies, was very low. In the 1980s, women organized themselves in special networks to improve their representation in order to highlight the issue through large-scale campaigns and manifestations. During the first fifty years after the emergence of voting rights for women, there were very few female ministers and women with important positions on committees in the parliaments. Politically, they were expected to deal with social affairs, and not with financial or industrial affairs and defense issues. In 1970, women constituted only less than 15 percent of the members of parliament. This number increased to 30 percent in the coming years and reached 38 percent in 1988. Since the 1980s, there have been dramatic changes. Compared to Anglo-Saxon countries, the Nordic countries have double the number of female parliament members.[2] Around 40 percent of the Nordic parliaments are women today. Female ministers in the Nordic region have responsibilities for all kind of issues, from defense to financial matters, as well as more traditional issues. The Nordic region has also seen a number of female political leaders, including the first female President of Iceland, Vigdís Finnbogadóttir, (1980–96) and the President of Finland, Tarja Halonen (2000–12).[3] Norway had its first female Prime Minister, Gro Harlem Brundtland, already in 1981. She served three terms in 1981, 1986–89, and in 1990–96. Also today the Prime Minister of Norway is

---

[1] Iceland was still a part of Denmark. The country became independent in 1918 and a republic was declared in 1944.

[2] Henrekson, Magnus and Stenkula, Mikael (2009) "Why Are There So Few Female Top Executives in Egalitarian Welfare States?" *The Independent Review*, Vol. 14, p. 242.

[3] Nordic Council of Ministers (2010) "*Gender Equality—The Nordic Way*," ANP 2010:701, Copenhagen, p. 8.

female. Iceland had a female Prime Minister, Jóhanna Sigurðardóttir, who served from 2009 to 2013.[4] Denmark got its first female Prime Minister in 2011, Helle Thorning-Schmidt. Sweden has not yet had any female prime ministers.

Nordic Women and Education

The percentage of female students at Nordic universities is about 60 percent, similar to the rest of Europe. What do they study? Most generally, female students are concentrated in the fields of health, welfare, human and social sciences. Less than 20 percent of the students studying these subjects are male.[5] It is also very popular to study medicine and to become a veterinary surgeon. The Swedish government has even decided to offer a quota to male students. Earlier, female students were only 20 percent of the total number of students who studied at the Swedish technical universities. Several measures have been taken during the last ten years to attract more female students to these universities, and these efforts have produced positive results. Now the percentage of female students at, for example, Chalmers in Gothenburg is about 30 percent, and Chalmers has also an increasing number of female PhD students.[6] The same positive development regarding female students has also been the case for KTH Royal Institute of Technology in Stockholm: of all full-time students, 31 percent are women.[7] In the other Nordic countries, there seems to be a stagnation in relation to technical fields of study, especially engineering, manufacturing and constructing. Here, 20 to 30 percent of the students are female.[8]

Nordic Women and the Labor Market: Its Development Regarding Percentages of the Female Workforce

In a 2012 report, the World Economic Forum found that when it comes to closing the gender gap in "economic participation and

---

[4]Ibid., p. 10.

[5]Blades, Derek and Pearson, Mark (2006) "*Women and Men in OECD Countries*," Paris, p. 13.

[6]Chalmers International Reception Committee's homepage.

[7]KTH Royal Institute of Technology's homepage.

[8]Blades et al, *op. cit.*, p.13.

opportunity," the United States is ahead of not only Sweden, but also Finland, Denmark, the Netherlands, Iceland, Germany, and the United Kingdom. It states that Sweden's rank according to the report can largely be explained by its political quota system. Though the United States has fewer women in the workforce (68 percent compared to Sweden's 77 percent), American women who choose to be employed are far more likely to work full-time and to hold high-level jobs as managers or professionals. According to the same report, they also own more businesses, launch more start-ups, and more often work in traditionally male-dominated fields. As for breaking the glass ceiling in business, American women are well in the lead.

Of all the CEOs in Sweden in both the private and public sectors, about one-third are women. The trend is positive, but rather weak. The percentage of women CEOs is increasing more in the public units than in the private sector. This trend could also be explained through the dominance of women employed in the public sector. Women constitute about 80 percent of those employed in this sector. One-third of those employed in the private sector are women, but only 25 percent of the CEOs are women.[9]

Worth mentioning is also the difference between male and female employment rates. Sweden shows the best results. In Sweden the differences were only 5 percent in 2008, and about 7 percent in Denmark the same year, while the difference was roughly 12 percent in the U.S. Within the Nordic countries, with their developed welfare systems, public spending on family benefits as a percentage of GDP is higher than in the U.S. In Denmark it was almost 3.5 percent and a little less in Sweden, but less than 1.5 percent in the U.S. The Nordic countries did not top this list, as France and Britain spent more than Denmark and Sweden.[10]

In the outcomes of the comparison and observations in different studies it is often mentioned that a small proportion of Nordic women choose to work as managers and professionals. Most choose lower-paid, highly gender-segregated work. As Alison Wolf has written in her book *The XX Factor*, Scandinavian countries "hold the record for

---

[9]www.tillvaxtverket.se/download/18.../1369959456688/FVOV_12.pdf_ (visited 4/7/2014).

[10]"Women in the Workforce: Female Power," *The Economist*, Dec. 30, 2009.

gender segregation because they have gone the furthest in outsourcing traditional female activities and turning unpaid home-based 'caring' into formal employment."[11]

Despite vigorous efforts to stamp out gender stereotyping, most Swedish girls would still prefer to become day-care workers and nurses when they grow up. Boys would prefer to become welders and truck drivers. That's not all. To the extreme chagrin of social engineers throughout Scandinavia, mothers still take the bulk of the parental leave. Most men take parental leave only when a certain part of it is designated for fathers only.[12] These attitudes are changing step by step, as a result of additional financial advantages for families, where fathers are using more of the time allotted in the Swedish social insurance system, in combination with announcing more legal regulations to more or less force the fathers to take responsibility at home with their young children.

Women's Entrepreneurship in the Nordic Countries

Women's Entrepreneurship in Sweden

Development in Sweden has had the following characteristics. According to the Swedish Growth Authority—the Swedish governmental body responsible for following and analyzing all aspects related to entrepreneurship in Sweden—it is possible to get a clear picture of the situation for all kind of companies operating in the country. This body has to examine the conditions and the outcomes for entrepreneurship in order to present recommendations to improve the conditions. In 2012, it presented the current picture of female entrepreneurship in the country and the following description is based on this report.

Out of all the companies in Sweden, 23 percent are owned by women, but women's share of all recently established companies is higher—32 percent. Most female-owned companies are in the service sector, and constitute more than 90 percent of female-owned companies.

---

[11]Wente, Margaret. "Do Women Really Have It Better in Sweden?" *The Globe and Mail*, Nov. 22, 2013.

[12]Ibid.

Typical to Sweden is the very great number of small companies with fewer than 50 employees, and out of these companies, a large majority has one to ten employees. Together these companies constitute 99 percent of all Swedish companies.

More than half of the female-owned companies have no employees aside from the owner. About every fifth female-owned company is run by the woman together with her husband or another family member. This figure is a bit lower for male-owned companies. It is more common for male-owned companies to share the leadership with somebody outside the family (21 percent) compared to female-owned companies (15 percent).

From a legal point of view, most of the female-owned companies are neither limited partnerships nor joint-stock companies. Instead, they are set up based on a more simple legislation, which eases accounts and tax rules.

As already mentioned, most female-owned companies are in the service sector, where the most important business areas for female entrepreneurs are culture, pleasure and rehabilitation activities. This category constitutes more than half of all companies. Another important service sector is healthcare, where women own more than half of the companies. Also among education-oriented companies, women own a great share—40 percent. In some other areas, female-owned companies constitute very small shares, such as in the construction and transportation fields, as well as companies in the subsectors of information and communication.

Some other interesting aspects of female-owned companies in Sweden are that women who are running companies are in general younger than male entrepreneurs, and an increasing number of companies are run by younger women. Women entrepreneurs have in general higher levels education than male entrepreneurs.

It is rather common both among women and men that they run their companies part-time, but it is more typical for women to both have a full-time job in addition to a part-time managed company.

There are many success stories that could be highlighted when it comes to women's entrepreneurship in Sweden, but there is only space for a few examples. The person who could be named the queen of female entrepreneurship in Sweden is Antonia Axelson Jonsson, who inherited a large group of companies, among them multiple retail organizations, and managed to restructure and develop the group in a very dynamic and profitable way. She has increased the awareness regarding the environmental aspects, as well as the social conditions. Another great entrepreneur is Christina Stenbeck, who also inherited together with her brothers and sisters a group of companies in the information and communication sector, and has managed to develop this group of companies to become very competitive on an international level. There are many female entrepreneurs who have started from scratch and with very limited financial resources have managed to develop their companies. In this category there are also many women who have recently immigrated to Sweden, the so-called "new Swedes."

Development in Other Nordic Countries

The Nordic countries are among the highest-ranking in the world when it comes to entrepreneurial frameworks. They all have invested in entrepreneurial policies in order to enable growth.[13] At the same time, the Nordic countries are ranked high in most equality metrics, and are on the forefront when it comes to female employment rate.[14] Despite these factors, women's entrepreneurship in the Nordic countries is still proportionally low.

In a survey by the OECD from 2003, taking into consideration OECD member countries, the rate of self-employed women in Denmark, Finland, Iceland, and Norway is on a general level (22 to 33 percent) among OECD member countries. This can be compared to the countries with the highest rates of women's self-employment (Portugal, Canada, and the U.S., 38 to 40 percent).[15] According to Eurostat statistics, the Nordic countries rank only an average 21 to 26 percent for female business owners with at least one employee, whereas they

---

[13]Nordic Council of Ministers (2010) "Nordic Entrepreneurship Monitor 2010," ANP 2010:748, Copenhagen, p. 8.

[14]Sanandaji, Nima and Lepomäki, Elina (2013) "The Equality Dilemma: The Lack of Female Entrepreneurs in Nordic Welfare States," *Libera Papers*, p. 3.

[15]Denmark has the lowest number of self-employed women among the Nordic countries (22 percent). Finland has the highest, with 33 percent. OECD (2004) "Women's Entrepreneurship: Issues and Policies," *OECD Conference: Promoting Entrepreneurship and Innovative SMEs in a Global Economy: Towards a More Responsible and Inclusive Globalisation*, Paris, p. 16.

are ranked among the worst countries for women executives, with a rate of under 20 percent.[16] As for women employers, Nordic countries are again placed on an average scale.[17]

The question why the Nordic countries do not rate highly on female entrepreneurship is debated. On one hand, the Nordic states are known for their social-democratic welfare state models. These models enable women to enter the labor market in a higher rate than in other countries. On the other hand, the rate of self-employed women is proportionally low when compared to countries where social-democratic welfare state policies are not applied, such as the U.S. The correlation here between the rate of women entrepreneurs and the political system applied is far from straightforward.[18]

In a survey by the Nordic Innovation Center in 2007, the main obstacles female entrepreneurs face in these countries were considered to be lack of financing, work-life and family-life balance, and lack of information. Another obstacle that was also pointed out is the high alternative cost that high employment and high growth creates. These factors can be seen as obstacles by women in relation to childbirth. Gender-normative questions were also raised; women face obstacles in adapting to a business culture dominated by male norms.[19]

Another explanation is the importance of the emergence of a large public sector for women's employment and the high employment rate of women in the public sector. In the long run, this has had a negative effect on women's progress in work life. A further reason is that the sectors with a majority of women employees are under state monopolies or oligopolies.[20] One suggestion is to introduce policy changes, such as liberating sectors where women have prominent experience.[21]

---

[16]Sanandaji et al, *op. cit.*, p. 3.

[17]This can be compared to the highest-ranking country, Republic of Moldova, with a percentage close to 50 percent. OECD, *op. cit.*, p. 17.

[18]Ibid., p. 37.

[19]Nordic Innovation Centre. "Women Entrepreneurship—A Nordic Perspective," August 2007, p. 7.

[20]Such sectors are the health care and education sectors. Sanandaji et al, op. cit., p. 3.

[21]Ibid., p. 4.

The Nordic Council of Ministers addressed the issue of female entrepreneurship in 2008 by establishing a program. Before this, the question was not considered to the extent it is today by the member countries of the Nordic Council.[22] Today all countries with the exception of Iceland have a program or an action plan to support women's entrepreneurship.[23]

Today, most women entrepreneurs run small-sized companies in the Nordic region. The rate of female entrepreneurs in the Nordic region running companies with at least one employee is low,[24] indicating that most female-run companies employ only the founder of the company.

According to OECD statistics, the industries in which women in the Nordic region prefer to start their businesses are service-based.[25]

Comparison with North Africa and Countries in the Middle East

Although some positive developments are taking place in some countries in North Africa and the Middle East, the picture is still very gloomy, and in some countries, such as Libya and Syria, the conflicts have undermined the positions of women. In these countries' parliaments, the percentage of women is lower than in many other developing countries.

In Europe the percentage of female ministers is 15 percent. The Arab states remain the lowest from a global perspective with a rate of only 7 percent. By the end of 2011, women represented only 10.7 percent of parliamentarians in the Arab states—more or less the same proportion as that in 2010 and, despite the promising start to the year, the Arab region remains the only one in the world without any parliament that comprises at least 30 percent women.[26]

---

[22]For example, Denmark did not have any specific policy on the issue. Pettersson, Katarina (2012) "Support for Women's Entrepreneurship: a Nordic Spectrum," *International Journal of Gender and Entrepreneurship*, Vol. 4, p. 5.

[23]Ibid., p. 9.

[24]Sanandaji et al, *op. cit.*, p. 3.

[25]OECD (2012) "Entrepreneurship at a Glance," p. 95.

[26]Bachelet, Michelle. "Women's Empowerment in the Middle East and Worldwide," statement at the Women's Foreign Policy Group, 20 April 2012 in Washington, DC.

Some improvements exist, such as in Tunisia, where a law has been adopted securing parity on candidate lists, and in the case of Morocco, with the introduction of quotas for women parliamentarians, the policy shift has resulted in a 6 percent increase in women legislators last year. The backlash in Egypt is obvious. In January 2012's parliamentary election results there was a dramatic drop from 12 percent to only 2 percent of women now in parliament out of 508 members. There are many reasons to conclude that the so-called Arab Spring has yet to deliver for women in politics. [27]

The labor participation rate of women is also very low in many countries according to figures published by the World Bank.[28] The rate in 2012 was only 15 percent in Algeria, 24 percent in Egypt, 25 percent in Tunisia, 30 percent in Libya and 43 percent in Morocco. Worth mentioning is the importance of the agricultural sector in Morocco, where the role of women is very strong.

There are large groups of women, in particular, who are illiterate in the region. The rates, especially in countries like Egypt and Morocco, are very high. At the same time, the pattern on the university level has changed, and about 60 percent of all students are female students. The rate is even higher in some non-Mediterranean Arab countries like Qatar and the UAE.

Women's Entrepreneurship in North Africa

With the study "Women's entrepreneurship in MENA—Myths & Realities," Daniela Gressani[29] presented the outcomes of studies performed by the World Bank. She highlighted that there are remarkable similarities in terms of size, age location, sectorial distribution, export orientation, and overall performance between male and female-owned

---

[27]Ibid.

[28]The World Bank, "Labor Participation Rate, Female (percent of Female Population Ages 15+)."

[29]Daniela Gressani presented her paper in capacity of being Vice President of the Middle East and North Africa Region at the World Bank, at the Arab International Women's Forum Conference in Dubai December 9–11, 2007. Some of the conclusions presented by Gressani are presented in detail in the World Bank Report: *The Environment for Women's Entrepreneurship in the Middle East and North Africa Region*.

firms. It is, however, important to mention that only 13 percent of the companies in the region as such are owned by women.[30]

Moreover, if it was expected that the female-owned firms were small, the reality showed that the share of medium- and large-scale firms was higher among female-owned firms than male-owned firms. In the survey, more than 300 of the largest firms were owned by women, while only 8 percent of the firms owned by women were micro-firms employing fewer than 10 persons.

The common perception regarding the percentage of women who run their own companies is that they only own the company by name, but this is not true. More than half of the female-owned firms were managed by the women themselves.

Another myth concerns how well women-owned companies were integrated into the global market. The result showed that they are more likely to export than male-owned companies, in particular in Morocco and Egypt. Also, in the MENA region, the average professional competencies were a bit higher among the women (19 percent) compared to men (16 percent). Another important aspect is that female-owned companies hire more women (25 percent) than those owned by men (22 percent). There are some other interesting aspects that could be mentioned, for example the fact that Algerian business law is heavily androcentric and does not, for the most part, include references to women. The same observations were made regarding Egyptian legislation, as well as the Moroccan and Tunisian cases.

In several reports it was stated that the biggest barrier for improving female entrepreneurship in the MENA region is the business environment. This problem affects both women's and men's opportunities. Conclusions based on worldwide studies show that when investment procedures are simple and transparent, the start-up costs for new businesses are low and trade is facilitated through improved legislations and routines, the share of female-owned firms rises. On the other hand, women—due to social norms—still often meet negative attitudes and different treatment when they are working outside the home, although the laws are the same for men and women.

---

[30]In some Arab countries, such as Saudi Arabia, the figure is much higher: one third of the companies are owned by women.

Marianne Laanatza's opinion regarding the observations and conclusions presented above based on different international reports is that they reflect very well her own observations and conclusions. There is, however, one additional aspect that could be mentioned, namely the lack of risk capital for women and certain problems related to the possibilities of borrowing money from banks. These are relevant issues for women in North Africa and Jordan, but not as much of a problem for Arab women outside this region.[31]

Examples of Women's Entrepreneurship in North Africa

The common picture in Western media of women's conditions on the Arabian Peninsula is that they are to a great extent absent from the labor market and from the business arena, as well as from the economic sector in general. This picture is partly wrong. The above figures have been presented regarding the relative high percentages of women in the labor markets in Kuwait, Qatar and the UAE, and the high percentages of women in Saudi Arabia who own companies. But the picture is rather gloomy in North Africa . Most of the governments on the Arabian Peninsula are very eager to support female entrepreneurship, also to increase the influence of well-educated citizens both in the public and private sector in order to be less dependent on foreign experts and foreign workers in general. Every year important conferences on women entrepreneurship are held in Qatar and UAE, in order to strengthen female entrepreneurs, their networks and to improve mentorship for newcomers. Other Arab countries are doing the same, for example Lebanon and Morocco, but with limited resources.

In an article from July 2013, Alexandra Ma highlighted Arab women that are making such great progress as entrepreneurs in tech companies. She underlines that 35 percent of tech entrepreneurs in the Middle East and North Africa (MENA) region are women, a surprising statistic, considering the global norm of 10 percent. Nick-

---

[31]Throughout the years Marianne Aringberg Laanatza, one of the authors of this paper, has organized, cooperated and chaired several workshops and seminars for female entrepreneurs in the MENA region, in particular in cooperation with women from Morocco, Tunisia, Jordan, Egypt, Oman, Saudi Arabia and UAE.

named the "start-up spring," the number of small technology firms in the MENA region is on the rise, and more and more women are flocking to it at a faster pace than in the rest of the world. Ma presents three reasons for this. The first is that working in tech still allows women to conform to the traditional social norms. The second reason is that the virtual nature of the internet creates a safe haven, and the third is that women's own determination and drive are what spurs them on, and what ultimately makes them succeed.[32] Many more success stories could have been presented, but the one presented about women and tech can very much reflect the energy and efforts so many women in the MENA region are presenting, which all together can inspire and increase the expectations for woman entrepreneurship in the MENA region in other areas.

Comparison between Nordic Experiences and the Experience and Needs in the MENA Region

Women in the Nordic countries have managed much better in the political field than women in the MENA region. This strength for Nordic women has been important in order to develop the social and socio-economic legislation in the Nordic societies, in order to facilitate both husband and wife as part of the manpower outside the household. Through insurances and daycare, *inter alia*, there has been a very positive increase of women in the labor market. In the MENA region, upper-class and middle-class families have often at least one maid at home. This is not the case in the Nordic countries.

In the Nordic countries, there is a very segregated labor market. The same could be said for most MENA countries. Women are working in the public sector rather than in the private sector.

Regarding education, the situation in universities is the same. More than half of the students are female, both in Nordic countries and in the MENA region, although the percentages of female students are even higher in Qatar, UAE and Oman. Skills in information and communication technology seem to attract women in the MENA region

---

[32]Ma, Alexandra. "Why the Middle East is Beating Out the World in Female Tech Entrepreneurs," July 27, 2013, Policy Mic.

more than in the Nordic countries, and in particular on the Arabian Peninsula.

Female entrepreneurship in the Nordic countries is to a great extent concentrated to traditional areas for women, and to small-scale companies, with a great number of solo companies dominating the picture. In the MENA region there are relatively more medium- and large-sized companies owned by women, and with successful women entrepreneurs in the tech field; in this regard, the MENA region could present an inspiration for the Nordic region rather than the other way around.

From the Nordic side there are many tools offered and a favorable socio-economic context for women on the labor market, as well as for female entrepreneurship. Taking into consideration the relatively low percentage of women in the labor market and female entrepreneurs in countries in North Africa, there are obvious needs for reforms and structural changes. It needs to be added that even if some of the MENA countries have improved their legislation and administrative routines for investments and trade, there is much more to be done to facilitate— among other things—female entrepreneurship. In such a context, the Nordic countries have much to offer the MENA countries.

It is worth mentioning that in order to improve the climate for investments in the Middle East and North Africa, Sweden has financed the main part of the financial resources to the OECD project MENA-INVEST. In this project, female entrepreneurship is specially highlighted. Sweden also offers special training programs through the Swedish Institute for female entrepreneurship for women from the MENA region.

Conclusion

The question whether the Nordic experiences—and especially Swedish experiences—could be applicable and serve as inspiration in the MENA region was posed in the introduction of this text. An overview was presented of the participation of women in the societies through political influence, education, participation in the labour market and, in particular, on woman entrepreneurship.

Compared with the MENA countries, outcomes regarding the profiles and characteristics of women in the Nordic societies, participation in political institutions, the share of female students at universities, in the labor market and as owners of companies, show clear differences from many—but not all—points of view.

There are important aspects that could be considered to serve as inspiration for women in the MENA countries, namely the high percentage of women in the parliaments and other political related jobs in the Nordic countries. The ambitions of young women to get academic degrees are the same, although female students in the MENA countries seem to be relatively more interested in technical items than those in the Nordics.

There is a large gap between the percentage of Nordic women on the labor market compared with the situation on the MENA labor market, where the UAE and Qatar have the highest percentages (47 percent and 51 percent respectively). The Nordic countries could, together with some of the Arab countries on the Arabian Peninsula, inspire women in the rest of the MENA region to participate to a greater extent on the labor market, but the lack of public financial resources to facilitate women with day care services, insurance and so forth, is an obstacle. Another obstacle is the high rate of unemployment in the MENA region.

The percentage of women-owned companies is higher in the Nordic countries compared with the MENA countries in general, but neither the situation in the Nordic countries (25 percent) or in the MENA region (13 percent) are acceptable. Both Nordic women and their sisters in the MENA region need to make greater efforts to change this picture. It is, however, easier to start companies in Nordic countries, and such experiences could be used in the MENA countries, although the situation has improved there during the past few years as well.

On the other hand, women in the MENA region who have developed a relatively higher rate of large and medium-sized companies and managed better to establish and develop companies in the high-tech sector in comparison with the Nordic profiles, could inspire Nordic women entrepreneurs to follow their examples.

Chapter Fifteen

Glass Ceilings and Constitutional Barriers: Challenges to Effective Political Participation by Women and Others in Bosnia and Herzegovina

Valery Perry[1]

The participants in the November 2013 "Mediterranean Women in Leadership and Civil Society Conference" organized in Sarajevo did not have an inkling of the social protests that would hit Bosnia and Herzegovina (BiH) in early 2014. While a number of the BiH participants spoke openly and eloquently of the social, political and economic problems facing the country, the situation has in fact been deteriorating for years, with observers often asking how much worse the environment could get before something broke.[2] Some observers think that the events of February and the still unfolding aftermath could signal that breaking point; others see it as the latest in a line of short-lived bursts of civic activism that then recede with little substantial reform to show as a success; still others fret that the activity seems to be mostly limited to the Federation (and Brcko) leaving the RS relatively calm, suggesting once again the divided nature of the state.

At the time of this writing,[3] it is too soon to see how the situation could develop, which civic actions will flourish or disintegrate, or how decision-makers (BiH and international) might adjust their own

---

[1]The author would like to thank Lana Ackar, Kurt Bassuener, Helene Mastowski and Roska Vrgova for comments and suggestions. All opinions and any errors are those of the author alone.

[2]For background, see for example: "EU Policies Boomerang: Bosnia and Herzegovina's Social Unrest," by Kurt Bassuener and Bodo Weber. *Democratization Policy Council Policy Note*, February 14, 2014, available at http://democratizationpolicy.org/eu-policies-boomerang-bosnia-and-herzegovina-s-social-unrest; "Elite Driven Reform Will Not Save Bosnia," by Valery Perry, *Balkan Insight*, February 11, 2014, available at http://www.balkaninsight.com/en/article/elite-driven-reform-will-not-save-bosnia; "Bosnia Needs the Right Strategy for Change," by Raluca Raduta, *Balkan Insight*, February 25, 2014, available at http://www.balkaninsight.com/en/article/bosnia-needs-the-right-strategy-for-change.

[3]This document was drafted in mid-March 2014.

polices towards BiH in the wake of the visible and widespread manifestations of dissatisfaction. However, the unfolding situation does again provide an opportunity to highlight the core dysfunction of the post-war BiH system, and the Potemkin nature of its democracy.

In remarks made at the conference, this author noted that many of the structural, social and political obstacles minimizing and marginalizing women as full and leading actors in BiH are related to the core nature of the post-war, post-Dayton state. It is not difficult to understand why a country built upon a structure negotiated among the leaders of the formerly warring parties, with no women at the negotiating table, no civic approval or even discussion, and no subsequent parliamentary adoption, would be minimally friendly to, or welcoming for, women. In fact, as ultimately shown by the Sejdic-Finci case, the Dayton system which enshrined ethno-national principles at the core of the post-war state is at heart reactionary, putting presumed group interests above individual interests, ethnic prerogatives over civic prerogatives, and, as we have seen, political party concerns over citizen concerns.

This short contribution summarizes some of the issues that shape and constrain women's engagement in political and civic life, and which more broadly affect full citizen involvement. A brief review of post-war gender promotion efforts is followed by some highlights on civic activity in BiH generally. This is followed by a short review of top-down and bottom-up constitutional reform efforts. The concluding thoughts reflect on whether the system as it stands today is structurally capable of sustaining accountable, representative government for all citizens, including women and other oft-marginalized citizens (national minorities, demographic minorities, etc.) Can any set of laws or constitutional provisions overcome basic deficiencies in the rule of law and good governance? Can an electoral system built along ethnically gerrymandered election units encourage real accountability between the governing and the governed? Can political parties with little demonstrated internal democratic practice evolve in order to more effectively respond to the practical concerns of citizens? Thorough examination of each issue noted is impossible in the scope of this piece, but noted examples are indicative.

The evidence at hand is worrying, and it is fair to wonder how long BiH can muddle along, a frozen conflict characterized by existing and potential segment states, often characterized more as an oligarchy than a democracy.[4] However, if there is the will to re-examine the internal and external incentives for political reform vs. political stagnation or regression, then it would be possible to reimagine a structure that could provide for a more hopeful future.

The Political Glass Ceiling: Women in Post-Dayton BiH Politics

Women in post-Dayton BiH have been negatively affected by both the post-war transition, as well as the post-Cold War economic transition. Bosnia's history in terms of voting rights for women falls in between New Zealand first granting women the franchise in 1893, and Switzerland's near complete suffrage granted in 1971 (with one canton holding out until 1990). Women in Bosnia and Herzegovina gained the right to vote in 1945, and a quota system in Yugoslavia ensured that 30 percent of the delegates of regional and federal governments were women.[5] Over the next several decades, this led to more representation; in 1986, women made up 24.1 percent of the Assembly of the Republic of BiH, and 17.3 percent of municipal assembly mandates.[6] However, unlike the republics of Croatia and Serbia, Bosnia never experienced a feminist movement, and some point out that these numbers reflected *class*-consciousness rather than *gender*-consciousness, as gains for women were "understood only as a part of the emancipation of the working class, and most of the economic and social rights of women were connected to their status as workers."[7]

---

[4]Perry, Valery. "A 'Segment State' Vision of the Future of Bosnia and Herzegovina?" *Transconflict*. February 10, 2014, available at http://www.transconflict.com/2014/02/segment-state-vision-future-bosnia-herzegovina-102/

[5]Lithander, Anna (ed.). *Engendering the Peace Process: A Gender Approach to Dayton—and Beyond.* The Kvinna till Kvinna Foundation, 2000, p. 17, available at http://kvinnatillkvinna.se/en/files/qbank/55b37c5c270e5d84c793e486d798c01d.pdf

[6]*Women's Representation in Elections in Bosnia and Herzegovina: A Statistical Overview, 1986, 1990, 1996, 1997.* OSCE Democratization Branch, Political Party Development Program, January 1998. As cited in "A National NGO Report on Women's Human Rights in Bosnia and Herzegovina," International Human Rights Law Group BiH Project, May 1999, p. 181.

[7]Lithander, p. 17.

While the Dayton Agreement was the first major peace agreement adopted after the September 1995 World Conference on Women held in Beijing, the November Dayton negotiations definitely reflected the old way of doing business, and was at best gender neutral.[8] Perhaps because of the inherent dominant *realpolitik* of the constitutional development process and the constitution itself, or perhaps in a subsequent attempt to try to mitigate the results of the framework put into place at Dayton, there have been repeated—often remedial—efforts by external actors (donors, international organizations, etc.) to support and promote increased involvement by women in political life. For example, in 1998 the OSCE's Provisional Election Commission's *Rules and Regulations* required that at least 30 percent of candidates be women.[9] While admittedly just a first step, there were two key criticisms of this quota system approach. First, it applied only to the candidate list, and not to the number of women to actually *receive* mandates. Second, it would apply only to legislative positions, and not to executive positions.

In addition to attempts at structural reforms to increase gender balance in politics, institutional approaches were introduced. Gender Centers (one in the Federation and one in the RS) were established in the spring of 2000, with a mandate to monitor and encourage gender awareness and representation.[10] On March 5, 2003, the *Act on Gender Equality in Bosnia and Herzegovina* was adopted by the BiH parliament, with the stated aim of improving "equality between women and men, to ensure equal participation of women in all spheres of life and to prevent discrimination on the basis of sex."[11] Amendments were later made in 2009, including amendments providing for a minimum of 40 percent of the "under-represented gender," in line with Council of Europe recommendations.[12] Also in 2009, the country adopted an

---

[8]See Lithander for a thorough analysis of this issue.

[9]The OSCE was the primary international organization responsible for elections in BiH. The October 2002 elections were the first to be organized and administered completely by the BiH authorities.

[10]As noted in the Regulation on the Establishment of the Gender Center of the Federation of BiH, and the Regulation on the Establishment of the Gender Center of the RS, December 2000.

[11]The Act on Gender Equality in Bosnia and Herzegovina, Article 1.

[12]Council of Europe Committee of Ministers. "Recommendation Rec (2003)3 of the Committee of Ministers to member states on the balanced participation of women and men in public decision making." Adopted on March 12, 2003, available at https://wcd.coe.int/ViewDoc.jsp?id=2229.

anti-discrimination law. However, implementation has been dismal and economic and political marginalization continue, as shown in a survey of the situation in 2012-2013 noting 9 female representatives in the BiH House of Representatives, out of 42 (21.4 percent); 2 female delegates in the BiH House of Peoples out of 15 (13.3 percent),[13] and *zero* female Ministers (out of 9) in the state-level government, still at the time of this writing. It is clear that neither structural incentives nor cultural encouragement are resulting in more women in state-level government.[14]

The Civic Glass Ceiling: Post-Dayton Civil Society

A few words on post-BiH civil society can be useful to provide context on the potential for citizens—and women in particular—to engage in public life and impact political decisions and change in between elections. Post-war civil society development efforts in BiH have been extensive, beginning with immediate post-war humanitarian relief, and then expanding to include human rights initiatives, service delivery, advocacy efforts, reconciliation projects, educational ventures and more. While bringing ideas, opportunities and much needed cash infusions, however, one can argue that the scale of attention and money spent on such efforts resulted in a distorted environment or dependency trap.[15] Critics point out the often unintended effects of external initiatives and engagement: the emergence of civil society as service delivery; questionable domestic legitimacy; the focus on a project-based approach to civic action and subsequent competition among NGOs for funding; a focus on short-term international "trends" in at the expense of potentially

---

[13]Miftari, Edita. "Economic and Social Rights of Women in Bosnia and Herzegovina," *Sarajevo Open Center Human Rights Papers 1*, p. 2 (no date).

[14]*Analysis of Political and Public Participation of Women in the Republic of Srpska with Respect to the Application of Binding National and International Gender Equality Standards*. Republika Srpska Gender Center. June 2010. Available at http://www.vladars.net/sr-SP-Cyrl/Vlada/centri/gendercentarrs/media/vijesti/Documents/Analysis-of-Political-and-Public-Participation-of-Women-in-the-RS.pdf.

[15]Thomas Carothers, *Aiding Democracy Abroad: The Learning Curve*. Washington, DC: Carnegie Endowment for International Peace, 1999; Marina Ottaway and Thomas Carothers (eds.), *Funding Virtue: Civil Society Aid and Democracy Promotion*. Washington, DC: Carnegie Endowment for International Peace, 2000.

more relevant long-term local needs; and a focus on the urban-elites at the expense of more remote communities.[16]

While fair criticisms, NGOs *have* been able to make an impact, particularly at the micro-level.[17] Civic activities offer communities in particular opportunities for engagement that would otherwise not exist. However, in terms of targeted successes at the macro- or systemic level, big victories have been relatively few.[18]

Why have NGOs advocating for political reform been unable to make more of an impact? Organizational, technical and financial deficiencies play a role. However, so does the broader operating system in which civil society operates. A description of this environment written in 2001 still rings true in 2014: "The lack of transparency and accountability and the dearth of the rule of law and good governance

---

[16]See for example: Sebastian, Sofia. "Assessing Democracy Assistance: Bosnia," *FRIDE Project Report*, May 2012; Belloni, Robert. "Civil Society and Peacebuilding in Bosnia and Herzegovina." *Journal of Peace Research*. 38:2, March 2001, p. 178 (163–180); *Civil Society: Lost in Translation? Donors' Strategies and Practices in Civil Society Development in the Balkans*. Balkan Civil Society Development Network, Balkan Civic Practices #8, January 2012; *Civil Society in Bosnia and Herzegovina: Seeking the Way Forward*. United Nations Volunteer Program, 2011; Bieber, Florian. "Aid Dependency in Bosnian Politics and Civil Society: Failures and Successes of Post-War Peacebuilding in Bosnia-Herzegovina." *Croatian International Relations Review*. January–June 2002, pp. 25–29; Reich, Hannah. "'Local Ownership' in Conflict Transformation Projects: Partnership, Participation or Patronage?" *Berghof Occasional Paper* No. 27, September 2006, p. 7, available at http://www.berghof-conflictresearch.org/documents/publications/boc27e.pdf; *United States Agency for International Development, NGO Sustainability Index for Central and Eastern Europe and Eurasia* 74 (13th Ed. 2009), available at http://www.usaid.gov/locations/europe_eurasia/dem_gov/ngoindex/2009/; Catherine Barnes et al, *Civil Society Assessment in Bosnia and Herzegovina* ii (2004), available at pdf.usaid.gov/pdf_docs/PNACY559.pdf.

[17]See for example: Belloni, Robert. *Statebuilding and International Intervention in Bosnia*. London: Routledge, 2007, pp. 118–121; Sejfija, Ismet. "From the 'Civil Sector' to 'Civil Society? Progress and Prospects," in Fischer, Marina (ed.) *Peacebuilding and Civil Society in Bosnia Herzegovina: Ten Years After Dayton*. Munster: Lit Verlag, 2006, pp. 125–140, available at http://www.berghof-conflictresearch.org/documents/publications/daytone_sejfira_civilsoc.pdf.

[18]An advocacy effort for the direct election of mayors is often noted as an example of a significant success. However, some critics will point out that Center for Civic Initiatives (CCI) had much more practical and political support from the U.S. government and other international actors in this endeavor than is usual, which greatly increased the chances for success. See *Civil Society Assessment In Bosnia and Herzegovina*, prepared for the U.S. Agency for International Development, June 25, 2004; "Bosnia and Herzegovina Municipal Elections." *OSCE/ODIHR Election Observation Mission Report*, October 2, 2004, available at http://www.osce.org/odihr/elections/bih/41178.

make public scrutiny a chimera. Bosnian civil society has neither the leverage nor the potential resources to perform the task handed over by the international community."[19] The author goes on: "By fostering community isolation, mobilization and a general feeling of insecurity, ethnic elites legitimize each other and maintain a tight grip on their constituencies. At the same time, internal dissent, as expressed by those who question the existing social order by promoting and defending the possibility of a multi-ethnic polity, is often repressed and marginalized."[20] Others have written on the difference between civic activism in the RS vs. in the Federation, pointing out the impact of the more centralized and nationalized state on the quality of civic activism in the RS.[21] A World Bank report on the role of civil society in peace-building notes that, "Conflict is generally driven by macro-level factors,"[22] and "The assumption that many local peace initiatives will automatically influence peace building at the macro level has been proved wrong."[23]

The Constitutional Glass Ceiling:
Women and Constitutional Reform Efforts

All state-level constitutional reform efforts to date have failed.[24] There have been three main elite-driven efforts that unfolded from 2005 to 2009: the April Package, the Prud Process, and the Butmir talks. Later, negotiations aimed at constitutional reform to address the so-called Sejdic-Finci issue dominated constitutional reform discus-

---

[19]Belloni, Roberto. "Peacebuilding in Bosnia." *Journal of Peace Research*, vol. 28, no. 2, March 2001, p. 172.

[20]Belloni. "Peacebuilding in Bosnia." p. 173.

[21]Touquet, Heleen. "The Republika Srpska as a Strong Nationalizing State and the Consequences for Postethnic Activism." *Nationalities Papers*. Vol. 40, No. 2, March 2012, pp. 203–220.

[22]*Civil Society and Peacebuilding: Potential, Limitations and Critical Factors*. World Bank Social Development Department, Report No. 36445-GLB, December 20, 2006, p. 23.

[23]*Civil Society and Peacebuilding: Potential, Limitations and Critical Factors*. World Bank Social Development Department, Report No. 36445-GLB, December 20, 2006, p. 25.

[24]Only one amendment has been made, following the Prud Process; this clarified the status of the District of Brcko and its access to the BiH Constitutional Court. See http://www.ohr.int/ohr-dept/legal/laws-of-bih/pdf/001-Constitutions/BH/BH-Amendment-I-to-BH-Constitution-25-09.pdf.

sions since a 2009 decision by the European Court of Human Rights; as of this writing both BiH and international actors appear to have given up this effort.[25] All were focused on certain key political party leaders, with varying levels of international support and engagement, and with little to no civic involvement. Thus, they were limited to the country's male political leaders, with women again absent from the process.

A number of civil society efforts have also failed to gain traction; however, they did demonstrate a more participatory process. Three packages of reform proposals largely in line with recommendations of the Venice Commission were drafted. One was developed by the Alumni Center for Inter-disciplinary and Post-graduate Studies (ACIPS),[26] a second by the Young Lawyers Association, later renamed the Law Institute (LI),[27] and a third by *Forum Gradjana Tuzle* (Forum of Citizens of Tuzla).[28] In addition, an "expert group" tasked to consider reform of the Federation's constitution, heavily supported by the U.S. Embassy, delivered a set of 181 recommendations in spring 2013, and drafted these into a new constitution in autumn 2013.[29] Each of these bottom-up efforts to develop packages of reform were more inclusive than the noted top-down efforts, engaging women in consultations and drafting, and reflecting much broader civic consultation.

There have also been efforts among some women to draft constitutional reforms with an explicit focus on gender. In winter 2012, 13 women's NGOs working with a Swedish women's initiative (*Kvinna till Kvinna*) began to seek ways to involve women in developing constitutional reform proposals. Another women's initiative organized by the TPO Foundation had a similar objective.[30] The two networks

---

[25]The Sejdic-Finci case refers to a judgment from the European Court of Human Rights that found that the BiH Constitution's limitation of participation in the three-person presidency to a Bosniak and Croat (from the Federation) and a Serb (from the RS), and similar provisions in the House of Peoples, is discriminatory to those who do not identify as one of these three peoples.

[26]See Alumni Association of the Centre for Interdisciplinary Postgraduate Studies (ACIPS), http://www.acips.ba/eng/.

[27]See Law Institute of Bosnia and Herzegovina, http://www.lawinstitute.ba/.

[28]See Forum Gradana Tuzle (FGT), www.forumtz.com.

[29]Available at http://ustavnareformafbih.blogspot.com/.

[30]Transkulturna Psihosocijalna Obrazovna Fondacija.

launched a platform and set of amendments for "gender sensitive" reform, which also addressed broader political reform needs.[31] In some initial discussions with members of the Parliament on the proposals it is interesting to point out the surprise or chagrin of some MPs to see that their proposals were not limited to "women's issues" but addressed the need for broader political reforms as well. This again shows the tendency to ghettoize women in political life.

Breaking through the Ceiling?

This essay will close with a review of some specific challenges women face in order to break through as full participants in BiH public life. This will then be followed by broader challenges in the political system that affect *all* reform-minded activists. Taken together, while one may argue that women can be a catalyzing factor to change the broader political environment, one can also see the challenges to women's engagement that exist within the status quo.

Three specific challenges to women—out of many—are discussed first.

First, BiH did not experience a feminist movement before the war as did other parts of the former Yugoslavia (such movements were present in Belgrade and Zagreb, for example). When one adds the less developed nature of the economy even before the war; the impact of the war and the particular nature of sexual violence as a wartime tactic; and the rise of nationalist political often combined with the rise of religious/clerical political and social power bases- the position of a genuine movement for equality seems daunting. In this sense, feminist movement faces many of the same combination of political/ social/clerical pressures as the LGBT movement.[32] A lot of change *has* happened, but there is still a long way to go.

---

[31]The reform proposal is available at http://tpo.ba/inicijativa/dokumenti/P-Ust -proCol-Final-Web-.pdf. A previous gender sensitive reform effort, limited to gender issues, was prepared in 2008 with the support of UNIFEM.

[32]See Miftari, Edita. "Economic and Social Rights of Women in Bosnia and Herzegovina," *Sarajevo Open Center Human Rights Papers 1* (no date).

Second, it was noted above that post-war international and domestic humanitarian and development efforts in BiH have assisted in the establishment of many NGOs being run by and for women. Many of these provide critical support and services related to women's health issues, domestic violence and economic support for rural women in particularly marginalized positions. Many of these have also managed to secure important legislative victories on some targeted women's issues. However, there remains the risk of being stuck in a "pink ghetto," with women expected to address a narrow set of "women and children only" issues, while men continue to dominate the broader talks on issues like constitutional reform, privatization, security, and EU integration. It is this author's opinion that this is a long-term challenge not unrelated to the broader need for bigger democratizing reforms in the political and possible electoral systems.

On a third related note, women face the challenge of seeking ways to engage on the "toughest" political challenges while not risking the gains that they have made. On the one hand it is a positive step for services such as the provision of safe houses for battered women to have transitioned (in part or in full) from international funding to line items in relevant domestic budgets. However, this also then presents the risk of the group being held hostage by threats to such funding if they step over any red lines; one can understand the hesitance of certain women's groups, particularly in the more repressive RS, to engage in reform politics if they fear losing funds needed for critical women's health services.

There are many more specific challenges. They are not insurmountable. Women activists themselves could more actively seek to ensure that efforts aimed at bringing together "women activists" reach out not only to those women working in or on specific gender issues, but also women who are working for or leading policy groups, or other women who are "mainstreamed." The *Inicijativa F5* effort is one example of this being done; many more are needed.[33] Women could also resist efforts to pigeon-hole themselves in traditional "soft" corners, possibly by themselves making the policy links to broader political dysfunction and the inability of public administration to be able to fulfill their responsibilities in any sector. Women could encourage

---

[33]See http://www.inf5.info/o-nama/.

donors to stop drawing such distinct lines between soft women's projects, and bigger political project initiatives. The international community could also raise the profile of women by engaging in a more high profile way with female leaders on *all* issues; this, however, is complicated by the fact that embassies and international organizations tend to prefer to deal with political officials—and particularly in the case of BiH, with political party leaders—where again, no women are present.

Next, women *and* men who are dissatisfied with BiH's current reality face many challenges in determining how to break 18 years of gridlock. Several are highlighted below.

First, there are worrying signs that the BiH political arena could be on a track to become *less* transparent, democratic and accessible rather than more. Since 2006, BiH's state-strengthening and Euro-Atlantic integration processes have not only stalled, but they have in many ways even begun to reverse.[34] There have been active efforts among political parties and coalitions to make deals that would very likely limit the quality of (already weak) democracy. For example, in 2012, SDP and SNSD unveiled a package of proposals they sought to push through that would have weakened the conflict of interest law, made the freedom to access information more difficult and weakened a number of aspects of reforms implemented to strengthen judicial independence.[35] It also would have returned to closed-list voting in elections—purportedly to ensure greater representation of women, though in practice it is well known that closed lists facilitate tightened party discipline. While the package was not adopted in full, its component parts *have* remained on the radar screen. For example, changes to the law on conflict of interest were made in autumn 2013, and met with many concerns.[36] However, more broadly there has been a sense of indulgence among international actors; that the parties were at least

---

[34]McMahon, Patrice C. and Jon Western. "The Death of Dayton: How to Stop Bosnia from Falling Apart." *Foreign Affairs*. September—October 2009, pp. 69–83; Chivvis, Christopher. "Back to the Brink in Bosnia?" *Survival: Global Politics and Strategy*. Vol. 52, no. 1, February-March 2010, pp. 97–110.

[35]"Agreement on Program/Project Cooperation in Legislative and Executive Powers in BiH 2012-2014."

[36]Jukic, Elvira. "Bosnia's Conflict of Interest Reform' Causes Outrage." *Balkan Insight*. 8 November 2013.

agreeing on *something*, even if the point of agreement was a weakening of the democratic system.

Second, the election system, and the political parties that have managed to thrive therein, has over the course of the past 18 years demonstrated a weak link in terms of ensuring the accountability of political leaders. Particularly at the cantonal, entity and state levels, while there may be consistently poor results in terms of the provision of public services and jobs creation, there have been few if any significant changes in personnel or policy. While there have been shifts among ruling parties (with the introduction of parties like SNSD, HDZ 1990, SBB, etc.), there have been no shifts in terms of the political party platforms as ultimately implemented. This again shows the lack of mechanisms to ensure accountability.

In the 2012 municipal elections, for example, SNSD lost 26 municipalities, and while the SDP picked up three small municipalities, it lost 100,000 votes compared with 2008. However, the leaders of the two parties (Milorad Dodik and Zlatko Lagumdzija, respectively) remained at the heads of their parties. One would expect that significant electoral losses would result in political party changes in personnel or policy or both; this did not happen. This could be attributed to a serious lack of intra-party democracy.[37] It could also be attributed to a system in which political accountability matters less than one might assume. The main accountability present is based less on results, and more on corruption fueled patronage, breaking the back of public finances (pensions to privileged groups), and in many cases leading to a corrupt and non-meritocratic public administration.

Such electoral patterns are not unrelated to the structure of the country—to its electoral system, which in turn is based on the constitutional structure. There is no election in BiH in which all citizens are voting for the same set of candidates. Even the Presidency is selected

---

[37]In 2012 Roska Vrgova prepared an MA thesis at the University of Bologna-University of Sarajevo entitled *Intra-party Democracy in Consociational Democracies: The Cases of Bosnia and Herzegovina and in Macedonia*, that explores these dynamics. Vrgova cites Panebianco (Panebianco, Angelo. *Political Parties: Organization and Power*. Cambridge, England, Cambridge University Press, 1988) and others to explore the Balkan-specific manifestations of the tension between the normal defeat at the ballot box and pressure for party organizational change, and the tendency for parties to desire greater centralized control when they are in office.

on entity-lines; the inherent problems of this have been visible in terms of Croat efforts to ensure that "they get their" preferred Presidency member through some sort of weighting or gerrymandering of the Federation into electoral units or areas.[38] However, this focus fails to illuminate the bigger core problems—why can't a Serb living in the Federation vote for the member elected from the RS? Why—especially when the entities hold so much power in moving the country towards or away from EU integration—don't Federation residents affected by decisions in Banja Luka have the right to influence this choice?

Electoral systems affect electoral outcomes, in every country, either by directly shaping the rules of the game, or by creating an environment in which voters' choices and strategies reflect the demonstrated rules. Duverger's Law is well known. (Simply put, voters in the U.S. who might at heart want to vote for a third party Presidential candidate often decide not to, fearing that such a choice would dilute the outcome in a system that favors two parties.) In the BiH case, Hulsey explains the connections between party fragmentation and the country's electoral and constitutional structure.[39] Mujkic and Hulsey examine the success of nationalist parties in election after election in spite of voter frustration with their performance, as citizens are locked into a structural prisoner's dilemma.[40] Further, parties continue to be leader-dominated.[41] In BiH, there is no incentive for parties to seek to campaign for votes beyond their sole ethno-national base; the result is a bias to campaign to the poles, to demonstrate not a record of service but one's nationalist credentials. (A phenomenon by no means limited to BiH, but very dangerous in a still-divided post-war state.) The list

---

[38]For a review of this issue, see "Bosnia's Gordian Knot: Constitutional Reform," *International Crisis Group Europe Briefing No. 68*, July 12, 2012, available at http://www.crisisgroup. org/en/regions/europe/balkans/bosnia-herzegovina/b068-bosnias-gordian-knot-constitutional-reform.aspx.

[39]Hulsey, John. "Party Politics in Bosnia and Herzegovina," in Keil, Soeren and Valery Perry (eds.). *Statebuilding and Democratization in Bosnia and Herzegovina*. Ashgate, 2014 (forthcoming).

[40]Mujkic, Asim and John Hulsey. "Explaining the Success of Nationalist Parties in Bosnia and Herzegovina." *Politicka Misao*, Vol. 47, no. 2, 2010, pp. 143–158.

[41]Mavrikos-Adamou, Tina. "Leader-Dominated Ethnic Parties and Dysfunctional Institutional Design in Bosnia-Herzegovina and Kosovo," in Keil, Soeren and Valery Perry (eds.). *Statebuilding and Democratization in Bosnia and Herzegovina*. Ashgate, 2014 (forthcoming).

goes on, and these problems will not be solved by returning to closed lists, or by new gender balance quotas. They are inherent to the system, and again reflect the weak state of the country's democratic fabric.

Third, dysfunction and associated corruption are not an unintended byproduct of the status quo, "it is built into the system's DNA."[42] The Dayton structure builds numerous and overlapping "safeguards" into the state, entity and cantonal levels of government to persuade the warring parties that their groups' interests would also be paramount. This includes an asymmetric mix of ethnic and territorial federalism,[43] a vital national interest veto, an entity veto,[44] and both formal and informal ethnic quotas. The resulting problems are well known, summarized by the Venice Commission and countless policy reviews and reports.[45] While in theory, any system can work if there is political will to make it work, in practice we have seen that this is impossible; political leaders are making rational choices based on the present rules of the game.

It is understandable to seek to focus on local community problems in an effort to improve life on the ground while bypassing the bigger political straitjackets. The municipal level of governance could potentially provide interesting "laboratories of democracy," in part as they are run by directly elected mayors, so citizens know whether or not their mayor—with a specific name and face—has managed to pick up the trash, install street lights, etc. This approach has been taken by countless donor-funded municipal development programs, by many NGO-driven local community efforts, and has also to date been the focus of plenum discussions. However, over the course of 18 years it has been clear that both a) the success of municipal leaders is to at least a certain extent predicated on bigger political and structural

---

[42]The author would like to thank Kurt Bassuener for this observation and quote.

[43]Keil, Soeren, *Multinational Federalism in Bosnia and Herzegovina*. Ashgate, 2013.

[44]See Birgit Bahtic-Kunrath's, "Of Veto Players and Entity-Voting: Institutional Gridlock in the Bosnian Reform Process," for an excellent review of this issue. *Nationalities Papers*. Vol. 39, No. 6, November 2011, pp. 899–923.

[45]Venice Commission (European Commission for Democracy Through Law). *Opinion on the Constitutional Situation in Bosnia and Herzegovina and the Powers of the High Representative*, , CDL-AD (2005) 004 2, Mar. 11, 2004, *available at* http://www.venice.coe.int/docs/2005/ CDL-AD(2005)004-e.pdf; Foreign Policy Initiative BH (FPI). *Governance Structures in BiH: Capacity, Ownership, EU Integration, Functioning State*, 14 (2007).

forces;[46] and b) that local political structures are not succeeding in grooming a significant cadre of reform-minded, forward-looking, young mayors that might rise up through the system.[47] While horizontal linkages among municipalities are important, one cannot deny the currently negative impact of the dysfunctional vertical linkages.

Skeptics will say that constitutional reform is a non-starter; that reform minded people should aim for lower-level changes, for the harmonization of laws in the cantons and entities, and for coordination bodies and mechanisms. However, there is now ample evidence— nearly two decades worth—that there is no political will to make even sub-constitutional solutions work. For example, a Conference of Ministers of Education (modeled after a Swiss mechanism of the same name), is generally inert, as is a Ministry of Civil Affairs (MoCA) unit mandated to ensure (minimal) educational coordination. One need only consider the failure of BiH's authorities to meets the terms required for its young people to qualify for European ERASMUS scholarships as an example of this failure.[48] The government has been unable to agree on agricultural cooperative mechanisms, leading to the withdrawal of IPARD funds in 2013, and the inability of the country to export dairy products.[49] The inability of the police to respond to complicated public security threats—as witnessed in both the 2011 U.S. Embassy shooting incident and the February 2014 protests—suggests that existing "coordination" has proven itself to be ineffective.

---

[46]Municipalities have no legal definition in the state constitution, nor is the concept of local self-governance mentioned. Efforts aimed at improving inter-municipal cooperation for mutual economic benefit are often stymied by high level entity pressure (e.g., consider Herzegovina as a logical economic unit).

[47]Political parties would in fact like to see a return to indirectly elected mayors, as is the practice in neighboring Serbia, for example; so far this has not moved forward.

[48]Jukic, Elvira. "Bosnia Students Protest EU Scholarship Fiasco," *Balkan Insight*, December 18, 2013, available at http://www.balkaninsight.com/en/article/bosnian-students-plan-protests-over-eu-scholarships.

[49]"EU Freezes Funding for Two Agricultural Projects in Bosnia," *Intellinews*, June 6, 2013, available at http://www.intellinews.com/bosnia-and-herzegovina-1011/eu-freezes-funding-for-two-agriculture-projects-in-bosnia-7413/.

Final Thoughts

Many of these issues are likely to be discussed in a variety of fora in 2014. These issues will be on the formal BiH political radar screen, but as it is an election year, and as the political parties have been forming and dissolving coalitions and partners already for months, it is difficult to imagine them offering a new vision of a reform-minded future. The international community will also have these issues in mind. The EU—with Germany in the lead—is pondering options for a post-Sejdic-Finci approach in BiH, though it is too soon to tell whether it will create the incentive structured needed to press recalcitrant local officials to adopt a reform agenda and to make the legal or even constitutional changes needed to ensure progress. The United States is also increasingly aware of the unsatisfactory nature of the status quo, and is re-assessing its options for a new engagement. The results of the May European Parliament elections, and the unfolding Russia-Ukraine saga in Crimea, could also impact international community policy decisions. In terms of civil society, while the plenums are continuing it is unclear whether they will develop the leadership structures needed to evolve into an effective machine capable of effectively and strategically challenging the status quo. It is also uncertain whether the plenum participants will make the link between local demands and higher-level politics. The challenges are many. However, a process driven by citizen frustration and constructive engagement, and supported by a new set of external incentives to pressure politicians to reform, could provide a way out of a political stalemate that has victimized men and women for far too long.

Chapter Sixteen

Early Marriage in Morocco

Anissa Naqrachi

Early marriage in Morocco was the theme of a seminar organized by the Nour Association for Solidarity with Rural Women (ANSFR) on March 8, 2013, on the occasion of International Women's Day. The seminar highlighted the risks to women's health from pregnancies occurring before the age of 18 and was also an opportunity to reflect on early marriage and its harmful effects on young girls. Early marriage and pregnancy deprive girls of their childhood rights, including the right to education, to play, and to protection and tenderness, as well as natural development, but also exposes them to various physical, mental, and sexual violations.

Despite the fact that Morocco has signed international conventions and is committed to achieving their implementation—which has resulted in a major revision of legislation such as the *moudawana* (Family Code) and the Penal Code, especially as it concerns the fight against discrimination and the protection of children's rights as well as economic and social rights, it remains that there are still loopholes devoted to discrimination against women. We find many contradictions in the legislation, as is the case in Articles 19, 20, and 21 of the *moudawana*. Indeed, while the first items mentioned emphasize the sanctity of marriage, the joint participation of both spouses and dedicated capacity to marry at age 18, Articles 20 and 21 give a family judge the power to allow marriages before the legal age as an exception—an exception that revolted feminist associations.

Simply put, the exception has become the rule. The number of early marriages exceeded 47,000 in 2009 and continues to increase year by year, comprising 12 percent of marriages in 2011. In addition, judges grant leave in 92 percent of applications for girls not older than 14, which is unacceptable, as ANSFR castigates. "This is a crime that we all commit together. In most of these early marriages, the age difference between spouses is very important, whether the girl is married as a second wife or married (especially in rural areas), divorced during the first summer, and remarried the following year."

The marriage of minors has negative psychological effects on the girl. The wedding night alone should be considered rape. We must not forget that before age 18, the girl is still considered a child. Whether puberty has come does not make one a mature adult. Apart from psychological consequences, early marriage in general and early pregnancy in particular can be dangerous to the health of the girl. According to ANSFR statistics, it has been demonstrated that the first pregnancy, if occurring before the age of 18, may damage the young mother as well as her child. In addition to psychological and sociological effects of early marriage, early pregnancy may result in osteoporosis, anemia, increased risk of abortion and preterm births, hypertension, and increased cases of maternal mortality.

Following this presentation of the facts at the seminar, the ANSFR presented its recommendations in relation to marriage and early pregnancy. Indeed, the Association calls for coordination between national and international conventions ratified by Morocco and legislation to revise the Criminal Code and Family Code, the development of a law that protects women against all types of violence, awareness of the proper application of laws to recognize the responsibilities of the family, as well as companies, and conviction of parents who force their daughters to marry early.

Landmarks

- Article 19 of the *moudawana* reads: "Legal capacity is acquired for boys and girls enjoying their mental faculties at eighteen [18] Gregorian years."

- Article 20 reads: "The family judge in charge of the marriage may authorize a marriage of a boy and girl before the age of legal capacity to marry under Article 19 above, by reasoned decision specifying interest and reasons for this marriage, if he has first heard the minor's parents or legal representative. Similarly, he will arrange for a medical expert or a social survey. The judge's decision authorizing the marriage of a minor is not subject to appeal.

In 2006, judges agreed to 90 percent of requests for underage marriage. Thus, 12 percent of girls between the ages of 15 and 19 have the status of wife in Morocco—a very disturbing trend. Underage marriages comprise 8.34 percent of all marriages, or 21,660 out of a total 259,612 in the country. The response of the previous Minister of Justice, the late Mohamed Bouzoubaâ, in 2006 was meant to be reassuring: "This phenomenon is an exception. The increase in marriage applications is due to a transition period characterized by the entry into legal force of the *moudawana*."

Several years on, the new provisions do not appear to be well understood. The Democratic Women's Association of Morocco (ADFM) does not hide its concern. In a statement issued on the occasion of International Women's Day (again on March 8th) in 2008, the NGO noted that marriage licenses issued to minors in Morocco could seriously undermine the Family Code, adopted in 2004. However, the law is clear. Article 19, as noted earlier, states that "men and women enjoying their mental faculties and 18 Gregorian years of age, have the ability to acquire [sic] marriage."

Both sexes are therefore placed on an equal footing, unless an exemption age is provided for in Article 20 of the Family Code. Many parents take advantage of this age exemption despite the complexity of the process. Marriages of minors are in fact subject to prior judicial authorization, dependent on the interest and reasons involved. The judge must hear the mother and father to ensure the marriage is not a danger to the girl—hence the importance of expert medical and social investigation.

But women's rights activists openly criticize this exception. The basis on which authorizations are granted—especially as many violations in procedures are identified—is not well understood. According to a 2005 report by the Democratic League for Women's Rights, the conditions under which hearings are conducted and investigations with minors do not allow them to explicitly express their will, in violation of Articles 10 and 11 of the Code. The medical report usually replaces the demand for medical expertise stipulated by Article 20 of the Family Code. There is no precise and thorough investigation that would identify any pressure or the existence of material or moral constraints. Most of the time, impressions emerging from the statements of the father of the minor are the most critical. The same report lists the reasons given by the judges to allow the underage marriage. They are frequently associated with the physical capacity to bear the obligations of marriage, social and economic conditions of the minor, the existence of a relationship between the engaged, and dominant traditions in some regions. The causes of rejection of applications are limited, in turn, to the extreme immaturity of the minor and physical disability preventing entrance into marriage.

Violations

To prevent abuse, women's rights activists assert that child marriage should simply be banned, as in their view it is "hidden, authorized pedophilia." UNICEF argues the same: "It violates their rights to personal freedom and growth," insists Carol Bellamy, former UNICEF Executive Director. Presumably, lawyers are reluctant to go against tradition. It was not so long ago, in the minds of families, that the most obvious outcome for girls was intended to be marriage. And the earlier it occurred, the more it was worth—especially since even the girls who had the opportunity to pursue graduate studies and enter the labor market faced marriage imposed by their parents.

Poverty is also on the minds of the accused; in addition, marriage is a way to preserve virginity, which is fundamental in rural areas. In Taounate in the region of Fez, the average age of girls at marriage is 15 years—a practice not without consequence. It cuts at the root opportunities through study and personal growth opportunities. In addition, in girls, early marriage is almost always synonymous with pregnancy, the cause of high rates of maternal mortality and premature births as well as a lifetime of domestic and sexual servitude. Teenage girls are also more likely than mature women to acquire sexually transmitted diseases.

In its latest report on the situation of children in the world in 2011, UNICEF paints an alarming picture, starting with the marriage of adolescents. In Morocco, 11 percent of girls between ages 15 and 19 are married. In this regard, UNICEF noted in its report that "girls run the risk of ending up in a situation of powerlessness within the family home of their husbands away from their friends of the same age and other sources of support. This inability makes them even more vulnerable to abuse and they can be ordered to carry a disproportionate share of the housework." Attitudes toward violence and pregnancy are affected by this climate. The paper highlights that 64 percent of adolescents between ages 15 and 19 in Morocco believe that a husband is justified in hitting his wife under certain circumstances. With regard to HIV, only 12 percent of 15- to 19-year-old Moroccans have any knowledge of the disease.

According to UNICEF, Moroccan adolescents (aged 10-19 years) number 6.2 million, comprising 20 percent of the total population. The report also provides an overview of child labor in Morocco. Nine percent of boys aged between 5 and 14 years work compared to eight percent of girls. "Teenagers performing an excessive number of hours of work or working in hazardous conditions are unlikely to complete their studies, thereby reducing their chances of escaping poverty," the report says. As in most developing countries, Moroccan adolescents face many challenges, particularly related to the current economic downturn, climate change and environmental degradation, rapid urbanization and migration, aging societies, the rising costs of health care, and escalating humanitarian crises. According to the report, if one invests in favor of the 1.2 billion adolescents aged 10 today to 19 years, it will be possible to stop the cycle of poverty. "Adolescence is a crucial period—it provides an opportunity to consolidate the gains made during infancy but it is also a time during which these assets may volatilize," said Anthony Lake, the Director General of UNICEF. He added, "We need to focus more on how to reach adolescents—especially girls—on investments in education, health and other measures to engage them in the of process improving their own lives.

Conclusion

When, then, will be the end of this charade? At age 15, a girl or boy should be at their school desk. Youth in Morocco face all of the challenges listed above; the added pressure of early marriage is a threat to their life chances. Early marriage also affects debate and building social understanding of related issues like divorce, polygamy, sharing responsibility between spouses, and property rights. Suspicions about divorce and co-responsibility in marriage encourage male resistance to change. Early marriage is an impediment to progress.

The statistics are sobering, and rates of child marriage are rising. Morocco is not the only country facing early marriage as a social issue, and there is opportunity to tackle the problem together across borders. The Mediterranean Women in Leadership and Civil Society Conference helped draw attention to the issue in the Mediterranean Basin, and ANSFR will continue to work with partners in the United States, including the Middle East Partnership Initiative (MEPI), to eliminate early marriage.

Chapter Seventeen

Tunisian Women: Political Role, Gains and Challenges (The Case of Parity)

Najla Abbes

2011 was the year where Tunisian history suddenly witnessed a significant turnout by the outbreak of the popular uprising in Tunisia causing the fall of the authoritarian regime. That revolutionary movement led to free elections of the National Constituent Assembly (NCA) responsible for drafting the new constitution, which should be the symbol of a break with the past. For the first time, people of Arab countries, proclaiming their desire for democracy and without any outside help, managed to cause the downfall of an authoritarian regime and become masters of their own destiny. Hence, the hope of building an egalitarian society and a democratic state is finally allowed.

Ironically, 2011 was also the year when the story seemed to go back at least half a century for Tunisian women with a threatening public debate on women's rights. The questioning of the legal and social status of women has become systematic, recurrent and accepted.

Women's rights are part of the great achievements of independent Tunisia. President Bourguiba ensured since independence—and even before—the promulgation of the Constitution of June 1, 1959 to codify the right of the family in a reformist perspective, through the Personal Status Code (PSC), adopted August 13, 1956. This code is the result of a reformist movement that began in the late 19th century and defended the idea of a modern society and state.

Other laws and policies recognizing women's civil and political rights were adopted to fight any resistance to equality. Tunisia has ratified almost all international instruments on women's rights, including the International Convention on the Political Rights of Women and the International Covenant on Civil and Political Rights and the Convention on the Elimination of All Forms of Discrimination against Women (CEDAW), but with reservations and general statements.

However, a reading of the period from independence in 1956 to January 14, 2011 shows that Tunisia witnessed two phases: one was Bourguiba's reign (1956–87), which was marked by "the feminism of the state." Being a product of political will of those in power, embodied by the leader Bourguiba, the emancipation of women was part of an overall project to modernize Tunisian society. The period from 1987 until January 14, 2011 was characterized by political recovery of the emancipation of women in the new government and by the use of their assets for the purposes of political propaganda. In the absence of a real project of society, a feminist state mainly granted legal equality to show how the country was advanced and gave a real value to Tunisian women.

During the uprising (December 2010–January 2011), women were able to experience equal citizenship, which resulted in a very strong participation in the protests both in real and the virtual space. Hence, women were the human rights activists, the trade unionists, the opposition politicians, the bloggers, the protesters, etc... In this vast laboratory of transition, deconstitution and reconstitution, the range of possibilities is enormous.

The struggle for parity in the electoral lists was one of the major challenges for the cause of gender equality. But the elections results of the NCA demonstrated the limits of the campaign and the risk of regression endangering the Tunisian modernist project. In this context marked by political positions and ideological conflicts, attitudes towards gender equality ranged from defenses, threats and new conquests.

During the pre-election period of the NCA, the crises were numerous, but the concerns of institutions of this period were political, administrative, revolving around the management of crises and the establishment of a democratic pluralistic legislative arsenal in accordance with the objectives of the revolution. The debate about religion was virtually absent. The "highest authority of the objectives of the revolution, political reform and democratic transition" (HIROR) involving political actors and civil society, was developed and adopted between April and September 2011 with "five liberating country laws: the electoral law, the law on the independent electoral authority, the law on political parties, those concerning freedom of the press, and the law on freedom of the media."

However, all the instances of transition that were implemented during the transitional period before the elections of October 23, 2011 had a gender-unequal composition and were directed by men without exception. Within the HIROR, progressive activists and feminists fought for the inclusion of gender equality in the electoral law of the NCA to ensure adequate representation of women in the assembly in charge of drafting a new social and political pact for Tunisia. In addition, women's participation was considered as the best defense against obscurantism. This mobilization was successful with the adoption of the Decree of May 10, 2011 where Article 16, instituting parity and alternation in the electoral lists, marked a significant step forward in Tunisia, in the region, and in the image of the revolution. On the other hand, parity continued to be the subject of debate and did not seem to produce the desired quantity and quality effects. A negative message for gender equality in Tunisia emerged from the results of the October 23 elections.

If Tunisian women could not vote in the elections of the first Constituent Assembly in 1956, they were able to do it starting from the municipal elections of 1957, with a decree on the election excluding any gender discrimination against women voters. It is the same for the Electoral Code of 1966, which ensures equal rights for women and men. However, Tunisian women remained under-represented in public and political life. Power remained in the hands of men belonging to the hegemonic party.

To break with this discriminatory phase, it was important that the first real elections in Tunisia be pluralistic, transparent, credible and democratic under the control of the Independent High Authority for Elections (ISIE).

The Decree Law of May 10, 2011, concerning the election of the National Constituent Assembly, was characterized by an innovative element according to which Article 16 of the Act establishes parity in candidacy between men and women, alternating male and female names in the electoral lists and cancelling the lists that do not respect this rule.

Ignored by the media, the parity of nominations witnessed many objections. For some, parity is a "standard set" and detrimental to small parties of inland areas. It is "an illusion," a mere "decoration of participation" that does not match the "natural" skills of women because they are "unable to work in the political field." For others, the parity is "unworthy if it humiliates women."

Hence, the participation of women in the first democratic elections after the revolution was as follows:

- The female enrollment rate is 45 percent.

- There were 5502 women candidates.

- 128 lists are headed by women, 85 are lists of parties and 43 independent candidates.

- No list headed by a woman in the constituencies of Jendouba Kairouan, Sidi Bouzid, Kébili.

- Only 7 percent of the electoral lists were headed by women.

Feminists were disappointed. Only the coalition Democratic Modernist Pole (PDM) applied parity at the heads of lists with 16 women at the head of its 33 lists. The Ettakatol party of Mustapha Ben Jaafar has meanwhile managed to have four lists among its 33 presided by women. The Congress for the Republic (CPR), Moncef Marzouki's party, has presented one woman at the top out of its 33 lists. The Democratic Progressive Party led by Maya Jribi presented three women at the top of its lists. The Nahda movement, meanwhile, has placed one non-veiled woman as a head of list. This symbolic gesture reveals the absence of a genuine conviction of parity within the party, which seems rather to respect the parity but in second position.

Not everyone was necessarily prepared for parity, but this requirement has truly put the civil society up to a new challenge, a new way of looking at politics. The women were at the front of the stage. Attitudes have not always accepted this participation.

It is precisely against the political marginalization of women and in order to increase their participation in the process of transition that the Tunisian Association for Democratic Women (ATFD) led the campaign "Do not let them steal your voice"[1] and the League of Tunisian Women Voters was born in August 2011.

---

[1] http://www.femmesdemocrates.org.

However, social practices and sexist stereotypes against women in political leadership persist. Many men and women do not envision women as leaders in the political or public sphere. Some activists of the feminist cause were present on the electoral lists and as they carried the project of an egalitarian society, they have been more exposed to campaigns of defamation. The campaigns of intimidation and denigration against progressive women since January 14, especially in social media, played against those candidates.

It is also important to point out that the lack of media coverage for women during the elections campaign was significant. Women political actors, or party candidates or heads of lists, occupied a small space in the media coverage. It was 2.02 percent in the press, 4.92 percent on radio stations, and 2.02 percent on television channels. The media marginalization of women is not new, this is unfortunately a tradition in Tunisia. Before January 14, the former president's wife was "the only Tunisian woman to hold the media scene by appropriating the question of women's issues as being the president of the Basma Association and president of the Arab Women's Organization."

From this warm euphoria, parity seemed to be an illusion, as the elections results suggest that the battle for gender equality will be tough.

Election Results: The Time of Disenchantment

The elections of October 23, 2011 were the first democratic, free and fair elections in Tunisia. Despite the criticism of the composition of the ISIE and/or lack of efficacy in the control of the elections campaign, no party has been able to challenge the election result.

The Nahda party won 89 out of 217 seats. The Congress for the Republic won 29 seats, the Popular Petition (Al Aridha) 26 seats. Democratic Forum for Freedom and Work, or Ettakatol, had 20 seats. Fifty-nine women made it to the Constituent Assembly. They represent 27 percent of the 217 elected.

Because it won several seats in each constituency, the Islamist Nahda party is the one who brought the most women to the Chamber. Among the 59 women elected, 42 are members of the party. They represent 47 percent of the 89 women elected members of the party.

As for women's participation in the constituencies within the six NCA commissions, only the Commission on Human Rights and Freedoms is chaired by a member of the parliamentary group of Nahda.

At the government level, the Nahda party, not having an absolute majority of seats, was forced to deal with the CPR and Ettakatol to form a coalition government, the "troika." Despite inflation at ministerial portfolios, the representation of women is poor.

Based on this under-representation of women in the NCA and the government, the risk of regression for women's rights emerges in particular from the general political context and the profile of the winner.

Furthermore, after January 14, 2011, and especially after the victory of the Nahda movement in the NCA elections, both the risk of regression and citizen vigilance increased. Despite the differences between the Islamist and democratic parties, including the civil nature of the state and gender equality, these two faces of Tunisia coexist in the society and in the NCA and even called to find a compromise for the new constitution. Beyond the battle for egalitarian legal texts, another battle loomed, the resistance to the creeping radicalization against individual, cultural and political freedoms, pluralism and social peace.

This anxious climate that the Tunisian society in transition lives with identity fears, sharpened by the trends of political Islam, is projected on the female body and the passions are exacerbated to the point of obscuring the real social challenges and policies. In post-January 14 Tunisia, the battle between democrats and Islamists looked tough. Its battleground is definitely women and their rights.

2014 will be a decisive year for the future of Tunisia and Tunisian women and men. The adoption of the new constitution and the holding of legislative and presidential elections will determine the direction of Tunisia for several generations. Citizen vigilance and mobilization of the civil society and the democratic parties played an important role to defend the humanist and egalitarian message of the revolution.

The best example is the amendment to Article 45 that the NCA passed in the constitution protecting women's rights and seeking to ensure gender parity in elected government. The Assembly accepted an amendment to Article 45, outlining the protection of women's rights under the new constitution. The amendment passed, with 116 members in favor, 40 opposed, and 16 abstentions.

It was the most challenging article that created a controversy in the voting process. The difference in number between the deputies for and against the amendment was very close. Nine women deputies from the Islamist party Nahda voted against. The amended article reads: "The state guarantees the protection of women's rights and supports the advances therein. The state guarantees equal opportunities for women and men to take on various responsibilities across domains. The state strives for gender parity in all elected councils. The state takes all necessary measures to eradicate violence against women."

This amendment is the fruit of a very strong advocacy campaign conducted by the civil society with significant participation from the League of Tunisian Women Voters (LET). Together with a number of other feminist associations, we (the League of Tunisian Women Voters) developed a group of recommendations among which was parity in all elected councils, given that the constitutional draft did not make any reference to parity in the first place.

A day before the voting on women's rights in Article 45, the League of Tunisian Women Voters with other associations that defend women's rights organized a demonstration in front of the NCA to ask for constitutionalizing the equality between men and women and parity in all the elected councils.

During the demonstration, a group of women activists was allowed to enter the NCA and present the recommendations to a large number of deputies and journalists.

The following day, Article 45 was positively amended as stated above. We consider this a successful step towards the gain of parity. Despite the wording of "the state strives to…" instead of firmly establishing it, we acknowledge that it is now the role of the civil society to advocate for applying parity as a must and not an option.

Chapter Eighteen

Political Parties in Algeria: The Position of Women in Operation and Representation

Nadia Ait-Zai

In modern democracies, political parties have a very important political role: the principle is to allow individuals or groups sharing similar objectives to join forces to promote a common agenda. Algerian law under the different constitutions amended by laws on the creation of 1989, 1997 and 2012 political parties has led to the creation of political parties by defining them as (according to Article 3) a grouping of national citizens sharing the same ideas and who gather in order to implement a common political project and have access, through democratic and peaceful channels, to the exercise of powers and responsibilities in the conduct of public affairs.

Obviously, access to the exercise of power cannot be done without the involvement of women. However, it can be noted that women are underrepresented in politics. Despite equal rights enshrined in the constitution (Article 29), despite the right of women to vote and stand for election, the difference between the number of elected men and the number of elected women is a significant problem. Some would argue that if there is an overrepresentation of men elected, this is not a problem, as the interests of the whole population will be taken into account—both men and women. Others argue that equal representation is necessary, since there is equality before the law. Some even say that since women can stand for election there is no discrimination.

Equal rights are not enough—we must strive to achieve de facto equality. One of the main functions of political parties is to train, designate and support their candidates logistically and often financially, which makes them an essential part of the steps necessary to an election. The selection process of candidates is thus crucial to ensure the representation of women. Nevertheless, many parties have no specific approach to encourage women to stand as candidates. Only the Labor Party uses equality of opportunity and alternating on lists it proposes.

Political parties do not make much effort to encourage women to practice politics. In an interview, party member Mr. Hachid says that "parties do not like women," yet "they are found everywhere." He adds, "When it comes to women, parties of all persuasions, whether Democrats, Republicans, conservatives or Islamists, speak differently about them, but they unanimously grant them a secondary role.... Despite their role in Algerian society today, women seem to be a topic of discussion for politicians," he concludes.

The construction of de facto equality and the fight against prejudice, against the secular yoke, will feed political discourse but not achieve their eradication.

Evolution of the Law and Practices

The Single Party State

The 1976 Constitution provided that the Algerian institutional system was based on the principle of the single party. The National Liberation Front (FLN) was the only party in the country. Since 1962 the policy of the FLN against women was both aggressive and lax. When I say aggressive, I am referring to the campaign undertaken by the FLN in 1979 to encourage women to run for municipal elections. The UNFA sections, mass organization of women linked to FLN, traveled around the country and visited domestic firms to encourage women to stand as candidates in municipal elections held in 1979. We thought it would persist over time, but this was not the case.

Although the FLN has more activists, very few of them have emerged. The number of candidates elected to parliament fluctuated but has not exceeded ten: ten women in 1963, ten in 1977, only four in 1982, and eventually ten in 1986.

The Multiparty State

The 1989 Constitution declared a multiparty state by not introducing the term party, but rather "political association." It is clear that this formulation could cover only political parties. This marked the end of the one-party state, as the FLN disappears from the Constitution. Later, the 89.11 law of May 7, 1989 authorizes the creation of political associations. Article 5 of the law states, among other things, that these associations cannot be based exclusively on gender. Article 14 clarifies that the number of founders and leaders should not be less than 15. No reference is made to the presence of women in political parties.

Sixty parties were created, one of which was chaired by a woman. Due to the overly hectic and violent political activity, the parliament was then dissolved, to be replaced by the National Transitional Council in which 12 women would sit.

The 1996 Constitution put to referendum used the "political parties" formulation, and was followed by Order 97 / 09 of March 6, 1997 on Political Parties, in accordance with Articles 42, 123, 179 of the Constitution. Article 5 specifies again that no political party can base its formulation on gender or violence. The text makes no reference to women; it is simply written that Algerian women who have reached the voting age can join any political party.

In 1997, only 13 women from different political parties were elected to parliament. In the same year, out of over 1281 candidates, 78 women were elected to the People's Communal Assemblies. Yet if political parties have made no attempt to promote the representation of women, female voters could make a difference. Women constitute about half of the electorate. Of the 15,817,306 voters in 1997, 7,368,605 were women. The exercise of suffrage could theoretically make them acquire a fundamental political influence, but this did not happen.

In 2002, out of 3679 candidates, 147 women were elected to municipalities, and 113 of the 2,684 candidates were elected to the *wilaya* assemblies. For the legislative elections in May 2002, 27 women were elected out of 694 candidates. For the 2007 legislative elections, the former single party FLN lost 10 seats, while in 2002 there were 20 seats, the National Democratic Rally (RND) and the Democratic Cultural Rally (RCD) had only one woman elected.

The political will of the parties being in flux, the law will gradually evolve to finally pave the way for construction of a temporary mechanism likely to address female underrepresentation.

The Quota

The debate on the representation of women in politics was reintroduced by civil society, which in 2002 began to ask the question of why so few women were emerging in politics. Women are out in force in all sectors, health, education, public service, except in politics and decision-making positions. The parties are the vectors of the representation of women but also their visibility, therefore solutions must be found to correct the imbalance noted in the representation, and to encourage political parties to promote the emergence of women. In 2005, the public authorities were sensitive to this issue, and began the ratification of international conventions, particularly those relating to women's political rights. This allowed legislators in 2008 to amend the constitution by introducing Article 31(a), asserting the political rights of women. Article 31(a) provides that the "state works to promote the political rights of women by increasing their chances to have access to representation in elected assemblies. The rules shall be determined by an organic law."

The president of the republic said that "the constitutional reform will encourage more women to enter politics." It will be a giant step towards ending discrimination, surely opening the field to a large number of women who aspire to enter politics."

Organic Law No. 12-04 of January 12, 2012 on Political Parties[1] has been more proactive in introducing the reference to women. Hence the role and tasks of the party will be to train and prepare elites able to assume public responsibilities, to work dedicated to democratic action and alternation of power, and promotion of political rights of women, according to Article 11.

It is the obligation of the founding members of the party to bring among them a representative proportion of women, by Article 17. At the meeting of the constitutive congress including at least 400 to 500 delegates, a representative quorum of women must be included so that the latter will be valid.

A question arises about how to calculate the representative proportion of women. In fact, it must be at least 30 percent, if not 50 percent, women.

---

[1]*Official Journal of the Algerian Republic,* January 15, 2012.

Today it is difficult to get the exact number of activists of the existing political parties. Moreover, these provisions seem rather to address the new political formations that have emerged recently.

The legislative measures contributing to women's representation end with difficulty through the adoption of the Organic Law No. 12-03 of January 12, 2012 "setting the modalities to increase the chances of access of women to the representation in the elected assemblies."

The number of women on the lists of candidates, whether independent or presented by one or more political parties, shall not be less than a proportion of the number of seats; this varies from 20 percent to 50 percent, going through 30 percent, 35 percent, and 40 percent depending on seats to be provided. It is therefore an obligation on parties to mention on the electoral lists women under penalty of rejection thereof, by Article 5.

Some parties in parliament resisted the adoption of this law. The designated government representative, the Minister of Justice, had to go himself within the walls of the lower chamber to defend the bill.

The law setting the modalities to increase the chances of access of women to representation in elected assemblies has enabled the introduction of 147 female parliamentarians among 462 MPs in the legislative elections that took place on May 10, 2012. Political parties, according to law, benefit from specific financial aid from the state depending on the number of candidates elected to people's municipal assemblies, *wilayas* and to parliament. The arrival of 147 women upset many parties, if we refer to the reactions of some of them.

After the vote and the implementation of the law in March 2013 Aboudjerra Soltani from the Social Movement for Peace (MSP) advocated "the removal of Article 31(a) in the next constitutional amendment," stating that "this article has actually imposed a number at the expense of quality. Mediocrity has thus been favored, as can be noted in the assembly." He calls upon to get back to Article 29 of the constitution and remove quotas to return to equality.

The FLN won the elections by improving its performance from 136 to 220 seats, including 68 women. RND won six additional seats including 23 women. Islamist parties grouped in a coalition suffered a major setback by finishing third.

FLN now holds 47.81 percent of the seats of the People's National Assembly (221 of 462) while winning only 14.18 percent of the votes cast, that is to say, only 6 percent of registered voters. It owes this success, among other things, to the legalization of 17 parties on the eve of parliamentary elections. This fragmentation of the opposition electorate and a majority vote in two rounds led to this kind of representation.

At the municipal elections, two FLN female candidates were elected. They are the only ones to have been elected from 1521 municipalities. One of them (the elected mayor of El Mouradia) said, "Some political parties have presented women not out of conviction but to complete lists."[2]

Measures to Strengthen the Role of Women in Politics

Law and political will have forced political parties to use the mechanism put in place to increase the chances of representation of women in politics. However slowly, and with the impetus of female activists, political parties will get more familiar with the law. The rejection of the list that does not contain the proportions required by the organic law will lead them to implement organizational, educational or logistical measures. These measures will encourage the participation of women in politics and public life. Certainly within their national structure, women are co-opted, but at the lowest political level; parties have established women's sections to do this.

Women's Sections

All Algerian senior parties have a women's section: FLN, RND, MSP, RCD, FFS. A National Women's Council has been launched to contribute to a better representation and promotion of women.

It is difficult to assess the impact of women's sections due to the highly variable importance given to these sections in different parties. There is no direct relationship between the existence of these sections and an increase in the number of women, either candidates or elected. However, this organizational approach is often the only measure taken

---

[2]Personal interview.

to help women in politics. Female activists operating in these sections should develop training activities.

The educational aspect is translated by courses especially designed to prepare women for the role of activists, candidates or elected. Conferences and seminars are organized by parties, but is this aimed at encouraging women to stand for election?

Female activists themselves should draw up a work plan for the elections. This would avoid co-optation or the contested choice of non-party candidates. Many women activists have complained that the candidates chosen are not representative or have never been active within the party.

The currently existing women's sections must be revitalized and create work plans to encourage women's applications, which will allow them to go beyond mere figuration or controlled use or even direct support to men. These women's sections should not be used to transmit the policy of the party officials to women. Women's sections must serve women and not be just an additional structure in a party.

Women's sections enable women activists to impose their views and encourage the participation of women in political life through training. They could even create enthusiasm for women to join the party. But we must admit that this is not so easy, because the parties will be reluctant to the educational aspect that would encourage the female participation in political life through training. Many political parties do not wish to see women go beyond mere organization.

Sharing Power:
Give Women Their Rightful Place In All Parties

Open Making Decision Positions for Women in Parties

The reluctance of political parties lies in the fact that if there are more women, if women are equally represented or even comprise a third, then men's "overrepresentation" is reduced. This requires that some elected officials leave their positions, which can lead to conflict and explanations why this equal representation should be applied. It is actually the sharing of political power that is behind the difficulty of achieving either equality or the one-third measure in the representation of men and women in politics. The issue of monopoly of political power in the hands of a majority of men is often evaded, if not forgotten. We are talking about under-representation of women without referring to the fact that it arises from the presence of a majority of men. That is why it is important to note that the organic law on political parties in 2012 introduced the requirement that "among the founding members of a party there must be a representative number of women." This is where the political work begins; this is where we engage women as equal to trace a common political program.

The sociologist Nacer Djabi said the political party is not the ideal location for the woman; she is present as a member but not in decision-making structures.[3] And when she is present in this structure, it is to look after the office. This is shown through the duties assigned to women members of party political offices.

A woman in the Politburo of the FLN deals with social work, women and children; of the two women in the MSP, one of them runs the secretariat to the family; there are three women in the secretariat of the RCD and eight women in the TEJ's, and almost all of them deal with social matters, women, children, and/or human rights.

Adapt Logistics

Djabi goes on: "Women are very few in these organs, as the meetings of these bodies are held either in the evening or the weekend."[4] This requires that political meeting schedules be arranged according to family responsibilities. Can we hope—as is done by the Austrian People's Party—that parties would fund or make nurseries available? Members of the women's sections should think about it. In any event, meeting schedules must be changed to allow women to assume family responsibilities.

Offering training and childcare for children and changing meeting times to allow women to assume family responsibilities are explicit measures that face the existing social and political culture whose primary beneficiaries are women, not both genders. This is why parties

---

[3]Personal interview via telephone with Nacer Djabi.

[4]Personal interview, Djabi.

are so reluctant to adopt organizational and educational measures for women. The new law on political parties in Article 11 obliges parties to train elites able to assume public responsibilities and to promote women's political rights.

Review the Internal Selection Process of Parties

Some parties have established criteria for selection of electoral candidates without having to give any conclusive results in terms of female representation. Seniority, volunteer political work, skills, and long-term political training are criteria that normally give equal opportunities to women to be selected. But the 2007 legislative election results surprised more than one party, made aware of the quota mechanism by civil society and called upon by the recommendations of the meeting held in Parliament in March 22, 2007 to use the quota. Parties considered that "it was not a gender issue that arose before the participation of women, but of skill." The Labor Party, led by a woman, stated, "The Algerian electoral system, by proportional rates, guarantees diversity of representation while reserving seats for women among the five or three first places."[5] Equality of opportunity is a criterion used by the Labor Party. Other conservative or liberal parties who used the skill criterion put women on electoral lists in ineligible places. The RND and MSP confessed they had left the choice of candidates to *wilaya* committees, and at this level men are frequently misogynistic.

During the 2012 elections, some selected candidates were challenged for having never been active in the party that put them forward to be elected. Selection criteria should be reviewed to reduce gender discrimination. Women's sections of political parties should consider what is beneficial to them and to their party.

Recognize and Strengthen the Activities of Associations

Associations help encourage women to take part in elections. Some have specialized in the training of candidates as well as capacity building of newly elected women. Since 2006, many candidates have been trained and some of them elected. The work of these associations is to

---

[5]Louiza Hanoune in *Horizon*, March 22, 2007.

Table 1. 2012 Algerian Parliamentary Elections

National Summary of Votes and Seats (Number of Women Elected in Parentheses)
Registered Voters: 21,645,841
Votes Cast: 9,339,026
Invalid Votes: 1,704,047
Valid Votes: 7,634,979

Party	Votes	Percent	Seats
Green Algeria Alliance (AAV)	475,049	6.2	47 (15)
National Republican Alliance (ANR)	109,331	1.4	3 (1)
Future Front (FA)	174,708	2.3	2 (0)
Front for Change (FC)	173,981	2.4	4 (1)
Front for Justice and Development (FJD)	232,676	3.1	7 (1)
Algerian National Front (FNA)	198,544	2.6	9 (3)
National Front for Social Justice (FNJS)	140,223	1.8	3 (0)
Front of Socialist Forces (FFS)	188,275	2.5	21 (7)
Front for National Liberation (FLN)	1,324,363	17.4	221 (68)
Generation of 1954 (G54)	120,201	1.6	3 (0)
List of Independents (LI)	671,190	8.8	19 (5)
Movement of Free Citizens (MCL)	115,631	1.5	2 (1)
National Movement of Hope (MNE)	119,253	1.6	2 (0)
Algerian Popular Movement (MPA)	165,600	2.2	6 (2)
New Dawn (NA)	132,492	1.7	5 (0)
Algerian Party of Light (PAL)	48,943	0.6	2 (1)
Party of Dignity (PD)	129,427	1.7	2 (1)
Party of Youth (PJ)	102,663	1.3	2 (1)
National Party for Solidarity (PNS)	114,372	1.5	4 (1)
Workers' Party (PT)	283,585	3.7	17 (10)
Algerian Rally (RA)	117,549	1.5	2 (1)
National Rally for Democracy (RND)	524,057	6.9	70 (23)
Patriotic Republican Rally (RPR)	114,651	1.5	2 (1)
Union of Democratic and Social Forces (UFDS)	114,481	01.5	3 (2)
Others	1,743,734	22.8	4 (2)
Total	7,634,979		462 (147)

Adapted from Adam Carr's Election Archive, http://psephos.adam-carr.net/countries/a/algeria/alge-ria2012.txt.

educate candidates to the concept of gender equality and to think on the development and egalitarian content of the bills. Associations raise awareness among them so they will be visible at the forefront to gain political gravitas, not to provide an electoral argument that would ensure the woman's co-optation and promotion, often at the cost of her agency.

Conclusion

Saying things, putting oneself forward, and claiming seats do not mean that women will put men in the shadows. Politics should not be a hostile environment for women—they must be recognized as an equal partner.

Politics is a constant battle for women, if they have no desire to fight for their place and defend their ideas, they will soon be relegated to subordinate positions. They must therefore be aware of the role they will play by engaging in politics and win in the political field.

Three new parties are headed by women; the presidents of these parties must use equal opportunities and alternation on electoral lists to further reduce the gap between the males elected and the females elected. Women should be visible and make themselves known by citizens.

About the Authors

Najla Abbes is a Fulbright alumna. She was a Fulbright Language Teaching Assistant at Pfeiffer University, North Carolina from 2007 to 2008. She has a Master's degree in English Literature from The Higher Institute of Languages in Tunisia. She is currently working as a MEPI administrator at the U.S. Embassy in Tunisia. In this position she advises civil society actors in relation to the writing of funding proposals. She conducts field research and reports on MEPI-funded projects. She has also worked as an Arabic language instructor at the Foreign Service Institute Tunisia (FSI) and the School for International Training (SIT). Her main duties were to teach different levels of Modern Standard Arabic and conduct lectures and workshops on Tunisian identity, education, and women in Tunisia. Najla is the co-founder, treasurer, and program coordinator of the League of Tunisian Women Voters (LET). The league aims to improve Tunisian women's ability to participate effectively in public affairs, especially in politics and electoral practices, as voters and candidates based on the principles of human rights and social gender. As a program coordinator, Najla developed project proposals on women empowerment strategies and helped to implement an exchange program between Tunisian female potential candidates for the coming elections and Danish female MPs.

Nadia Ait-Zai, born August 5, 1952, holds a Master of Laws degree. She was elected vice-mayor of the municipality of Alger in 1979 and she held this post until 1984. She also held the post of Head of Department of the Direction Général des Nouvelles Galeries Algériennes. From 1984 onwards, she has been working as an attorney. She is also a lecturer at the Faculty of Law, University of Algeria. In 2004, she was awarded a diploma for her achievements as an educator of human rights. In 1993, Nadia became a member of an INSP-financed research group, which researches violence. In 1999, Nadia carried out a study for the Center of Women's Rights in Palestine: "L'Exclusion des Femmes de la Protection Internationale." In 2004, she carried out a study for UNICEF: "L'Impact de la Convention des Droits de l'Enfant sur le Droit National Algérien." In 2005, she presented a report on the situation of Algerian children for the Children's Rights Committee. In 2007, she gave an expert opinion on the Algerian national plan for the children to UNICEF and the Ministry of Women Affaires. The same year, she also carried out a study for the TESEC on the situation of Algerian women. In 2002, Nadia founded the Documentation Center for Women's and Children's Rights (CIDDEF). She is also the author of several books on women's and children's rights. Nadia is also a member of the Collectif Maghreb Egalité.

Intisar Azzuz holds a PhD in Environmental Design in Architecture from Texas A&M University and an MS in Architecture from the University of Oklahoma. She was previously the head of the Architecture Department at

Tripoli University in Libya. Dr. Azzuz is a civil society and community activist who has participated in, advised, and founded many organizations in Libya since 2011, including the International Egyptian Libyan Friendship Society, of which she is vice president. She was commissioned by the Deputy Minister of Health to work with people who were imprisoned and injured by Gaddafi's troops during the revolution, and interviewed more than 25 people and prepared files in ongoing research. She served as the keynote speaker at the Your Right conference, hosted by the organization 1Libya, to promote women's rights. She has also worked with Gender Concerns International, the Divorcees and Widows Society, the International Peace Organization for Human Rights, the International Women's Organization, and One Voice, among others. Dr. Azzuz also advised and trained NGO leaders in advance of meetings with the President of the General National Congress of Libya, resulting in presentations of written recommendations. She was also responsible for developing the curricula of the newly-formed International Libyan University's School of Architecture. During her stay in the U.S., Dr. Azzuz was co-founder and board member of the Middle Eastern Women Empowerment Center, President of the Oregon Chapter of the American Muslim Society, and an interfaith organizer for dialogue and understanding.

Ghazi Ben Ahmed is the Director of the Mediterranean Development Initiative in Tunisia and the Coordinator of the LEND Initiative for Tunisia. He is also the founder of the Club de Tunis, a Tunisian based think tank aiming to help policymakers to devise strategies for economic growth and regional development, and to empower both the private sector and NGOs in Tunisia and North Africa as an engine for regional integration, job creation and shared prosperity. Previously he was the Lead Trade Expert in the African Development Bank (AfDB) working in the private sector department of the Bank. He was in charge of the $1 billion Trade Finance Initiative of the Bank. He received the "Highly Commended" prize for the Best Development Finance Institution (DFI) in Africa at the Trade Finance Magazine 2010 Awards for Excellence, the Trade Finance Deal of the Year 2010 and the Trade Finance Bank/House of the Year Award 2010. Before joining the AfDB, he was employed at the UNCTAD, the United Nations Agency for Trade and Development, in the Africa and LDC Division, as Senior Advisor, providing support to African trade negotiators in multilateral trade negotiations and regional trading arrangements. He provided economic studies and reports; elaborated the Diagnostic Trade Integration Studies and assisted the countries in mainstreaming trade into the national development plans under the Integrated Framework. He has also worked for almost 10 years in the European Commission in Brussels, in several Directorates-Generals. He was also responsible for the task force on market access and non-tariff barriers and the High Level Dialogue between the EU and China. He holds a PhD in Economics from the University of Montpellier I (France).

Adel Awni Dajani is the founder of several specialist Maghreb-related financial companies, including The International Maghreb Merchant Bank (the Maghreb's first licensed investment bank, established in 1995 with the IFC, European banks, and finance professionals from Tunisia, Libya and Algeria). Mr. Dajani was IMBank's first Managing Director and was a member of the Executive Board of the Bank from its inception to 2003. Maghreb Venture Partners, a specialized and Maghreb-focused private equity vehicle established by Mr. Dajani in 2004 that acts exclusively as a corporate finance advisory vehicle and packager of private equity opportunities in Algeria, Libya, Morocco, Tunisia and Mauritania. Mr. Dajani is an independent board member at the Aman Bank, one of Libya's leading private banks, owned by private Libyan investors and Banco Espirito Santo of Portugal. He has also been a private equity principal investor in several start-up companies in Libya, Tunisia and Morocco. Mr. Dajani was educated at Eton College and the Universities of London and the Sorbonne. He is a qualified barrister at law and a member of the UK, Hong Kong and Libyan Bar Associations. Mr. Dajani has had published several articles on banking, investment, and the post-Arab Spring challenges in leading business journals and has spoken at many international investment conferences on the Maghreb. Mr. Dajani is the Alumni Representative for the Maghreb Chapter of the School of Oriental and African Studies of the University of London and a founder of the Old Etonian MENA Association. Mr. Dajani co-wrote *The Islamic Frontiers of China, Peoples of the Silk Road*, first published in London in 1990, based on his extensive travels in China with How Man Wong, an acknowledged authority on Chinese minorities and President of the China Research and Exploration Society. The book was updated and republished by IB Tauris in London in 2011.

Emily Dyer joined the Henry Jackson Society as a researcher in January 2012. She is currently researching women's rights in Egypt having recently returned from Cairo. Beforehand, she co-authored *Al-Qaeda in the United States: A Complete Analysis of Terrorism Offenses* and helped present its findings to policy makers on various platforms, including the British Parliament, the White House and the National Counterterrorism Center. Emily previously worked as a Higher Executive Officer for the Preventing Extremism Unit at the Department for Education, where she wrote several papers on extremism within educational settings. Beforehand she was based at the Policy Exchange think tank. Emily has written for publications including *The Observer, The Telegraph, The Huffington Post, City AM, The Atlantic, World Affairs, CTC Sentinel* and *Standpoint* magazine, largely on women's rights in the Middle East, extremism, and human rights. Emily studied International Relations from the University of Birmingham, where she produced a First class dissertation on Islamic feminism in Iran, and has travelled widely within Syria and Turkey.

Dajana Džindo is a Visiting Scholar at the Center for Transatlantic Relations at Johns Hopkins University SAIS. She was Project Manager for the Women in Leadership and Civil Society Conference held in Sarajevo in November 2013. Dajana received a Master's degree in Business Communication with Honors from the Faculty of Political Sciences of the University of Sarajevo in 2011. She is also a Humanity in Action Senior Fellow and a European Fund for the Balkans Fellow. Dajana gained significant communication and management experience at the foundation Humanity in Action, the Creative 24/7 Marketing Agency, the Municipality Centre of Sarajevo, the Sarajevo Faculty of Political Sciences, the Media Plan Institute Sarajevo, the Friedrich Ebert Stiftung, the Youth Forum of Igman Initiative, and elsewhere. Since 2007, she has been active in the civil society sector in Bosnia and Herzegovina and other former Yugoslav countries, representing the interests and rights of young people, establishing active cooperation among youth in the countries signatory to the Dayton Agreement, promoting BiH's EU integration, and especially promoting respect for human rights and equality of women in Bosnia and Herzegovina. Dajana is also the co-author of a number of articles, including "Politics in Media and Media in Politics—BH Media Accuracy Perception," published by the University of Sarajevo; "The Importance of Internet and Social Networks in Humanitarian Actions", presented at the University of Novi Sad (Serbia); and "Social Networks and the Leadership Concept" presented at the University of Tuzla (BiH).

Leila Hadj-Abdou joined the Center for Transatlantic Relations SAIS as an Austrian Marshall Plan Foundation Fellow, where her research analyzes immigrant integration policies in Europe. She obtained her Ph.D. from the European University Institute in Florence, Italy. Her doctoral thesis, "Governing Urban Diversity," assessed immigrant integration policies and discourses about immigrants in the European capital cities of Vienna and Dublin. Her thesis was supervised by Rainer Bauböck and Donatella della Porta. Leila has worked as a researcher, project manager, and lecturer at the Institute for Political Sciences at the University of Vienna and as a lecturer at the Institute for European Studies and International Relations at Cormenius University in Bratislava, Slovakia. She started her academic career as a researcher and project manager at the Austrian Institute for East- and Southeastern European Studies within the Department of Social Sciences in Vienna. Leila has published on a wide array of topics including: international migration, multiculturalism and cities, managing religion in Europe, Islam, politics of recognition, politics of belonging, and populist right-wing parties. She has also participated as a researcher and project manager in several international, interdisciplinary research projects. Notably, she participated in the European Commission-funded project entitled "Values, Equality, and Differences in Liberal Democracies: Debates about Female Muslim Headscarves in Europe" (EC/6FP). Leila has taught courses on migration, political systems, qualitative methods, gender relations, and racism. Previously, Leila was a visiting researcher at University College Dublin, UMR Cultures and Urban Societies, CSU, CNRS Paris, and the Institute for Higher Studies in Vienna.

Samra Filipović-Hadžiabdić is the Director of the Agency for Gender Equality of Bosnia and Herzegovina. She also established and initiated other institutional mechanisms for gender equality in Bosnia and Herzegovina, including the Gender Center of the Federation of Bosnia and Herzegovina, the Gender Center of Republika Srpska, and committees in the legislative bodies. In that role, she developed governmental strategies to mainstream gender issues (National Action Plan as per the Beijing Declaration, the Gender Action Plan of BiH, Strategy for Preventing and Combating Domestic Violence, and the Action Plan for the Implementation of UN Security Council Resolution 1325) and led the processes of development and adoption of the Law on Gender Equality in BiH. Ms. Filipović-Hadžiabdić is an approved UN and Council of Europe expert and leads BiH delegations to UN sessions and constructive dialogues with UN treaty bodies. As the director of the Gender Equality Agency of Bosnia and Herzegovina, Ms. Filipović-Hadžiabdić took a leading role in the development of the Regional Declaration on Cooperation of Institutional Mechanisms for Gender Equality in Western Balkan countries and has organized a number of regional initiatives. Ms. Filipović-Hadžiabdić also initiated the establishment of a Master's degree in Gender Studies at the University of Sarajevo, where she lectures. Ms. Filipović-Hadžiabdić holds a BA in Law, and a MA in State and International Public Law from the University of Sarajevo, where she is a doctoral candidate.

Olivier Guitta is the Director of Research at the Henry Jackson Society, responsible for setting the strategic agenda for the research department and overseeing the Society's academic focus, as well as conducting his own research on geopolitics in the MENA region. He is an expert on security and counter-terrorism, having briefed the European Union, the United States Congress and NATO, as well as U.S. presidential candidates, SOCOM and Europol. He is a regular speaker at international security conferences and has lectured at the National Defense University and the Joint Special Operations University. Born in Morocco, raised in France and educated in Cologne and Paris, Mr. Guitta spent twelve years in New York as a Portfolio Manager for two major financial firms. Following the attacks of September 11th 2001, he left the world of finance to work as a geopolitics and risk analysis consultant in Washington DC and then France, before joining The Henry Jackson Society in July 2013. Olivier has appeared on numerous international broadcasters including the BBC, CNN, France 24, Canadian TV, Fox News and NPR. His writing on geopolitics and security issues has been published in a range of outlets, including *Le Monde*, *Weekly Standard*, *Jane's Defense Weekly*, *The Examiner*, *Jamestown Terrorism Monitor*, *National Post* (Canada), *Valeurs Actuelles* (France), and *Asia Times* (Hong Kong). He has also written in-depth studies on Hezbollah for the Brookings Institution and on Euro-U.S. cooperation on terrorism for the American Legislative Exchange Council. His daily reading of the Arabic, European, Israeli and U.S. press, combined with his business experience, give him a unique perspective on world events.

Camilla af Hällström is an entrepreneur based in Helsinki, Finland. She is a graduate of the University of Helsinki and the University of London, having obtained law degrees from both universities. She was affiliated with the Center for Transatlantic Relations SAIS in fall 2013 and helped to coordinate the Mediterranean Women in Leadership and Civil Society Conference in the framework of the Mediterranean Basin Initiative at the Center. Camilla runs two companies and a charitable foundation.

Edward P. Joseph is a highly experienced field practitioner and expert/lecturer on conflict, stabilization and reconstruction. In April, 2012, as Deputy Head of the OSCE Mission in Kosovo, he led the 'technical team' of OSCE negotiators and forged an eleventh hour breakthrough to run Serbian elections in Kosovo, averting a brewing crisis between Serbia and Kosovo. Secretary of State Hillary Clinton specifically acknowledged Edward's contribution in this role. In more than a dozen years of experience in the Balkans, Edward compiled other notable distinctions, including wartime experience on every conflict front, playing a vital role in the arbitration of Brčko District in Bosnia and Herzegovina, and coordinating the evacuation of the Žepa 'safe area' as UN civil affairs officer in July 1995. He has been published in *The New York Times*, *Foreign Affairs*, and in other leading outlets. Joseph was a helicopter pilot in the U.S. Army Reserve, and holds a J.D. from the University of Virginia and a B.A. and M.A. from Johns Hopkins University and the School of Advanced International Studies, respectively.

Marianne Laanatza is an expert on the Middle East and North Africa, and she is a Senior Lecturer and Researcher associated with Lund University, Stockholm University as well as Uppsala University in Sweden. Her research is within empirical conflict research and economics with a focus on international trade policy. She is also a frequent guest lecturer at several universities in the Middle East, North Africa, other EU member countries, as well as in the U.S. During the last ten years, Laanatza has been a member of a team responsible for a great number of international advanced training programs related to WTO issues and obligations in free trade agreements. In this capacity she has trained a great number of the staff in the Ministries of Trade, other Ministries and governmental institutions in the Middle East and North Africa, as well as in several Asian and Sub-Saharan African countries. Women's perspectives are especially highlighted in these programs. Other programs target the private sector, with as many women representatives as possible. She has also, as a consultant, performed case studies for the World Bank and other international institutions and organizations.

Andy Mullins is a Visiting Scholar at the Center for Transatlantic Relations at the Johns Hopkins University Paul H. Nitze School of Advanced International Studies. He is a Project Manager for the Mediterranean Basin Initiative at the Center. He is the author of *Reconciliation or Reckoning? Massacres, Memory, and Politics in Independent Slovenia* (2011), a study of the collective memory of the 1945 post-war massacres in Slovenia and use and abuse of memory in contemporary political and social discourse. He is a graduate of the University of Washington's Jackson School of International Studies, where he was a Title VI Foreign Language Area Studies Fellow. He has worked as a translator and correspondent for Sarajevo's *Oslobođenje* newspaper and is published in Bosnian-Herzegovinian media regularly. Andy is a member of the Supervisory Board of the Mediterranean Development Initiative in Tunis, a member of the Executive Board of the America-Bosnia Foundation, and was a founding member of Seattle's Slovenian cultural society, *Slovenska miza*.

Anissa Naqrachi is the founder and president of the Nour Association for Solidarity with Rural Women (ANSFR), a group of approximately 1,900 female members in southern Morocco. She is also the president of the Amal Arab Group to Eradicate Early Marriage (AAGEEM), a network with member states Egypt, Lebanon, Yemen, Palestine, Saudi Arabia, Mauritania, and Jordan. Ms. Naqrachi is secretary-general of the Morocco Foundation and international vice-coordinator of the Union of Moroccan Women's Associations (NUWO), a Personnel and Professional Master Coach at the No Limit Coaching Academy in Paris, France, and a mentor at Kvinvo Denmark. A microbiologist by profession, she holds certificates and diplomas in NGO Management (2005, U.S.); the promotion of education for girls and women at the Institute for International Cooperation in Tokyo (2006); equal status and human rights of women in the Middle East and North Africa from Lund University in Sweden (2006) and Denmark (2006); the empowerment of rural women in the Afro-Asian region: opportunities and challenges from Japan (2007); and the advanced international program on human rights and disability from Sweden (2008). She is currently the SIPU Local Partner for Gender Equality Training, financed by SIDA (2009–2012), and a graduate of the Middle East Entrepreneur Training (MEET) program in Egypt (2009). She is the Algeria and Morocco liaison officer for the Foundation for the Future. She is a committee member on the National Initiative for Human Development, an innovative and ambitious project aimed at eliminating poverty, vulnerability, precarious situations, and social exclusion, and is a trainer.

Aylin Ünver Noi is Assistant Professor in the Faculty of Economics and Administrative Sciences, Department of International Relations, and Vice-Director of the European Union Application and Research Center, at Istanbul Gedik University. She is also associate researcher at European Institute for Research on Mediterranean and Euro-Arab Cooperation MEDEA, Brussels. She holds a PhD and an MA from the Department of European Union

Politics and International Relations, European Union Institute, Marmara University, Istanbul and a BA from the Department of International Relations, Faculty of Economics, Administrative and Social Sciences, Bilkent University, Ankara. She is author of *The Rise of Nationalism in Europe* (published in Turkish by IQ Publishers, Istanbul, 2007) and *The Euro-Mediterranean Partnership and the Broader Middle East and North Africa Initiative: Competing or Complementary Projects?* (published in English by the University Press of America, Lanham MD, 2011) as well as several articles on the Arab Spring. She is also editor of the book titled *Islam and Democracy: Perspectives on the Arab Spring* (published in English by the Cambridge Scholars Publishing, New Castle, 2013).

Slim Othmani has headed the NCA-Rouiba Juice company, owned by his family, since 1999. Prior to NCA-Rouiba Juice, he spent seven years as operations manager at Fruital-Coca-Cola, a business also owned by his family and shared today with Equatorial Bottling Company from Catalonia, Spain. Prior to returning to Algeria and his family-owned business, he served as Regional Sales Manager for North Africa for Alis Technologies, a Canadian technology venture. He holds a computer science and engineering degree from the University of Mathematics and Computer Sciences in Tunis, Tunisia, and an Executive Master of Business Administration degree from the Mediterranean School of Business in Tunis. Othmani is member and co-founder of major Algerian entrepreneurial associations, including Forum des Chefs d'Entreprises (FCE), Club d'Action et de Reflexion autour de l'Entreprise (Club CARE), the Algerian Drink Producers Association (APAB), the Maghreb Economic Forum (MEF), and Hawkama Al-Djazaier a project of Injaz Al-Arab of which he is the former president. He was born in Tunis on March 3, 1957, and is married with two children.

Valery Perry first worked in Bosnia and Herzegovina (BiH) in 1997 as an election supervisor. She has lived in Sarajevo since 1999, conducting research and working for organizations including the NATO Stabilization Force (SFOR), the European Center for Minority Issues (ECMI) and several NGOs. She worked at the OSCE Mission to Bosnia and Herzegovina in Sarajevo from 2004–2011, as Deputy Director of the Education Department, and Deputy Director of Programs in the Human Dimension Department. She currently works as Chief of Party for the Public International Law and Policy Group (PILPG) in Sarajevo, implementing a project to increase civil society engagement in constitutional reform processes in Bosnia and Herzegovina. Valery received a B.A. from the University of Rochester, an M.A. from Indiana University's Russian and East European Institute, and a Ph.D. from George Mason University's Institute for Conflict Analysis and Resolution, writing a dissertation examining democratization and peace building strategies in post-Dayton BiH. Valery has published numerous articles and book chapters, and has spoken at conferences and policy events in the United States and throughout Europe.

Rupert Sutton is a Research Fellow at the Henry Jackson Society, where he focuses on domestic extremism, global terrorism, and on security threats and political developments in the Levant region. He has written comment and analysis for *Haaretz*, the *Huffington Post*, and *New Humanist*, and has also spoken at the European Parliament. He also gives regular risk assessment presentations on the Levant to oil and gas, insurance, and financial firms on behalf of Strategic Analysis, the Henry Jackson Society's in-house risk consultancy, and has written a number of short briefings on these issues. Rupert has an MA in Terrorism and Security (with Distinction) from King's College London, during which he focused on sectarian violence in the Middle East and Northern Ireland, and a BA in War Studies from the University of Kent.

Sasha Toperich is a Senior Fellow at the Center for Transatlantic Relations. He is also President of the America–Bosnia Foundation, President of the World Youth Leadership Network, and a world-renowned pianist. Dr. Toperich has also held several diplomatic positions for Bosnia and Herzegovina. In 2002–2003, he was advisor to the Ambassador of Bosnia and Herzegovina to the United Nations, from 2003–2007, he was a Special Envoy of the Presidency of Bosnia and Herzegovina to the United States; and in 2009 and 2010, he served as a Counselor at the Permanent Mission of Bosnia and Herzegovina to the United Nations. He is a co-author of two papers in the book *Unfinished Business: Western Balkans and the International Community* (Brookings Institution/CTR, 2012) titled "The Regulatory Environment in the Financial System in Bosnia and Herzegovina and How to Improve It" and "A New Paradigm for the Mediterranean: U.S.–North Africa–Southeast Europe." Dr. Toperich is the Director of the Mediterranean Basin Initiative and chairman of the Supervisory Board at the Mediterranean Development Initiative in Tunisia.